The Social History of the Brazilian Samba

For Mum, Dad, Ian, John, Eddy and Alex, with love

The Social History of the Brazilian Samba

LISA SHAW

Ashgate

Aldershot • Brookfield USA • Singapore • Sydney

Published by
Ashgate Publishing Limited
Gower House
Croft Road
Aldershot
Hants GU11 3HR
England

Ashgate Publishing Company
Old Post Road
Brookfield
Vermont 05036-9704
USA

British Library Cataloguing in Publication Data

Shaw, Lisa
    The Social History of the Brazilian Samba
    (Ashgate Studies in Ethnomusicology)
    1. Sambas. 2. Ethnomusicology—Brazil—History—20th
    century. 3. Music and society—Brazil—History—20th
    century. 4. Brazil—Social conditions. 5. Brazil—Social life
    and customs—20th century.
    I. Title.
    306.4'84'081

Library of Congress Cataloguing-in-Publication Data

Shaw, Lisa, 1966-
    The social history of the Brazilian samba/Lisa Shaw.
        (Ashgate Studies in Ethnomusicology)
    Includes bibliographical references and index.
    ISBN 1-84014-289-8 (hardcover)
    1. Sambas—History and criticism. 2. Music and society—
    Brazil. 3. Composers—Brazil. I. Title.
    ML3417.S53 1998
    784.18'88—dc21   98-36992
                                                       CIP
ISBN 1 84014 289 8   MN

This book is printed on acid free paper

Printed and bound in Great Britain by MPG Books Ltd, Bodmin, Cornwall

Contents

Ashgate Studies in Ethnomusicology
General Editor's Preface

The aim of this new series is to encourage ethnomusicological study (with 'ethnomusicology' defined very widely), which has significance for all those involved in it. The series is interested in work which emphasizes the relationships between people and music in cultural context, as individuals within communities, and which acknowledges a varied range of contributions and looks to beneficial outcomes for those 'being researched' as well as for the 'researcher'. To this end it supports what might be regarded as a dialogic praxis, of collaborative discursive action and reflection, in which the researcher might become part of the facilitation of a particular focus, in time and place. It is also an intention to enable the investigation and problematizing of ethnomusicological practices, and to discuss ways of clarifying such issues and addressing them.

There is a place in the series for the 'traditional' studies of particular musical practices, where these are related to cultural and functional significance, and where they give an insight into modes of representation and transmission. This is particularly true where the research process gives those sharing the information a new and useful view of their own activities. Innovative and experimental work that is appropriate to the principal aims of the series is also encouraged.

Malcolm Floyd

King Alfred's University College, Winchester

Acknowledgements

Writing this book has been a source of immense enjoyment, and has left me with many debts to friends, relatives and colleagues. It was thanks to my great friend Professor John Gledson that I first became interested in the work of Noel Rosa and subsequently in Brazilian popular music from the 1930s and 1940s as a whole. Without John's expert guidance, constant encouragement and generous assistance there is no doubt that I would not have completed the doctoral thesis on which this book is based. He was also kind enough to proofread the final draft of the manuscript, a truly thankless task. I am very grateful for the many hours of conversation and laughter that I have enjoyed in the Gledson-Thompson household over the last eight years or so.

Ever since embarking on this project back in 1990 I have been able to count on the support of my family and many close friends, as well as a number of colleagues in the Department of Spanish and Portuguese at the University of Leeds. I would like to thank Professor John Macklin, in particular, for granting me study leave at a vital moment, which enabled me to complete the thesis, and also for excusing my absences from the Department as the final manuscript of this book took shape. It was thanks to a scholarship from the Anglo-Brazilian Society and BAT Industries/ Souza Cruz that I was first able to visit Brazil in 1991, and to begin to collect the song lyrics and other published material on which this study is based. My extended visits to Rio de Janeiro would not have been possible without the selfless hospitality and kindness of Elmar Pereira de Mello and Hilda White Rössle de Mello, who have always taken a great interest in this project. This book has also benefited from the informed comments and suggestions made by Dr David Treece and Professor James Higgins, the examiners of my PhD thesis. Finally, I would like to thank Alex Nield for helping me to overcome my fear of technology.

Introduction

Between 1930 and 1945 Brazil and its people witnessed a series of dramatic social transformations, which irrevocably altered their identity. The revolution that brought Getúlio Vargas to power in 1930 was followed by the establishment of his authoritarian *Estado Novo* or New State in 1937, the regime which governed Brazil until Vargas's overthrow in 1945. A transition period in Brazilian society, which moved from a rural to an urban structure, centred on the changing capital of Rio de Janeiro and the rapidly growing city of São Paulo, it witnessed the birth of industrialization and the continued attempted integration of ex-slaves and their descendants, as well as European immigrants, into mainstream society.

The 1930s also saw the culture industry take shape in Brazil, with the rise of the radio, the talking cinema and the record industry. In the course of this book the evolution of samba will be examined in detail against this social and historical background, giving full consideration to the way the songs were written, the lifestyles and social position of the *sambistas* or composers, the impact of commercial and political constraints, and the respective position of each *sambista* in relation to the power structure of the regime. Samba lyrics constitute highly significant historical documents since they were initially the sole mouthpiece of uneducated blacks, and thus provide a unique record of their experiences and views. As samba became more commercialized in the 1930s, and was taken on board by the emerging middle class, the lyrics bore witness to the social and political changes taking place within *carioca* (Rio) society. The first three chapters of this book outline the social, cultural and musical origins of the samba genre, and explore the historical context of the Vargas era in greater depth.

In the remaining three chapters the work of three *sambistas* is analysed in detail, providing a revealing illustration of how popular music has traditionally articulated changes in community and identity in Brazil. Ataúlfo Alves and Ari Barroso, although born in the state of Minas Gerais, were adoptive *cariocas*, and along with Noel Rosa their music was inextricably linked to the Rio society of the 1930s and 1940s. Ataúlfo was a poor, black musician, and on his arrival in Rio at the age of 18 he lived in the Rio Comprido area of the city, near the district of Estácio de Sá. It was in the shantytowns of Rio that he met fellow popular musicians and participated in the carnival groups or *blocos*. Despite his humble origins, Ataúlfo perfected a highly professional, sophisticated image, and adapted successfully to the demands of the burgeoning radio and record industries and their middle-class audiences. In contrast, Ari Barroso came to Rio at a similar age to Ataúlfo to study law at university, with the help of a family inheritance. A gifted pianist, he became involved in the city's musical scene by performing in local cinemas, and later by composing songs for the theatre. A white university graduate, Ari became a media celebrity, as well as one of the most famous and accomplished singer-songwriters of the era. His image was that of a respectable, patriotic, well-liked family man, who nevertheless enjoyed Rio's night life to the full and was courted by the filmmakers of Hollywood in the 1940s. Finally, Noel Rosa came from a similar background to Ari, in that he was white, from the lower-middle-class northern suburb of Rio, Vila Isabel, and also attended university. His penchant for the bohemian night clubs and bars of Lapa, the city's then red-light district, however, took precedence over his studies and he soon dropped out of the faculty of medicine. In the bars of the socially mixed district of Vila Isabel he came into daily contact with other popular musicians and songwriters, and with the black *malandros* or spivs, who were part and parcel of the underworld of samba that so fascinated him in the late 1920s and 1930s. It was the *malandro*'s marginal, alternative lifestyle that Noel adopted himself, and despite his relatively privileged background and widespread popularity he remained closely involved with the milieu of Rio's poorer quarters and never lost his irreverent attitude towards the authorities. His precarious health, which led to his untimely death in 1937, and a physical disability no doubt helped him to identify with society's outcasts.

Chapter Four examines the work of Ataúlfo Alves, since it is the most typical of the time and thus serves to establish many of the tacit thematic and stylistic conventions of the samba genre. Chapter Five explores the unrivalled linguistic richness and complexities of Noel Rosa's sambas, for Noel toyed with these unwritten conventions and, socially, he bridged the gap between the ambitious, poor, black composers like Ataúlfo, and the educated, white *sambistas*, such as Ari Barroso. Finally, Chapter Six studies the discourse of Ari's lyrics, which helped definitively to establish samba as a respectable musical form, attuned to the refined palates of its new, middle-class audience.

CHAPTER ONE

Samba: its Roots and Conventions

Samba is widely thought to be directly descended from the *batuque*, a circle dance performed by the slaves of Brazil's colonial plantations, which was imbued with a spiritual force. It is thought that in the early seventeenth century African slaves began to perform rhythmic dances in order to disguise their religious rituals. The accompanying displays of percussion were given the generic name of *batuques* by the Portuguese. The slaves went on to perform *calundus* or *lundus* in the eighteenth century, dances which also had a religious significance and were often used to bring good luck.[1] Various regional offshoots of these *batuques* evolved, which all appeared to have a common feature - the *umbigada*, or 'bump with the belly button'. This was a movement taken from the dances of the Congo and Angola, where it was the culmination of the marriage ceremony.[2] The term samba is thought to have originated in Angola, where the Kimbundu word *semba* was used to refer to the *umbigada* dance step. By the beginning of the nineteenth century, whilst slaves continued to participate in the *batuque*, free blacks had developed an accompaniment to the dance played on the *viola* (a type of Portuguese guitar taken to Brazil by the Jesuits).[3]

Samba has always been intrinsically linked to the annual carnival celebrations held in Brazil, especially in the city of Rio de Janeiro. Both samba and *carnaval* emerged from a long process of cultural miscegenation, which brought together European influences from the Portuguese, and African influences from the slaves transported to the northeast of Brazil to work on the sugar plantations, and later moved south to provide labour in the mines of Minas Gerais and the coffee plantations in the state of Rio de Janeiro. The roots of carnival can be traced back to ancient Egypt, Greece and Rome, where the Roman festival of Lupercalia was celebrated on 15 February in honour of the god Pan. In Brazil, some kind of pre-Lenten celebration has existed since the mid-sixteenth century, after the arrival of the Portuguese in 1500. The early carnivals in Brazil were based on the *entrudo*, a tradition which originated in the Azores and became popular in Portugal in the fifteenth and sixteenth centuries. The *entrudo* involved various kinds of pranks and riotous antics, such as the throwing of stink bombs, and was outlawed in 1853 in Brazil. This form of celebration finally died out at the beginning of the 1900s.

In the early years of the twentieth century three separate carnivals were held in Rio: firstly, that of the poor in the central Praça Onze district of the city, secondly, that of the middle class in the Avenida Central (now the Avenida Rio Branco), and thirdly, that of the wealthy, white élite with their lavish costume balls and processions. There was still no single carnival music, and the samba and the *marcha carnavalesca* (carnival march) were created to provide a carnival rhythm. The *marcha*, often referred to as the *marchinha*, was of bourgeois origin, and was inspired by Portuguese marches, passed on to the colony via music hall. The samba, on the other hand, is believed to have grown out of the primitive rhythms of the *batuques* and *lundus* of the slaves of the sugar plantations, many of whom had been moved to the coffee plantations of the state of Rio after the decline of the sugar trade and gold mining. With the end of the coffee boom in the valley of the Paraíba do Sul at the close of the nineteenth century much of this workforce settled in the city of Rio, and by the second decade of the twentieth century a small Afro-Brazilian community existed in the port area and other central districts of the city. It was within this group that samba music evolved.

The Afro-Brazilian religious cult of *candomblé* has close links with samba, and both were outlets for black self-expression at the beginning of the twentieth century. Hilária Batista de Almeida, or Tia Ciata, as she was known, was the most famous *mãe-de-santo* (priestess) in Rio at that time. As well as being a religious leader in *candomblé*, she promoted meetings between musicians in her home, just off the Praça Onze, the square that became the centre of social life for Rio's poor black inhabitants in the second decade of the twentieth century and around which many *terreiros* or cult centres grew up. Tia Ciata allowed her home to be used for parties where 'decent' dance games and music were performed in the front rooms, but at the back of the house samba and religious ceremonies worshipping the African deities or *orixás* were practised in secret. The fact that she was married to a policeman no doubt enabled her to host such clandestine activities. It was in her home that a heterogeneous group of musicians and enthusiasts met and performed music, including semi-literate Bahian popular composers, whites and mulattos from Rio's lower middle class, such as the dance hall pianist and self-taught composer Sinhô, and the popular musician Pixinguinha, as well as civil servants and other professional people, like Mauro de Almeida, who is thought to have written the lyrics of the first samba '*Pelo telefone*' ('On the Telephone'), allegedly the outcome of these get-togethers. This song, registered in Rio's National Library in 1916, was credited to Ernesto dos Santos, usually referred to by his nickname of Donga, although there was considerable controversy over the true authorship of the composition, and heated opinions on this matter were aired in the *carioca* press by the parties concerned. Informal gatherings like those that gave rise to the writing of this song, where both samba and *choros* were performed, were held in various districts of the city, such as Saúde at the end of the nineteenth century, and later in Lapa, Cidade Nova, and Riachuelo. It was on the *morro*, literally 'the hill' but long since synonymous with Brazil's hillside shantytowns, that samba developed, among blacks who were forced to flee to the outlying districts, in the face of police repression. Thus the *morro* became inextricably linked to samba and its creators.

This early samba acted as an identity marker for the poor, largely black community, whose physical territory was frequently taken away. In 1904, under the direction of the then *prefeito* (mayor) of Rio, Pereira Passos, and President Rodrigues Alves, Rio's city centre was the object of a massive renovation campaign, part of the savage urbanization of the city known as the *'bota-abaixo'* (literally 'knocking down'), which drove out the poor to the hillside shantytowns. Between 1904 and 1906 641 buildings and 21 streets were demolished in order to create space for the Avenida Central. Under the slogan *'O Rio civiliza-se'* ('Rio is becoming civilized') the poor were forcibly moved from central areas of the city, that were becoming valuable, to the *favelas* or shantytowns and the suburbs of the humble *Zona Norte* (North Zone). Hence the *bairro* (neighbourhood or district) became a central part of the identity of the lower classes, as distinct from the *cidade* (city) as a whole.[4] Furthermore, unemployment and underemployment among blacks were exacerbated by the influx of European immigrants to Brazil in the first decades of the twentieth century, spurred on by government incentives. The Brazilian élite's belief in the racial superiority of whites and the *branqueamento* or 'whitening' ideology, gave rise to the myth of the *operário ideal* (ideal factory worker), of white, European origin. Brazil's blacks and mulattos, who had proved highly skilful in a whole host of trades and crafts prior to the abolition of slavery in 1888, were subsequently stigmatized, the implication being that they were unsuitable for modern life and progress. Forced into a marginal existence, they accounted for the vast majority of Rio's poor, *morro* inhabitants.

Throughout the 1920s, samba was written and performed by ex-slaves and their descendants, and it gradually divided into two strands. On the one hand, there was the samba of the *sambistas* of the central area of the city, where *'Pelo telefone'* was created, which was tolerated by the authorities and given the respectable label of *'cultura afro-brasileira'* ('Afro-Brazilian culture'). On the other was the samba of the musicians of the *morros*, who were persecuted by the police and considered to be part of a marginal underworld. Two such individuals were Ismael Silva and

Nilton Bastos, from the Estácio de Sá district, who founded the first *bloco carnavalesco* or samba school in 1928, called 'Deixa Falar' ('Let Them Talk').

At the end of the 1940s, 95 per cent of the population of Rio's *favelas* were black or mulatto, as opposed to 27 per cent in the overall population of the city. The shantytowns provided the perfect breeding ground for black cultural manifestations, including samba.[5] On the *morro* blacks could isolate themselves totally from the pervasive ideals of the white élite, and it became a spiritual refuge, as well as a physical hideout for petty criminals and persecuted *sambistas*. Internal harmony on the *morro* was paramount, and there existed a moral code of practice. Each member of the community had a particular role to play in maintaining the status quo, such as the peace-keeper or *valente*. The community as a whole took precedence over the individual, and the street rather than the makeshift shack became the centre of life.[6] *Lá fora* (out there) was considered an entirely different world by the inhabitants of the *morro*, and any contact with the alien *cidade* was treated with some apprehension. It was a closed society, and access to outsiders, other than in the form of police raids, was mostly denied.[7] The *morro* allowed Afro-Brazilian traditions to be preserved and to flourish, and it had its own social structure and means for economic survival.

The similarities between the evolution of the Brazilian samba and the Argentinian tango from the 1920s to the 1940s are striking. Up until 1917 tango had been the marginalized song and dance form of the suburbs of Buenos Aires, where the rural population settled, its lyrics centred on the denunciation of social conditions. However, when it migrated to the city, these social themes were replaced with a more personal, emotional content. The macho, violent *compadrito* character, the peasant newly arrived in the city, ceased to exist, as did the references to prostitutes and violence. As in Brazil, the new media, chiefly radio and cinema in Argentina, brought this form of popular music into mass culture. Like samba, tango became popular in the three main senses of the word, that is, quantitatively by reaching a mass audience, qualitatively by still retaining some of its oppositional elements *vis-à-vis* the dominant élite culture, and yet also becoming a populist form, part of the process of popular mobilization. Perón, like Vargas, although some years later, sought to coopt support for a capitalist path of development among the poor, and under his rule the cultural production of the lower classes, such as tango, was given increased exposure on a national stage.[8]

The thematics of samba lyrics

Malandragem: *a lifestyle of idleness and roguery*

In broad terms samba dealt with two main themes in the 1920s, '30s and early '40s - women and love affairs, and the figure of the *malandro*, a black spiv or hustler with a horror of work and a love of women, gambling and carousing.[9] By the early 1900s, the real-life *malandro* had made his presence known in Rio de Janeiro, and in the 1920s he entered samba lyrics and became the protagonist of a poetic text that was just beginning to be heard outside its original community.[10] The *malandro*'s negative attitude to manual labour directly flouted the work ethic of the Vargas government. He parodied bourgeois values and lifestyle in his dapper, white, linen suit, which formed an ironic contrast to his dark skin, his jauntily tilted straw hat, two-tone shoes, silk shirt and scarf, and spurned the manual labour (*trabalho no pesado* or *o batente*) that was so closely associated with exploitation and the institution of slavery, which was only finally abolished in Brazil in the late nineteenth century. The figure of the *malandro* is epitomized in the following extract from a samba by Noel Rosa. Here he is from Salgueiro, a Rio shantytown and stronghold of samba, he lives from gambling and is obsessed with his smart appearance, as is suggested in the reference to the *tintureiro* or dry cleaner's in the third line. However, *tintureiro* was also the 1930s' Rio slang term for the police van used to arrest vagrants, and this reference is a reflection of the police harassment suffered by these marginal characters and by *sambistas* themselves:

'*Mulato bamba*', 1931, Noel Rosa

Este mulato forte
É do Salgueiro
Passear no tintureiro
Era seu esporte
Já nasceu com sorte
E desde pirralho
Vive à custa do baralho
Nunca viu trabalho

'Cool Mulatto', 1931, Noel Rosa

This strong mulatto
Is from Salgueiro
Hanging around in the dry cleaner's
Was his favourite sport
He was born lucky
And since he was a kid
He's lived from a pack of cards
He's never seen a day's work

The ethos of *malandragem* constitutes one of the poles of Brazilian national identity, and the figure of the *malandro* has been explored in depth by the great Brazilian literary critic Antonio Candido de Mello e Souza. He traces the evolution of this character back to Manuel Antônio de Almeida's novel *Memórias de um sargento de milícias* (*Memoirs of a Militia Sergeant*), published in 1853-54, and beyond, and more specifically to one of the characters of this novel, Leonardo, whom Candido calls: '... o primeiro grande malandro que entra na novelística brasileira ...' ('... the first great *malandro* that appears in the Brazilian novel ...'). According to Candido, elements of the ethos of *malandragem* are also to be found in the works of the seventeenth-century poet Gregório de Matos, and the figure of the *malandro* reemerged in the twentieth century in Mário de Andrade's novel *Macunaíma*. Nevertheless, the *malandro* is not peculiar to Brazilian society, but is one example of the generic type of the picaresque adventurer.[11] There is an obvious similarity between the Brazilian *malandro* and the figure of the *curro* in Cuba, who appears in the nineteenth-century novel *Cecilia Valdés* by Cirilo Villaverde.[12] Parallels can also be drawn between the *malandro* and the characters of Nicolás Guillén's poetry from the 1930s, who also wear *sapato de do tono* (two-tone shoes). It is no coincidence that the slave-based societies of both Brazil and Cuba should produce a mythical black figure who rejects demeaning manual work and challenges his inferior social position. Antonio Candido also states that the *malandro* character bears traces of other popular heroes found in Brazilian folklore, such as Pedro Malasartes, a similarity which Roberto Da Matta embroiders on in his book *Carnavais, malandros e heróis: para uma sociologia do dilema brasileiro* (*Carnivals, 'Malandros' and Heroes: Towards a Sociology of the Brazilian Dilemma*). Here he shows Pedro, a figure from popular literature, to be a rural *malandro*, who lives by cheating the system (his bosses) and compensates for his lack of power with his cunning, thus turning his fortune around.[13]

Nevertheless, it was in the lyrics of *carioca* samba that the mythical Brazilian *malandro* found his true identity. The *sambista* found his greatest source of inspiration in the ethos of *malandragem*, and in the 1920s and early 1930s the so-called *samba malandro*, with its anti-establishment discourse, predominated. Although seemingly self-obsessed and concerned, above all, for his own well-being, the *malandro* is, nevertheless, vehemently opposed to the exploitation of his social class. He challenges any form of manipulation by the state, and thus is worshipped by the rest of his community. He does not want to become a middle-class city dweller, preferring to indulge in small acts of *malandragem*, rather than make any serious attempt to climb the social ladder. The samba '*O que será de mim?*' ('What Will Become of Me?'), written by Ismael Silva in 1931, clearly illustrates the spiv's aversion to honest toil:

'*O que será de mim?*', 1931, Ismael Silva

Se eu precisar algum dia
De ir ao batente
Não sei o que será
Pois vivo na boemia
E vida melhor não há

Não há vida melhor
E vida melhor não há
Deixa falar quem quiser
Deixa quem quiser falar

O trabalho não é bom
Ninguém deve duvidar
Trabalhar, só obrigado
Por gosto ninguém vai lá

'What Will Become of Me?', 1931, Ismael Silva

If one day I have to
Go out to work
I don't know what will happen
'Cos I live a bohemian life
And there's no better way to live

There's no better life
No better way to live
Let people say what they want
Let them say what they like

Work isn't good
No one should doubt that
I'll only work if forced to
Nobody works for the fun of it

The myth of the *malandro* had much more power than the real-life black spiv, and helped preserve the socio-cultural identity of his community. He came to symbolize the marginal world of the poor *bairros* and *morros* of the city of Rio. It was in these areas that many impoverished blacks did, in fact, spurn poorly paid, manual labour, in favour of a lifestyle that often transgressed the law, revolving around gambling, petty crime and organized prostitution. As Sam C. Adamo explains: 'The popular association of the Afro-Brazilian with crime is embodied in the image of the *malandro* or vagabond who never works and survives by using his cunning and wits'.[14] This criminal stereotype of blacks and mulattos was reinforced by the ideas of Social Darwinism, but the *malandro* was, in reality, the product of an economic structure incapable of absorbing all the male workforce available in urban Rio.[15]

The *malandro* and the *sambista* became synonymous, with the performance of samba being outlawed by the authorities in the first decades of its existence. During this clandestine period in samba's history, when its performance was closely associated with the Afro-Brazilian cult practice of *candomblé* in the minds of the authorities, the state feared the potentially subversive group solidarity engendered by informal musical or religious gatherings. Police repression was used to try to stamp out both activities until the 1930s, and as Adamo says:

> What were considered the 'uncivilized' and 'barbarous' practices of non-whites provided a means for a powerless group of social and economic outcasts to organize and become a threat to the established socio-economic order. Unification of non-whites in urban areas would have been a threat to traditional society.[16]

Until 1930, public order offences like drunkenness, vagrancy and begging were used to control those outside mainstream society. Fights, sometimes involving knives and guns, would occasionally break out between rival samba groups, but it was an unlawful minority of participants that stigmatized all *sambistas* and contributed to the *malandro*'s violent image. Such disturbances prompted a police response in the form of arrests and the confiscation of musical instruments. Maria Júlia Goldwasser states that she heard of many cases of samba schools competing in carnival that left a trail of wounded and even dead behind them, and of *baianas* (black women wearing the typical dress of those from the city of Salvador in the northeastern state of Bahia), sometimes men in disguise, who would hide an arsenal of weapons under their clothes.[17]

Around 1920 there had been a perceptible shift in the cultural establishment's attitude to Brazil's African heritage. Most intellectuals no longer rejected it as a dangerous menace to society, and instead began to view it as an integral part of Brazilian culture. As Dain Borges says:

> ... this new attitude toward the Afro-Brazilian heritage coincided with the mobilization and commercialization of festive aspects of Afro-Brazilian urban popular culture between 1910 and 1940. This mobilization undermined the formal and informal discriminatory policies of the First Republic. By making Afro-Brazilian practices more visible, less clandestine, it abated some of their connotations of polluting menace. Slyly or sincerely renamed as 'schools', *samba* societies and *capoeira* martial arts circles sought and won police permission to meet and perform on the streets. Record companies commercialized *samba* marches, legitimating Carnival music as a product. ... Eventually, in a variety of ways, Brazilian intellectuals unbarred access to Creole popular traditions, to symbols and ideas that had previously been stigmatized and cast out.[18]

With the establishment of Vargas's provisional government in 1930, a totally new tactic was employed by the authorities. Repression was replaced, to a large extent, by tolerance and cooption. Samba and Afro-Brazilian cult practices were permitted, provided that their participants abided by certain rules laid down by the regime. Non-white institutions such as these were 'Brazilianized', and their potential for subversion was defused. In 1932, for example, Rio's largely Afro-Brazilian carnival was brought under government sponsorship and became a national festival. The same process of appropriation by the state took place a few decades earlier with *capoeira*, the warfare dance game of Angolan origin, developed by Angolan slaves on the plantations of the state of Bahia in the eighteenth and nineteenth centuries, possibly as physical training for slave insurrection. After emancipation, *capoeira* gangs continued to exist in urban areas, often armed with knives, and naturally posed a threat to law and order. In the late nineteenth century, politicians dealt with this problem by forming alliances with these gangs. In return for favours and patronage, the latter were encouraged to channel their energies and violence into intimidation, with the aim of ensuring electoral success for their patrons. Thus, the threat that gangs of blacks posed was attenuated, and an impression of leniency on the part of the ruling élite was maintained. As Gerhard Kubik states: 'It was a result of the same process of "emancipation" which turned *capoeira* from a prosecuted activity into a harmless manifestation within a presentable white category: *Folclore* (Folklore).'[19]

As carnival grew in importance, samba became increasingly acceptable in the eyes of the white élite. Its force as a vehicle for ethno-cultural expression was reduced by encouraging its adoption by other sectors of society. Originally a symbol of black identity, samba gradually became a symbol of the Brazilian nation as a whole.[20] The appropriation of samba by Vargas's authoritarian regime clearly fits the pattern identified by Eduardo Diatahy B. de Menezes, which divides the process of cultural domination into three stages, as follows:

1. The rejection of 'offensive/disorderly' elements by the repressive apparatus of the state. (In the case of samba this took the form of the eradication of overt references to the ethos of *malandragem* via censorship, and greater incentives for *sambistas* to deal with uncontroversial, eulogistic, pro-establishment topics.)
2. Domestication by separating these dangerous elements from the 'exotic/decorative', which can be used in a process of symbolic domination. (The innocuous, patriotic features of samba were foregrounded to create a symbol of national as opposed to ethnic or class identity.)

3. Recuperation. The culture industry and the ideological apparatus of the state transform these desirable elements into cultural expressions of the dominant class, for the purposes of ideological education, national marketing for the tourist industry, and suchlike.[21] Samba, like other Afro-Brazilian cultural forms, such as *feijoada* (Brazil's national dish)[22] and *candomblé*, was to become a national symbol, produced and consumed by a cross-section of Brazilian society and projected abroad as a reflection of Brazil's mythical racial democracy.[23]

As a result of the restrictions placed on *sambistas* by the censors, the *malandro* was replaced in song lyrics by his respectable counterpart, the *malandro regenerado* (reformed spiv). Cláudia Matos believes, however, that the ethos did not disappear entirely, but rather became increasingly ambiguous. She says that songwriters managed to evade censorship and seemingly to toe the official line, yet still put across elements of the counter-culture of *malandragem*. The *malandro*'s vision of life became more realistic and a critical view of society was covertly expressed.[24] Matos quotes Noel Rosa's samba '*Rapaz folgado*' ('Laid-back Guy') of 1933, which triggered off a famous polemic between Noel and Wilson Baptista, as an example of this transformation. In this song, Noel is giving Wilson advice, telling him to be more subtle in his advocacy of a life of *malandragem* if he wants to survive as a *sambista*:[25]

'*Rapaz folgado*', 1933, Noel Rosa

Deixa de arrastar o teu tamanco
Pois tamanco nunca foi sandália
Tira do pescoço o lenço branco
Compra sapato e gravata
Joga fora esta navalha
Que te atrapalha

Com o chapéu de lado deste rata
Da polícia quero que te escapes
Fazendo um samba-canção
Já te dei papel e lápis
Arranja um amor e um violão

Malandro é palavra derrotista
Que só serve pra tirar
Todo o valor do sambista
Proponho ao povo civilizado
Não te chamarem de malandro
Mas sim de rapaz folgado

'Laid-back Guy', 1933, Noel Rosa

Stop dragging your clogs[26]
'Cos clogs have never been sandals

Take that white scarf from around your neck
Buy some shoes and a tie
Throw out that knife
That gets in your way

With your hat tilted like that
I want you to escape from the police
By writing a *samba-canção*
I've given you a pencil and paper
Find a lover and a guitar

Malandro is a defeatist word
Its only function is to take
All value away from the samba writer
I propose that civilized people
Don't call you a *malandro*
But a laid-back guy instead

Matos believes that *sambistas* could ostensibly write about the reformed *malandro regenerado*, while at the same time using him as a mouthpiece to make ironic comments about daily life.[27] Deliberate chinks in the reformed spiv's armour allow us to glimpse his former lifestyle and origins, along with his true attitude towards the new work ethic that he appears, on the surface at least, to espouse. The spiv's linguistic dexterity is crucial to his existence. Many *sambistas* chose this '*falar macio*' ('smooth talking'), as opposed to the '*pisar macio*' ('smooth walking'), as Gilberto Vasconcelos puts it.[28] Instead of extolling the virtues of *malandragem* in their lyrics, they directed their efforts into creating a language of *malandragem*, which would embody the ethos in its irony, ambiguities, word play and satirical humour. In the samba '*Bastião*' by Wilson Baptista and Brasinha, for example, the eponymous hero is an exemplary manual worker, who has embraced the work ethic of the Vargas regime wholeheartedly, it would appear. However, it is telling that he always catches the *bonde errado* (the wrong tram), as a result of his illiteracy, and his error lies, perhaps, in his failure to pursue the more enjoyable and more profitable existence of *malandragem*, and in his willingness to allow himself to be used by a capitalist system that, in reality, cares little about his welfare and social advancement:[29]

'*Bastião*', Wilson Baptista and Brasinha

Bastião
Valente na picareta
É um covarde
Quando pega na caneta
Que tempo enorme ele consome
Quando tem que assinar o nome

Bastião
Foi criado na calçada
Não viu cartilha
Nem tabuada
Bastião
Sempre toma o bonde errado
Não sabe ler
Nem bilhete premiado

'Bastião', Wilson Baptista and Brasinha

Bastião
Brave with a pickaxe
Is a coward
When he picks up a pen
He takes an enormous amount of time
When he has to sign his name

Bastião
Was brought up on the street
He never learned to spell
Or to do sums
Bastião
Always catches the wrong tram
He can't read
Not even a winning ticket

Bastião has become the antithesis of the *malandro*, the ingenuous, down-trodden, exploited worker, often referred to as the *otário* (mug or sucker), who made his appearance in the lyrics of samba in the early 1940s in particular. Likewise, Pedro Malasartes, the archetypal *malandro* of Brazilian folklore, has a brother who is his complete opposite - he is honest and hard-working yet is always abused and cheated in reward for this. Roberto Da Matta calls this type of character the *caxias*. This law-abiding citizen '... denota o mundo da estrutura, das leis e do autoritarismo' ('... denotes the world of structure, of laws and authoritarianism'). Da Matta explains how this character is just one step away from becoming the naïve, obedient *otário*, who is the favourite victim of the *malandro*.[30] Frequently a loser in love and a figure of pathos or ridicule, the *otário* is also a conscientious worker and upstanding citizen. In many sambas, earning an honest living is seen to be the only way forward, both for the individual and for Brazil as a nation. Irrespective of the power of censorship and the incentives offered to popular musicians to support the state in their work, the effects of Vargas's support among the lower classes and the success of his attempts to mould working-class consciousness cannot entirely be disregarded.

Women and affairs of the heart

The other main theme of samba lyrics from the 1930s and early 1940s was that of women and romantic love. The profession of *sambista* was a male-only bastion, as was popular song writing in Brazil, by and large, until the 1950s.[31] The lyrics of samba were therefore written from a totally male perspective, which excluded any female voice. Within the discourse of samba lyrics from this period women fall into three distinct categories: firstly, that of the cunning, faithless *femme fatale* or *malandra*, secondly, that of the dreary, long-suffering domestic drudge, and, finally, that of the deified fantasy woman.[32] These three stereotypes have obvious parallels with universal representations of women, such as those identified by feminist critics in western literature of male authorship, according to which womanhood is either represented by the angel woman or the she-devil.[33] The drudge shares many qualities with the self-sacrificing, virginal, ideal mate, and the *malandra* is the archetypal whore, an autonomous, sexually active deviant, who is rejected by society. Yet they also fit into a more specific Brazilian context.

In Brazil's literary tradition stereotypical portrayals of black and mulatto women predominate. The Naturalist School depicted the dusky, sensual *mulata*; for example, Aluísio Azevedo's novel *O cortiço* (*The Tenement*), published in 1890, has as one of its protagonists Rita Bahiana, a mulatto girl who is faithful to no one but who has an almost bewitching power over men, which she manipulates to her own ends. David Brookshaw states that she is entirely controlled by her fickleness and sensuality, and is thus a typical naturalistic heroine. The '*Mulata* Myth' also embraces an element of danger; she poses a threat to the established order and harmony. In Coelho Neto's novel *Turbilhão* (*Whirlwind*), published in 1906, to quote one example, we see the havoc caused by a mulatto woman's seduction of a man from a white family striving to keep its position within the urban middle class, and the reader is implicitly warned against such contact. Later in the twentieth century, the novels of Jorge Amado took up this same traditional theme; the best illustration is *Gabriela, cravo e canela* (*Gabriela, Clove and Cinnamon*), published in 1958, in which the *mulata* is the incarnation of the white man's sexual fantasy. As David Brookshaw affirms: 'She is not allowed to exist either as a wife or as a mother, for she is a symbol of sexual license. She is respected neither as a woman nor as an individual. Her function is to attract men, to be exploited by them, and to exploit in turn by obtaining her own ends through sex'.[34] Such stock types as that of the lascivious mulatto woman find their historic origins in the slave system. As Sônia Maria Giacomini observes, slave women were seen as sex objects by the masters of the plantations, free of any kind of religious or moral impediment, alien to roles reserved for the white women of the plantation house, such as procreation. Slave women, particularly the more desirable half-castes, thus became the target of the hatred and jealousy of the white women of the *casa-grande* (plantation house). Cases of the latter inflicting hideous torture and mutilations on their black rivals were not uncommon. Their husbands and legitimate sons sought to excuse their infidelities and over-active libidos by stressing the wanton nature of the black and mulatto women. Thus the myth of the manipulative mulatto sex goddess was engendered.[35]

The *malandra* is the mulatto temptress *par excellence* and, as her name suggests, she represents the female equivalent of the debauched, lazy *malandro*. She is characterized in countless sambas by her treachery, dishonesty and lascivious lifestyle. Like the *malandro*, she exploits the opposite sex for her own ends. Sometimes her victim is the naïve, hard-working and long-suffering *otário*, whose heart she easily breaks. At other times it is the like-minded *malandro* himself who falls prey to her womanly wiles. She belongs to no one man and like the *malandro* she rejects domesticity and honest employment in favour of living off her wits and indulging her every desire. The *malandro* cannot live without her and vice versa, and yet both distrust the opposite sex and shield themselves from emotional involvement and commitment. The *malandra* is a challenge to male domination since she exposes the one weak point in the character of the *malandro*. This otherwise wordly Romeo lays himself open to exploitation by falling for her charms, thus running the risk of becoming his antithesis, the *otário*. Male *sambistas* openly confessed to this Achilles' heel in the figure of the *malandro*, despite the fact that he was the mythical hero of the *morros*. The *malandro* is dependent on the *malandra* in order to justify his habitual distrust and callous treatment of women, since she has caused him to be constantly on his guard against emotional trauma and financial exploitation. She is exemplified in the following samba by Sinhô:

'Não quero saber mais dela' (*'Samba da Favela'*), 1927, Sinhô

A mulher que eu mais amava
Foi morar lá na Favela
Eu não quero saber mais dela
Pois brigava todo dia
Sem eu nada lhe fazer
E caía na orgia
Da noite ao amanhecer
E dizia a toda gente
Que era livre, e era só
Era filha de serpente

Neta de cobra cipó
Com a boca na botija
Lhe peguei no feiticeiro
Fazendo grossa cuxiva[36]
Com o próprio meu dinheiro
Dês aí lhe fiz a trouxa
E mandei levar a ela
Que pra se vingar de mim
Foi morar lá na Favela

'I Don't Want Anything More to do with Her' ('Shantytown Samba'), 1927, Sinhô

The woman I loved most
Went to live in the shantytown
I don't want anything more to do with her

She fought all the time
But I did nothing to her
And she joined in the orgy
From dusk 'til dawn
And she told everybody
That she was free, that she was alone
She was the serpent's daughter
The cobra's granddaughter

I caught her swigging from a bottle
With the sorcerer
Making witchcraft
With my money
So I packed her bags for her
And sent them to her
To get her own back
She went off to live in the shantytown

Typically, the *malandra* character in this samba has a penchant for heavy drinking, witchcraft and other carnal pleasures, the double meaning inherent in the term *orgia* (orgy) reflecting the association made by *sambistas* between female independence and sexual promiscuity. The hackneyed image of her as the snake-like *fin-de-siècle* temptress is given a particularly prosaic treatment here, in keeping with the status of samba in the 1920s, when the genre was still stigmatized as a cultural manifestation of poor blacks (Sinhô himself was a mulatto) and *sambistas* had not yet begun to adapt their lyrics for the more sophisticated tastes of the record-buying radio listeners who emerged in the 1930s.

The figure of the domestic drudge is the antithesis in terms of behaviour and fidelity of the *malandra*, and is epitomized in the famous samba '*Ai, que saudades da Amélia*' ('Oh, How I Miss Amélia'), written by Ataúlfo Alves and Mário Lago in 1941, and in the samba '*Emília*' ('Emília') of 1941, by Wilson Baptista and Haroldo Lobo, the protagonist of which is an exemplary, good-hearted, acquiescent housewife:[37]

'*Emília*', 1941, Wilson Baptista and Haroldo Lobo

Quero uma mulher que saiba lavar e cozinhar
Que de manhã cedo me acorde na hora de trabalhar
Só existe uma
E sem ela eu não vivo em paz
Emília, Emília, Emília
Eu não posso mais

Igual a ela ninguém sabe fazer meu café
Não desfazendo nas outras Emília é mulher
Papai do céu é quem sabe a falta que ela me faz
Emília, Emília, Emília
Eu não posso mais

'Emilia', 1941, Wilson Baptista and Haroldo Lobo

I want a woman who knows how to wash and cook
Who wakes me early when it's time for work
There's only one
And without her I cannot live in peace
Emilia, Emilia, Emilia
I can't take any more

Nobody can make my breakfast like she can
Without offending others, Emilia is the woman
God above knows how much I miss her
Emilia, Emilia, Emilia
I can't take any more

Submissive, passive and altruistic, the drudge is ready and willing to pander to her partner's every whim. She is the ideal mate of the honest, hard-working *malandro regenerado* who appeared in the 1940s, and she features predominantly in sambas from the beginning of that decade. She is a one-dimensional home-maker who is denied any sexuality of her own. Her sole functions are to hold the family and home together, and to uphold the double standards of the macho world that *sambistas* recreated.

José Ramos Tinhorão argues that the social transformations brought about by industrialization led to a change in the attitude to women expressed in samba lyrics. He uses the sambas '*Emília*' and '*Ai, que saudades da Amélia*', cited above, to illustrate this change. He proposes that until 1942 (both these sambas featured in the Rio carnival celebrations of that year) such naïve female characters were exploited by the cruel *malandro* since they would tolerate his wanton ways and support him financially in his hand-to-mouth existence. However, Tinhorão observes that as Vargas tried to bring about a turn-around in the attitude of the lower classes to manual labour, and integrate them fully into the workforce, the factory worker, a newcomer to the lyrics of popular song in Brazil, began his quest for a trustworthy female companion to take care of him and thus the figure of the housewife came to be venerated. Tinhorão views such a portrayal of women in a positive light, seeing it as an indication that the working man has at last learned to appreciate his selfless mate.[38]

Finally, the idealized, mythical goddess, although much rarer, is an important reflection of the ultimate dream of the macho *sambista*. She is the amalgam of the previous two stereotypes. She has the physical attractiveness and desirability of the *malandra*, but has none of her malice or treachery, and yet she too is synonymous with the home, which, like her, is barely recognizable as a humble shantytown dwelling, as shown in the following example:

'*A mulher dos sonhos meus*', 1941, Ataúlfo Alves and Orlando Monello

Tenho tudo que andava procurando enfim
Tenho o meu doce lar
E um amor que gosta muito de mim
Encontrei a mulher dos sonhos meus
Graças a Deus

Um doce lar
Que prazer
Que alegria
Alguém que me sabe amar
Isso mesmo é que eu queria
Um violão pra tocar pro meu amor
Teve fim a solidão
Teve fim a minha dor

'The Woman of My Dreams', 1941, Ataúlfo Alves and Orlando Monello

I've got everything I've been looking for at last
I've got my home sweet home
And my love who really loves me
I've found the woman of my dreams
Thank God

A sweet home
What pleasure
What joy
Someone who knows how to love me
That is just what I wanted
A guitar to play to my love
My loneliness has ended
So has my pain

It has been suggested that the *malandra* and the drudge are two sides of the same feminine ideal in a male-dominated society, and therefore that the alternating use of these female images corresponds not to any historical changes, but rather that these two disparate stereotypes sit happily side by side throughout this period.[39] It would also seem that at times these two divergent fantasies merge in the form of the dream woman we see here.

These female stock types and their characteristics are obviously seen from a male standpoint, and their relevance lies particularly in the way they contrast with the portrayal of the opposite sex in these lyrics. The *malandra*, unlike her male counterpart, is not praised for her free-wheeling, hedonistic existence, but is condemned, instead, for her heartless treatment of her lovers. She behaves unacceptably when she pursues an identical lifestyle to that which is perfectly respectable for and even expected of her male opposite number. Her activities, it is always implied, pose a threat to the fabric of society as a whole. In flouting patriarchal control such women become dangerous to society. The *malandro*, in contrast, provides an alternative lifestyle that helps to offer a solution to the pressures to accept poorly paid, demeaning, manual labour. Furthermore, the *malandro* stud is revered for his sexual prowess and control over women. The domestic drudge, epitomized by the characters of Amélia and Emília, is merely an extension of the cosy *lar* or home. The sole attributes she is given relate to her role as selfless, hard-working housewife, faithful partner and doting parent. Conversely, when these characteristics are present in the male they are ridiculed, and are embodied in the figure of the *otário* or *caxias,* the mug who works very hard for little monetary reward and remains faithful to his mate despite often being cuckolded in return. Furthermore, Amélia is venerated for her lack of vanity, yet one of the most vaunted qualities of the *malandro* is his dapper dress sense and his obsession with his personal appearance.

One of the consequences of Vargas's industrialization drive was the large-scale entry of women into the workforce, principally as factory workers. Furthermore, many black women from Rio's poor districts operated their own informal sector, providing for their children alone by cooking food to sell in the streets. A male presence in the home was often temporary, and such women had an independent income, as well as considerable social power. In many cases they used their informal network of contacts to find work for their male companions.[40] In spite of this, the issue of female employment is rarely tackled in samba lyrics, with the notable exception of Noel Rosa's '*Três apitos*' ('Three Whistles') of 1933 and his '*Você vai se quiser*' ('Go If You Want To') of 1936, the latter allegedly inspired by his wife's request to go out to work.[41] In addition, the portrayal of women in samba lyrics perpetuates the prevalent sexist attitudes of the time they were written. The countless sambas which deal with the subject of domestic violence provide a clear illustration of this. In 1924 the *sambista* Sinhô, in his samba '*Já-Já*', wrote:

'*Já-Já*', 1924, Sinhô

Se essa mulher fosse minha
Apanhava uma surra já-já
Eu lhe pisava todinha
Até mesmo eu lhe dizer chega

'Right Now', 1924, Sinhô

If that woman were mine
She'd get a hiding right now
I'd pound her all over
Until I'd said she'd had enough

This theme continued into the 1930s and the tone of such songs was light-hearted, and trivialized the issue. The total absence of taboo surrounding this topic would seem to suggest that it was just one more everyday occurrence, part of the banal *cotidiano* (daily life) that samba lyrics gave value to, and to which no outrage or even distaste were attached. It is rather a source of amusement in many cases. In such sambas the flirtatious antics or infidelities of women are seen as a just cause of this violence, or else women are portrayed as masochists who provoke it. In Noel Rosa's samba '*O maior castigo que eu te dou*' ('The Biggest Punishment I Can Give You') of 1934, for example, the male pours verbal venom on his fickle lover, threatening to punish her by not giving her a good hiding, because she enjoys such physical abuse:

'*O maior castigo que eu te dou*', 1934, Noel Rosa

O maior castigo que eu te dou
É não te bater
Pois sei que gostas de apanhar
Não há ninguém mais calmo do que eu sou
Nem há maior prazer
Do que te ver me provocar

'The Biggest Punishment I Can Give You', 1934, Noel Rosa

The biggest punishment I can give you
Is not to hit you
'Cos I know you enjoy a good beating
There's no one calmer than I am
And there's no greater pleasure
Than to see you provoke me

It is interesting to note that after 1937, the year of the installation of the protectionist and paternalist New State, the figure of the battered wife disappears from samba discourse.

Finally, it is apparent that sambas from the 1930-45 era on the subject of women and love are often tinged with allusions to money, or more frequently to a lack of it, as in the following example:

'*Não é economia*' ('*Alô padeiro*'), 1943, Wilson Baptista and Haroldo Lobo

Alô padeiro
Bom dia
De manhã em diante
Eu vou suspender o pão
Eu explico a razão
Não é economia
É que aqui em casa
Eu agora estou sozinho
Aquela morena já não
Me faz companhia

Avisa o quitandeiro
Que eu briguei com a Dulcineca
Sem ela pra que legumes?
Neca, Neca
Vendi o rádio, a nossa cama e o fogão
Eu vou comer de colher
Numa boa pensão

'It's Not To Save Money' ('Hello Baker'), 1943, Wilson Baptista and Haroldo Lobo

Hi there, baker
Hello
As from tomorrow
I'm going to cancel my bread
The reason is
Not to save money
It's just that here at home
I'm all alone now
That dark girl no longer
Keeps me company

Let the grocer know
That I broke up with Dulcineca
Without her what's the use of vegetables?
Neca, Neca
I sold the radio, our bed and the stove
I'm going to eat with a spoon
In a good boarding house

Here solitude and poverty go hand in hand, and the home has disintegrated as a result of the woman's act of desertion. In other cases the love of a good woman can compensate for an absence of material wealth. Conversely, the love of a grasping *malandra* frequently leads to a man's financial exploitation by her. The issue of poverty is rarely tackled overtly by *sambistas*, as one would expect given the watchful eyes of the censors, and the women/love theme predominates. It has therefore been suggested that conflicts in the love-life sphere, so often the theme of sambas, and particularly of the more morose sub-genre known as *samba-canção*, throughout this period, were sometimes used as a metaphor for the trials of financial hardship in the poor areas of the city.[42] It could be that certain composers sought to convey the real-life struggle for survival via the exaggeration of their love-life traumas.[43] This possible ambiguity would lend weight to the argument that the theme of *malandragem* was not eliminated by censorship, but rather that it found more subtle expression in the nuances of language and imagery.

In summary, the two thematic strands of *malandragem* and women/romantic love permeate samba lyrics from the 1930s and '40s, and form the backdrop against which the work of the three *sambistas* examined in this book must be viewed. It is only by setting their lyrics within the general context and tacit conventions of samba in this era that any meaningful analysis can be carried out, and it is in this way that the importance of intertextuality and the compliance with or, conversely, the flouting of traditions can be appreciated. The choice of illustrative songs by other composers from the period in this chapter is intended to establish the overall framework within which Ataúlfo Alves, Noel Rosa and Ari Barroso were writing.

Notes

1. Tinhorão, J. R. (1988), p. 37.
2. Ibid., pp. 46-7.
3. Gerhard Kubik remarks on the manner in which cultural manifestations may be persecuted or driven underground, but are still retained in the subconscious of their creators, until such time as they can resurface again: 'In a time of slavery and oppression some specific cultural traits may be forced to disappear among their carriers. They do not really disappear. They only "retreat" to a safer area of the human psyche. For example, if you prosecute drumming in an African community and even burn all the drums of the people, what will happen? The drums will perhaps really disappear and the drum patterns will not be sounded again, but they will still remain - in a silent shape. The drum patterns will just retreat into the "body" of the people. And there inside they will remain like on a micro-film. This has nothing to do with genetics, because the transmission is cultural, through human interaction. The drum patterns will be transformed into a set of "motional behaviour"; they will go back to their source. In this form they will continue to be transmitted from mothers and grandmothers to their children, from father to son during work, non-verbally, as an "awareness" of a style of moving. When a favourable moment in history comes, the drum patterns surface again, perhaps on some other instruments. Some young people suddenly "invent" something new.'

Kubik, G. (1979), pp. 49-50.
4. Sodré, M. (1983), p. 239.
5. Matos, C. (1982), p. 29.
6. Sodré, M. (1988), p. 146.
7. Such communication was largely considered unthinkable, as Maria Júlia Goldwasser makes clear in her study of the Mangueira samba school. 'No tempo em que a Escola era interiorizada no Morro, a ida de pessoas "de fora" constituía um acontecimento tão insólito no lugar, que até ia-se buscar e levar "lá fora na calçada" aqueles raros visitantes "ilustres"' ('In the times when the School was located within the hillside shantytown, the arrival of people from "outside" constituted such an unusual occurrence that someone was even sent "out there into the street" to bring up those rare, "illustrious" visitors'.) Goldwasser, M. J. (1975), p. 40.
8. Rowe, W. and Schelling, V. (1991), pp. 35-6, 171, 175.
9. Rowe and Schelling call this ethos '... a kind of counter-culture of play and leisure from which the petty-bourgeois values of work and respect for money and authority were excluded' and '... a counter-cultural idealization of idleness and of the body as a source of pleasure rather than as an instrument of work'. Ibid., pp. 130, 139.
10. Nestor de Holanda mentions two of the most famous *carioca malandros* of this era, known as *'Meia-Noite'* ('Midnight') and *'Mme. Satã'* ('Mme Satan'), in his book *Memórias do Café Nice*, pp. 156, 171.
11. Antonio Candido (1970), p. 71.
12. Villaverde, C. (1972).
13. Matta, R. Da (1979), p. 134.
14. Adamo, S. C. (1983), p. 28.
15. Tinhorão, J. R. (1990), p. 229.
16. Adamo, S. C. (1983), p. 187.
17. Goldwasser, M. J. (1975), p. 120.
18. Borges, D. (1995), pp. 70-71.
19. Kubik, G. (1979), p. 33.
20. See Fry, P. (1982), pp. 47-53 (esp. 52-3). For further information on this process of cultural cooption, particularly on the economic control of samba schools and carnival processions, see Rodrigues, A. M. (1984).
21 Menezes, E. D. B. de (1982), pp. 9-14.
22. *Feijoada* is thought to have been created by the slaves on the colonial plantations, who combined beans and other ingredients with the scraps of meat, particularly pork, discarded by their masters.
23. In the words of Peter Fry: ' ... a conversão de símbolos étnicos em símbolos nacionais não apenas oculta uma situação de dominação racial mas torna muito mais difícil a tarefa de denunciá-la. Quando se convertem símbolos de "fronteiras" étnicas em símbolos que afirmam os limites da nacionalidade, converte-se o que era originalmente perigoso em algo "limpo", "seguro", e "domesticado". Agora que o candomblé e o samba são considerados "chiques" e respeitáveis, perderam o poder que antes possuíam' ('... the conversion of ethnic symbols into national symbols does not only hide a situation of racial domination but also makes it much more difficult to denounce. When symbols of ethnic "boundaries" are converted into symbols that affirm the limits of nationality, what was originally dangerous is converted into something "clean", "safe", and "domesticated". Now that *candomblé* and samba are considered "chic" and respectable, they have lost the power that they once had'). Fry, P. (1982), pp. 52-3.
24. Matos, C. (1986), pp. 35-60 (esp. 40).
25. According to the popular musician and radio star Almirante, Noel did not yet know

Wilson when he wrote this song, but did so 'Movido por louvável interesse pela regeneração dos temas poéticos da música popular' ('Moved by a commendable interest in the regeneration of poetic themes in popular music'). Almirante (1977), p. 146.

26. *Tamancos* are translated into English as 'clogs', but only the sole was made of wood. The top of this type of footwear, which was worn by the poor, consisted of a leather strap.

27. Matos, C. (1986), pp. 51-2.

28. Vasconcelos, G. (1977), p. 102.

29. The samba *'Bonde da Piedade'* ('The Piedade Tram'), written by Geraldo Pereira and Ari Monteiro in 1945, provides a good example of the new, clean-living worker. Another example of this character can be seen in *'O bonde São Januário'* ('The São Januário Tram') of 1940, by Ataúlfo Alves and Wilson Baptista, p. 69. For more information on the tram as a theme in carnival music see Tinhorão, J. R. [n.d.], *Música popular: um tema em debate*, pp. 138-57.

30. Matta, R. Da (1979), p. 134, 208.

31. The notable exception was the female singer-songwriter Chiquinha Gonzaga (1847-1934). Her famous carnival *marcha 'Ó Abre Alas'* ('Make Way'), written in 1899, was the first registered *marcha*, as well as the first song to be written specifically for carnival. McGowan, C. and Pessanha, R. (1998), p. 37.

32. Berlinck, M. T. (1976), pp. 101-14 (esp. 101-2).

33. See Gilbert, S. and Gubar, S. (1979), *The Madwoman in the Attic: The Female Writer and the Nineteenth-Century Literary Imagination*. See also Ellmann, M. (1979), *Thinking about Women*, and Sharpe, S. (1976), *Just Like a Girl: How Girls Learn to be Women*, Chapter Three, on media stereotypes of women as sex symbols, domestic drudges or virulent harridans.

34. Brookshaw, D. (1986), pp. 27, 40, 65, 164.

35. Giacomini, S. M. (1988), p. 66. The *'Mulata* Temptress Tradition' is identified by Raymond S. Sayers (1956) in his book *The Negro in Brazilian Literature* , p. 49.

36. *Cuxiva* is a type of witchcraft associated with Afro-Brazilian cult practices.

37. *'Ai, que saudades da Amélia'* is examined in detail in Chapter Four, pp. 63-4.

38. Tinhorão, J. R. (1982), pp. 11-14.

39. Berlinck, M. T. (1976), p. 111.

40. Velloso, M. P. (1990), pp. 207-28 (esp. 211-13).

41. See pp. 133-5 for the entire lyrics of *'Três apitos'*.

42. Matos, C. (1978), pp. 5-7.

43. Borges, B. (1982), pp. 69, 94-5. Borges argues, with specific reference to *samba-canção*, that writing such songs performs a cathartic function for the composer and presumably, on hearing them, for the audience too. She claims that the male composers and protagonists of their songs may even be genuinely confused as to the exact cause of their material and emotional ills.

CHAPTER TWO

The Vargas Regime (1930-45): Cultural Policy and Popular Culture

When Getúlio Vargas came to power in 1930 the development of industrial production and of labour and social welfare legislation were two of his main objectives. In Vargas's opinion, industrialization was the key to a strong nation-state, and had to be accompanied by advances in social welfare and labour protection. He created two new ministries during the period of his Provisional Government (1930-33): the Ministry of Labour, founded in November 1930 and later expanded to encompass Industry and Commerce in February 1931, and the Ministry of Education and Health. The Wall Street Crash of 1929 and the ensuing Great Depression, which severely reduced the spending power of the USA, Brazil's principal export market, led the price of Brazilian coffee to plummet from 22.5 cents per pound in 1929 to just eight cents in 1931. Brazil's purchasing power abroad collapsed, but this was offset by maintaining a reasonable level of internal consumption via the government's support policy to coffee growers. Consequently, the conditions for industrialization were favourable in the early 1930s, and the surge in industrial output in the 1930s was a consequence of both governmental policy and the collapse of competition from overseas manufacturers. Between 1930 and 1939, 12,232 new industrial establishments were set up in Brazil, as opposed to only 4697 in the previous decade.[1] This transformation of the industrial landscape was most noticeable in São Paulo, a fact which may have helped redress the state's loss of political influence under Vargas.

Vargas strongly supported the legislation created by the new Ministry of Labour under Lindolfo Collor. In December 1930 the *Lei de Nacionalização do Trabalho* (Law of Nationalization of Labour) was introduced, by which two-thirds of the workforce of every firm had to be Brazilian nationals. Decrees were issued to regulate employers' and workers' bodies and to establish minimum holidays for employees. In March 1932 Pedro Salgado Filho became Minister of Labour, and he introduced legislation on female and child labour, and fixed an eight-hour maximum working day. Health and education were also prioritized by the Vargas administration, and throughout the 1930s various campaigns to stamp out diseases were promoted, including widespread vaccination against tuberculosis, and the reorganization of schooling. In the late 1930s and early '40s, the Minister of Labour, Valdemar Falcão, was instrumental in introducing trade union legislation, based on Fascist models (1939), labour tribunals to settle conflicts between workers and management, the improvement of pension facilities, and the widening of concessions for the poor (a compulsory minimum wage was introduced on 1 May 1940).

Nicknamed '*Pai dos Pobres*' ('Father of the Poor'), Vargas gained widespread support among the members of the nascent working masses. The year 1930 heralded a new era in terms of class relations, in which the state strove to create a dignified proletariat, proud of its contribution to the establishment of a better, more prosperous nation. There can be no doubt that Vargas was determined to coopt the labour force into a recognized place in Brazilian society and political life, and this pragmatic manoeuvre may or may not have been combined with a genuine sense of sympathy with the plight of the proletariat during the first years of industrialization. The policies of the authoritarian *Estado Novo*, established in 1937, aimed to represent the interests of capital, both industrial and agrarian, and to reorganize society. The middle and working classes were incorporated into the new social structure, but the intention was to neutralize the political activities of these new social forces. The dominant belief was that only a strong, centralized government could bring about true democracy, and nationalism went hand in hand with this autocratic stance since it legitimized the state's absolute sovereignty and its control over the whole country. Furthermore, nationalism presupposed that all Brazilians identified with a common destiny, with its roots in a shared past. The state was perceived as responsible for the morality of the nation, and capable of redressing Brazil's backwardness in relation to the developed world.

The *Estado Novo* maintained close, cordial links with Brazil's ruling classes, namely the rural oligarchy and the urban bourgeoisie, and thus Vargas was able to introduce sweeping political changes with the minimum of reaction. Vargas personified the state, and was credited with having established order to Brazil in turbulent times. The impact of his mythical image can be seen in the following quotation from the newspaper *Estado de São Paulo*, 19 April 1942:

> Graças a essa ordem admirável em que vivemos, de perfeito equilíbrio moral e material, é que nosso país se tornou exceção no mundo convulsionado de 1942. Sentimos da conflagração o menos possível ... Graças a esse homem providencial as comoções pelas quais o Brasil tem passado não deixaram manchas indeléveis. Ele é menos o presidente da República, que o chefe da família brasileira. Seu maior carinho é para os que mais sofrem (It is thanks to the admirable order in which we live, in perfect moral and material balance, that our country has become an exception in the turbulent world of 1942. We

feel the least possible repercussions of the conflagration ... Thanks to this man
of foresight the disturbances that Brazil has experienced have not left indelible
marks. More than just the president of the Republic, he is the head of the
Brazilian family. He shows most affection towards those who suffer most). [2]

The propaganda of the regime aimed to coopt the urban working classes
by addressing them in populist discourse which denied the existence of
social classes and stressed, instead, the role of the all-embracing,
benevolent state. Society was presented as being a homogeneous group,
and labour was portrayed as the key to human dignity. The labour laws
were a way of integrating the workers into society, and instilling in them a
sense of cooperation with the government in the development of the nation
as a whole. The regime's relations with the emerging working class were
improved by the upsurge in demand for Brazilian goods caused by the
outbreak of the Second World War, which took Brazil out of the industrial
crisis of the first years of the *Estado Novo*. The textile industry, for
example, had been in decline since 1938, and only returned to 24-hour
production in 1941. The size of the urban population and of the proletariat
grew rapidly from the 1920s to the 1940s. The government offered
incentives to the unemployed to return to the countryside, but migration to
the Rio-São Paulo axis continued unabated. In 1920 the number of
industrial workers was calculated to be 293,673, and in 1940, 781,185.[3]
The legislation introduced after 1930 to protect the rights of the proletariat
also had the effect of successively curtailing its independence. The *Lei de
Sindicalização* (Trade Union Law) of April 1931, for example, obliged all
trade unions to become affiliated to the Ministry of Labour, and their
leaders were gradually replaced by the government. *Peleguismo* involved
planting, in top trade union positions, hand-picked government supporters,
who obsequiously paid homage to Vargas and the state in their speeches to
their members. Communist sympathizers amongst the workforce were
pursued with ferocity by the chiefs of police of the federal district of Rio.
Physical torture was commonplace and the expulsion of workers' leaders
became a frequent occurrence. Government propaganda also helped to
create the image of an acquiescent workforce. In spite of these repressive
and coercive steps, illegal demonstrations and protests did take place, with
the communist movement reemerging in 1942, and in 1945 strike action
confirmed the continued ideological convictions of a small, politicized,
hard core of the working class.

Brasilidade and the forging of a national identity

The forging of a national consciousness, or *brasilidade*, and the creation of
an emblematic iconography of state were central concerns of the

Vargas administration, particularly in the aftermath of the 1930 revolution, and throughout the ensuing 15 years they were to mould cultural policy in response both to a need for national integration and to the challenges posed by Brazil's increasingly multi-ethnic demographic profile. In the period of political uncertainty and instability which followed the coup of 1930, the need for a strong, unifying identity was paramount. This was especially the case given the vast size of the nation and the importance of regional politics and regional identities. The traditional rivalry between the most powerful states, particularly São Paulo and Minas Gerais, and the exclusion of the northeast and the south from national politics, had aggravated the lack of national unity. Under the Old Republic the growth of a national consciousness had been inhibited by these factors. The waves of immigrants entering Brazil from Europe and Japan from the end of the nineteenth century onwards complicated the situation further. In November 1930 the Revolutionary Union was created as an attempt to establish a national political movement in support of the revolution. Although the idea of such a national party soon collapsed, it is significant that it aimed to emphasize the idea of *brasilidade*, as well as to act as a counterbalance to the army and to replace the regional parties.

The regime's fears of regional opposition were proved justified by the *Paulista* (São Paulo) civil war which began on 9 July 1932, when a popular movement took control of São Paulo in the name of a free constitution for Brazil, and ended with the surrender of the insurgents at the close of September. In order to consolidate Vargas's political position, which had been bolstered by the prestige he had acquired from this victory over the *Paulistas*, elections were held on 3 May 1933. The elections were carried out on a regional basis, as was the case before 1930, and with the notable exception of the state of São Paulo, the outcome was to the government's advantage. Between November 1932 and May 1933 a commission was hard at work on the draft of a new constitution. The final document contained a pronounced nationalist undercurrent, and it restricted immigration, ostensibly of Japanese nationals to São Paulo, but more significantly of Jewish refugees from Europe. The strict separation of church and state, inherited from the 1891 constitution, was modified in favour of the church, and divorce was made illegal. Further elections in October 1934 gave Vargas a comfortable majority at a federal level, but saw a considerable revival of the power of the regional oligarchies in the states. Throughout 1934 and 1935 there were fierce political battles, sometimes ending in violence. In response to the volatility of several states and the anti-communist reaction unleashed after left-wing revolts in the northeast, in April 1935 the government introduced its National

Security Law, institutionalizing wide-ranging powers of repression and extending the presidential powers. Although Brazil was officially governed by the liberal 1934 constitution until the establishment of the *Estado Novo*, this was a period of harsh repression, particularly of communist and other left-wing sympathizers.

Throughout the Vargas era, debates on the issue of identity had a profound impact on policy-making. The regime's immediate response to this concern was to tighten immigration policy. In the long term every effort was made to promote a self-consciously national culture, of which popular culture formed an important part, and to shape a new historical identity for Brazilians. The early 1930s witnessed a perceptible shift in Brazil's self-image. Whilst white European immigration and the ideology of *branqueamento* continued to be glorified and encouraged, the term *europeu* (European) ceased to embrace Jews or Arabs, who were now considered undesirable and portrayed in the press as a threat to the fabric of the nation.[4] The *brasilidade* campaign led to the closure of foreign-language schools, and the use of the Portuguese language was made compulsory throughout the Brazilian press. This wave of cultural nationalism particularly targeted the German and Italian immigrant communities of the south, and the Japanese and Italians who had settled in São Paulo state. As nationalism and xenophobia became powerful political tools, and the scientific, racialist doctrines of the dictatorships of Europe gathered credence in Brazil, the regime endeavoured to cultivate a new identity for the nation, based on a mythical, white European template.

President Vargas's personal fascination with the preservation and exhibition of Brazil's heritage manifested itself a little over two weeks after the 1930 revolution when he donated a flag used by the victors in the rebellion in the state of Paraná to the *Museu Histórico Nacional* (National Historical Museum), a hitherto highly traditional archive of historical relics, each with clear associations with national heroes, such as the emperors Pedro I (1798-1834) and Pedro II (1825-91), and Tiradentes, the leader of the failed independence movement of the late eighteenth century. Consequently, a blatant symbol of the armed struggle which brought Vargas to power became intrinsically linked to the centuries-old process of forging a strong, independent, unified nation-state. The Vargas administration went on to establish a network of institutions charged with the preservation of the nation's historical memory, such as the afore-mentioned museum, which was totally revamped on the orders of the new administration, and displayed an incongruous mixture of historical artefacts and contemporary objects. The museum conveniently overlooked the unseemlier aspects of Brazil's history, inviting visitors simply to marvel at the country's continuing successes. By foregrounding glories past and present the regime sought to justify its position as the next logical phase in a process of nation-building which dated back to the end of the colonial period.[5]

The quest for a national identity was also undertaken by the right-wing Integralists. As well as adopting regalia and paramilitary apparatus based on the models of Mussolini's Italy and Hitler's Germany, they greeted each other with the Tupi Indian term '*Anauê*', and their leader, Plínio Salgado, had learned the Tupi language in an effort to find a distinctive Brazilian nationality. Although the Integralists had helped create favourable conditions for the coup of 1930, the subsequent abolition of all political parties forced them to reorganize as a social and cultural entity. Nevertheless, on 10 and 11 May 1938 militant members of the party attempted a putsch in Rio de Janeiro, supported by some of Vargas's old liberal opponents, but it proved to be abortive.

The *Estado Novo*, announced by Vargas on 10 November 1937, was a response, in part, to his desire and that of the military, to create a strong nation-state and to overcome regional divisions. Throughout 1936 and 1937 Vargas's intentions remained unclear, but on 18 September 1937, the presidential plot was set in motion when he secured the approval of the War Minister, General Dutra, who helped to ensure the support of the military. When the establishment of the new regime was officially announced to the nation, the change was accepted calmly, with only one cabinet member tendering his resignation. Vargas explained his actions in a radio broadcast, emphasizing that in periods of crisis a democratic, multi-party system was a menace to the unity and stability of the nation. A new constitution was quickly introduced, and Article Two evidenced the New State's commitment to forging a national iconography. It prescribed that there should be only one flag, hymn and motto throughout the country, and in accordance with its directives there followed an emotional flagburning of the regional emblems in a Rio de Janeiro square. The new constitution extended Vargas's term of office by six years and on 2 December a decree abolished all political parties. The provision for a plebiscite to approve the new regime was abolished almost as soon as it was announced. Vargas stressed to reporters from democratic countries the essentially democratic nature of his regime, although to the Brazilian public he defended its authoritarian aspects. His stance was typically pragmatic, and he suggested to his close associates that it was simply a step aimed at dealing with the immediate situation, and that the end would justify the means.

The issue of Brazilian nationalism was placed high on the *Estado Novo*'s agenda. A reflection of the growing sense of nationality in the 1930s was the emergence of the military as a political force, yet despite military jealousy between Brazil and Argentina there was no real question of conflict with any of Brazil's Latin American neighbours. Consequently an internal source of patriotic sentiment had to be fostered. On 7 September 1938, at the end of the 'Week of the Fatherland and of the Race', Vargas announced in a radio address:

A prompt solution must be given to the problem of strengthening the race, assuring the cultural and eugenic preparation of the new generations ... The commemorations for the Fatherland and Race ought to be from now on an unequivocal demonstration of our effort to raise the cultural and eugenic level of youth ... For a Brazil, united, for a Brazil strong, for a Brazil great.[6]

In 1944 the *Departamento de Imprensa e Propaganda* (Press and Propaganda Department) or DIP organized a *Congresso de Brasilidade* (Congress on Brazilian Identity). Another aspect of *brasilidade* was the interest in opening up, developing and settling Brazil's vast interior, although the so-called '*marcha para o oeste*' ('march to the west') did not really take off until the 1950s, culminating in the inauguration of the new capital city, Brasília, in 1960. There can be no doubt that Vargas did foster a heightened national awareness among Brazilians and that he helped replace the local particularism of the Old Republic with a sense of nationalism in keeping with the twentieth century and the modern industrial state that he founded.

Edgard Carone says that the *Estado Novo* era was the first time in Brazilian history that deliberate attempts were made to endow the state with a mythical significance. This applied not only to the nation as a whole, but also to its individual representatives. Although these measures never succeeded in reaching the heights of the Fascist regimes in Europe, they managed to accentuate the supposed qualities of the president to a great extent, and to a considerable degree achieved the same results with lesser political figures. The state became identified with people of unique qualities and abilities, who nevertheless paled into insignificance alongside their great leader. In April 1940 whole pages of newspapers were dedicated to Vargas's life and personal attributes. The newspaper *Estado de São Paulo* of 19 April 1940, for example, described the 'coragem, magnanimidade e singeleza, traços característicos do perfil político do Presidente Getúlio Vargas' ('courage, magnanimity and simplicity, characteristics of the political profile of President Getúlio Vargas'). In the following day's edition of the same newspaper, the Minister of External Relations said of Vargas:

Homem sem ódio e sem vaidade; dominado pela preocupação de fazer o bem; servido por um espírito de tolerância exemplar, sistematicamente devotado ao serviço da Pátria, não é de estranhar a situação privilegiada que desfruta na família brasileira (A man without hate or vanity; concerned above all with doing good; blessed with an exemplary spirit of tolerance, systematically devoted to serving the Fatherland, it is thanks to him that the Brazilian family enjoys such a privileged position).[7]

Official commemorations and celebrations were employed to publicize the myths. From 1942 the *Dia do Presidente* (President's Day) had to be celebrated by radio stations, schools, recreational clubs, newspapers and professional institutions. Together with the singing of the national anthem, speeches on Vargas's life and personality had to be read out. Books and leaflets were also produced on these topics by the state and other publishers who were well aware that the government would buy the bulk of them.

Censorship and propaganda

The revolution of 1930 mobilized public opinion in Brazil and awakened a desire for participation in political life among the population. It was thus necessary for the nascent political regime to try to direct and control the opinions of the Brazilian people, and to obtain their support for further political changes. To this end the Provisional Government of 1930 established the *Departamento Oficial de Propaganda* (Official Department of Propaganda) on 2 July 1931, which was transformed into the *Departamento de Propaganda e Difusão Cultural* (Department of Propaganda and Cultural Diffusion) on 10 July 1934, which in turn was renamed the *Departamento de Imprensa e Propaganda* (Press and Propaganda Department) or DIP on 27 December 1939. Of the three bodies, the last was the only truly effective mechanism. The repressive organs of the new dictatorship included Filinto Müller's political information service and the DIP, under the direction of Lourival Fontes from 1939 to 1942, of Major Coelho dos Reis from August 1942 to July 1943, and of Captain Amílcar Dutra de Menezes until the Department was dismantled in 1945. Vargas himself was responsible for appointing the top functionaries of the DIP. The Department's principal function was '... a elucidação da opinião nacional sobre as diretrizes doutrinárias do regime, em defesa da cultura, da unidade espiritual e da civilização brasileira ...' ('... the elucidation of national opinion on the doctrinal directives of the regime, in defence of culture, of spiritual unity and of Brazilian civilization ...').[8] After the establishment of the New State, the DIP set about enhancing Vargas's personal image, and many homes and shops began to display his portrait. His public persona bore little relation to his true character, and with the assistance of the DIP his rather cold and reserved personality was transformed into a likeable, affable public image.

The media referred to him by a variety of nicknames, such as '*o homem de ação*' ('the man of action'), '*o homem do sorriso*' ('the man with a smile'), '*o homem do destino*' ('the man of destiny') and '*o maior trabalhador*' ('the greatest worker').

The media, under the control of the DIP, were used to reiterate and corroborate the ideology of the regime, and to obtain consensus and docility among the public. According to Silvana Goulart, the myth of the easy-going, cordial Brazilian temperament was emphasized, and was presented as the result of a gentle intermingling of races with no reference to the harsh realities of the nation's colonial history. Any aspects that did not confirm this harmonious notion were conveniently overlooked. Thus any unrest among the working class would be seen as unnatural and deviant since it did not correspond to this 'context of cordiality'.[9] The DIP actively encouraged artists and writers to create works that were national in character by means of subsidies, sponsorships and prizes.

The DIP's official publication, *Cultura Política* (*Political Culture*), was the main vehicle for transmitting and legitimizing the official doctrines and philosophies underpinning the *Estado Novo*. This magazine was written by and for intellectuals, and was used by the regime to coopt the intelligentsia into producing highly patriotic contributions, which dealt with national themes relating to contemporary Brazil. The Modernist movement in the Brazilian arts, for example, was interpreted by the editors of *Cultura Política* as an artistic reflection of the political changes begun in 1930, in that it signified a rupture with previous styles and canons and concerned itself with ideas and themes of national inspiration. Contributions to the magazine were made by the leading intellectuals who were linked to the regime, as well as ministers, representatives of the armed forces, and President Vargas himself.

Press censorship under Vargas took various forms, ranging from economic pressure on newspapers that refused to endorse the ideology of the regime after the establishment of the *Estado Novo*, to the seizure of editions and the compulsory inclusion of state-produced news items. No publication could go into circulation without the authorization of the DIP. The state had a monopoly on printing paper and put severe pressure on any opposition publications, with the result that 61 newspapers closed their doors in the face of such adversity. The DIP distributed money for state propaganda purposes, such as the printing of pro-establishment articles. Antônio Pedro Tota suggests that most material that actually reached the newsstands was supplied by the *Agência Nacional* (National Press Agency) or at least was the result of 'suggestions' made by this body.[10] The tone of such articles was characteristically solemn and grandiloquent, and the myth of a picture-postcard Brazil of endless riches was perpetuated. São Paulo was the 'metrópole das chaminés altaneiras' ('metropolis of proud chimney stacks') and the river Amazon gained the dimensions of 'um capítulo da história da civilização, força cega e de fertilidade extraordinária, que pelo trabalho viria a se transformar em energia disciplinada' ('a chapter from the history of civilization, a blind force of extraordinary fertility, that our efforts would transform into disciplined energy').[11] After 1937, journalists were treated like civil servants, and they were responsible for serving the interests of the nation and not of any other political or regional grouping. Furthermore, professional associations were created by the state, ostensibly to support cultural activity, such as the *Instituto Nacional do Livro* (National Book Institute) and the *Instituto Nacional de Cinema Educativo* (National Institute of Educational Cinema). In practice these institutions constituted a mechanism for regulating artistic production. Every cinema was obliged to show the *Jornais Oficiais* (Official Newsreels), and had to show at least one Brazilian full-length film and one short each year, as did casinos and sports clubs, in order to promote and protect the national film industry. The DIP participated in the making of Brazilian films at all levels, and all theatre productions had to undergo *censura prévia* (prior censorship). No forms of improvisation were permitted.

Radio and popular music

Radio and popular music were two principal targets of Vargas's clamp-down on the media. The radio played a crucial role in popularizing the regime since it enabled the state's ideology to reach rural areas outside the normal range of its populist discourse. In accordance with the nationalist fervour of the government, regional differences were attenuated by the power of the radio, which was used as a means of standardizing and integrating the politics and culture of the country as a whole. Radio had taken root in Brazil in the 1920s. On 7 September 1923 Radio Sociedade was inaugurated, and shortly afterwards Radio Clube do Brasil followed suit. This started the invasion of huge antennae throughout the city of Rio. Between 1923 and 1926 the number of radio sets rose from 536 to 30,000.[12] During the 1930s the regime installed radio receivers and loudspeakers in public squares throughout the interior, thus ensuring that radio reached as wide an audience as possible. The *Hora do Brasil*, broadcast daily between eight pm and nine pm by all radio stations in Brazil, was the flagship programme, designed to encourage social and political unity. It claimed to have an informative, a civic and a cultural function. Its civic role took the form of references to the nation's past, a source of pride and enthusiasm which could be channelled into the realization of current objectives. The cultural dimension entailed the promotion of Brazilian music and popular song. Seventy per cent of the music it broadcast was home-grown, and the work of Brazil's most famous popular composers and performers was transmitted to the entire nation.[13]

The *Estado Novo* was well aware of the importance of music as a way of inculcating ideas and reaching individuals on an emotional level. Its usefulness as a tool for achieving national unification and patriotism was often a topic of discussion in the DIP's magazine *Cultura Política*. The state encouraged choral singing in unison, believing that it fostered a sense of belonging, but it was popular music that constituted the ideal vehicle for reaching the illiterate masses and integrating them into the mainstream population. (In 1920, 65.2 per cent of Brazilians over the age of 18 were illiterate and by 1940 the figure was still 56.4 per cent.)[14]

The world-renowned classical musician and composer, Heitor Villa-Lobos, who began life as a popular musician, from 1932 onwards acted as intermediary between the state and popular composers and performers. He was responsible, for example, for the *Dia da Música Popular Brasileira* (Brazilian Popular Music Day), first celebrated at the *Estado Novo*'s national exhibition in January 1939, which brought together the cream of Brazil's popular musicians and performing artists. So-called competitions were organized by the DIP to promote the most prominent artists, but the results were usually rigged in favour of the most loyal and obliging songwriters. In the words of Sérgio Cabral: 'Nos concursos de músicas carnavalescas, nos desfiles de carnaval, nas estações de rádio, nas gravadoras de discos, em tudo estava a mão do DIP' ('In carnival music competitions, in carnival parades, in radio stations, in recording studios, the hand of the DIP was everywhere').[15] After 1935, samba schools were legalized and were obliged to enter the carnival competitions as official entities, each known as a *Grêmio Recreativo Escola de Samba*. From then on the annual parades were organized and financed by the state.

Censorship of radio broadcasts was intensified and in 1940 alone 108 radio programmes were banned by the DIP. In the same year the government took charge of Radio Nacional and thus began a monopoly of the radio audience of Brazil's main cities. This radio station then began to build up the biggest radio 'cast' yet seen in Brazil for any single station, employing many popular musicians, such as Ari Barroso, Lamartine Babo and Almirante. Of the 80 radio stations in Brazil in 1940 (by 1944 there were 110),[16] Radio Nacional thus acquired the greatest number of listeners by far. The DIP supplied both the press and radio stations with lists of forbidden terms, the use of which could result in prison sentences. From 1937 these lists were sent to newspapers every month, and included any reference to the regime before 10 November 1937. The term *'União Soviética'* ('Soviet Union') was also banned from use, yet often the choice of outlawed terms was somewhat idiosyncratic. The use of the term *'amante'* ('lover'), for example, even in phrases such as *'amante da música'* ('music lover'), was prohibited.[17] All radio stations had to broadcast news items supplied to them by the *Agência Nacional*, and all of them were dependent on the state for the concession to operate. As well as the official censors, an independent watchdog was set up by the growing number of radio stations. This was known as the *Comissão de Censura da Confederação Brasileira de Radiodifusão* (Censorship Commission of the Brazilian Confederation of Radiodiffusion) and its remit was to prohibit the transmission of certain pieces of music that had slipped through the DIP's net. One such composition was Wilson Baptista's samba *'Lenço no pescoço'* ('Scarf Around My Neck'), written under the pseudonym of Mário Santoro and recorded by Sílvio Caldas in 1933, which was to trigger Baptista's famous polemic with Noel Rosa. Tight control of the content of song lyrics was assured by the censors of the DIP, whose stamp of approval was required before lyrics could be reproduced on sheet music or recorded on disc.

These repressive measures were accompanied by the cooption of songwriters and performers. The DIP coerced popular composers into creating songs that were patriotic in character by offering attractive incentives, such as sponsorships, subsidies and competition prizes. If they toed the official line and espoused the new work ethic of the Vargas regime, publicly rejecting the traditional theme of samba lyrics, *malandragem*, which advocated a lifestyle of idleness, crime and debauchery, songwriters could receive considerable commercial rewards. The turnaround in the portrayal of the *malandro* is, without doubt, the clearest example of this cooption by the state. As Antônio Pedro Tota explains: '... aos poucos os compositores começaram a substituir o tema mais badalado da música popular - a malandragem e a boemia - pelo seu oposto, o trabalho' ('... gradually composers began to replace the most common theme of popular music - *malandragem* and bohemian living - with its opposite, work').[18] According to Silvana Goulart, after 1940 the DIP advised composers to exalt honest toil in their lyrics and to criticize bohemian lifestyles.[19] The DIP compiled its own record library and archive, and was instructed to record the voices of the 'grandes cidadãos da Pátria' ('great citizens of the Fatherland'), regional songs, and the most famous compositions by the leading popular composers of the day, in addition to any music which could serve as patriotic propaganda. It was thus responsible for assembling an archive of what was considered a very important aspect of national culture. There can be no doubt that the DIP was omnipresent and its impact on popular music immense. In the view of the musicologist Sérgio Cabral: '... o DIP, a partir do golpe de 10 de novembro, tinha absoluto controle da música popular brasileira e de qualquer tipo de manifestação a ela relacionada' ('... the DIP, from the coup of 10 November onwards, had absolute control of Brazilian popular music and of any kind of manifestation linked to it').[20]

The Second World War signalled the start of another phase in the Vargas regime's relationship with popular music and a turning-point in the repressive measures imposed on the latter. In the run-up to the conflict, Vargas had openly sided with the Fascist dictators of Germany and Italy, maintaining strong links with Germany in particular. In January 1936 sambas by the 'Estação Primeira de Mangueira' samba school were transmitted direct to Germany on the radio programme *Hora do Brasil*. Shortly after, Italy received a similar broadcast. Back in Brazil the radio also served Vargas's war propaganda purposes. In a country where there was no nationwide press, the radio was the perfect vehicle for reaching as wide a sector of the population as possible. According to Sérgio Cabral, Vargas:

> montou um esquema de propaganda nos moldes do que fora adotado por Goebbels, sendo o primeiro governante latino-americano a utilizar o rádio como Hitler estava usando (created a propaganda machine along the lines of that adopted by Goebbels, being the first Latin American leader to use the radio in the way that Hitler was using it).[21]

With the outbreak of the war in Europe, Brazil, with its Fascist-style *Estado Novo*, trade links with Germany, Italian and German immigrant populations, and strategic location, became a focus of international attention, particularly from the USA. If Brazil had sided with the Axis powers it could have threatened the supply of raw materials to the USA and British shipping in the South Atlantic. The possibility that some of the continent's nations might support the Axis powers led President Roosevelt to persevere with military agreements and with the Good Neighbour Policy, which promoted cultural exchange with Latin America in order to foster greater understanding and support for the USA's foreign policy. Brazil was officially neutral at the start of the war in Europe. However, German-Brazilian relations were upset by the drive to 'Brazilianize' the German immigrant communities of the south, and by the 1938 Integralist putsch, which prompted the stationing of troops among the German communities as part of the nationality policy. An important commercial deal was signed between Brazil and the United States at the beginning of 1939 and the entente between the two countries was strengthened in

September 1940, with the granting of a twenty million dollar loan from the Export-Import Bank of the USA to build the Volta Redonda steelworks in Brazil. Military agreements soon followed, which made Brazilian bases available in the event of an attack on the USA by a non-American power. By 1941 Brazil's foreign policy obviously hinged on its relations with the USA, and Brazil finally declared war on Germany and Italy on 21 August 1942, in response to torpedo attacks on Brazilian shipping off the northeastern coast. Vargas used Brazil's involvement in the international conflict to press on with industrialization under strict governmental control, and to call for national unity in the face of a common enemy. By sending Brazilian troops to fight in Italy he probably hoped to inspire national pride. He also seized the opportunity offered by wartime conditions to extend his mandate. Along with the DIP's existing censorship of all the media - press, radio, cinema, books, theatre - postal censorship was also imposed with Brazil's entry into the world conflict in 1942.

Paradoxically Brazil's involvement in the war brought with it greater freedom for the nation's popular songwriters, enabling them to criticize and even denounce the *Estado Novo*. As Sérgio Cabral says:

> As brechas contra a censura do DIP só iriam surgir com a entrada do Brasil na guerra, quando, a pretexto de se espinafrar os nazistas, os compositores arranjavam um jeito de exaltar a democracia (The loopholes in the censorship of the DIP would only emerge with the entry of Brazil into the war, when, on the pretext of criticizing the Nazis, composers found a way of praising democracy).[22]

Other composers still preferred to eulogize their leader, providing him with rousing, patriotic numbers.[23] Censorship loosened its grip in Brazil as pressure mounted against the Vargas dictatorship, both within the military and the general public. The year 1942 proved to be the key date in the history of repression and censorship under Vargas. Before then, personal and artistic freedom had been entirely suffocated but, with the change in the course of the war in favour of the Allied powers, the *Estado Novo* became less dictatorial, having little choice but to allow for a redemocratization process. Throughout the media, cases of attacks on the regime and of composers duping the censors grew in number in 1944 and 1945, as the social base of the state began to crumble, and particularly as support among the dominant social classes diminished. In this two-year period newspapers began openly to attack the authoritarian nature of the regime and to question its economic policies. Furthermore, clandestine leaflets and newspapers calling for the fall of the regime sprang up, such as the tabloid *Liberdade* in Rio de Janeiro. As the war reached its end the agricultural and industrial oligarchies, as well as the upper middle class, began to demand redemocratization that would bring about regeneration for the country.

Censorship was, naturally, a pivotal issue in Vargas's relationship with popular music, and thus coloured the portrayal of him and his regime within the lyrics of popular song. However, there were many positive developments instigated by Vargas, particularly his labour laws, and there can be little question that he did enjoy widespread popularity among the masses. As Jairo Severiano says:

> Muitas composições foram dedicadas ao presidente durante o período. Naturalmente, em todas elas só há lugar para o elogio, requisito sem o qual não passariam pelo crivo da censura. Seria injusto, porém, negar o fascínio da personalidade de Getúlio que, não obstante sua posição de ditador, deve ter sinceramente cativado diversos compositores (Many compositions were dedicated to the president during that period. Naturally, in all of them there is only room for praise, the pre-requisite for escaping the scrutiny of the censors. It would be unjust, however, to deny the fascination with Getúlio who, despite his position as dictator, must have sincerely inspired various composers).[24]

One such composition was the samba 'O sorriso do Presidente' ('The President's Smile'), written in 1942 by Alberto Ribeiro and Alcir Pires Vermelho, which takes its lead from one of Vargas's nicknames, 'o homem do sorriso':

'O sorriso do Presidente', 1942, Alberto Ribeiro and Alcir Pires Vermelho

Quem já sondou o teu céu
E já viu o teu mar
Eu sei que não poderá querer
Outro céu, nem outro mar
E sob a benção do azul
E aos beijos do mar
Vive sempre a sonhar
É bem maior que o próprio céu
E maior que o próprio mar
O meu amor por ti
Há um sorriso feliz
Alegrando o país
Onde eu nasci

'The President's Smile', 1942, Alberto Ribeiro and Alcir Pires Vermelho

Whoever has looked into your sky
And has seen your sea
I know that they cannot want
Another sky, nor another sea
And blessed with the blue
And the kisses of the sea
They live in a dream
It's much bigger than the sky itself

And bigger than the sea itself
My love for you
There is a happy smile
Delighting the country
Where I was born

Ultimately, the Second World War was to bring about the downfall of the Vargas administration. At the beginning of 1945 the conflict was reaching its climax, and the *Estado Novo* suddenly lost the support of the Brazilian military, who began to fight amongst themselves to promote Vargas's successor. This weakening of the President's hold on the state apparatus was exploited by journalists and intellectuals to voice their demands for complete freedom of speech and democratic elections. As the year wore on Vargas's plans remained ambiguous. At times he seemed willing to retire to his native Rio Grande do Sul, at others he appeared to be encouraged to stay by his friends and supporters in the so-called '*queremista*' movement (a title coined from the phrase '*Queremos Getúlio*' or 'we want Getúlio'). Much of the working class, who had been drawn into the government's populist pact, adhered to this movement. However, unlike in 1937, Vargas no longer enjoyed the support of the military, who were also committed to free elections. In August and September his popularity rose temporarily with the return of the expeditionary force from Europe, but the crisis gathered pace on 10 October when he suddenly changed the electoral rules by bringing forward the date of the proposed state elections to 2 December. Fearing that he could do the same again, a group of army generals, under the leadership of Pedro Gois Monteiro, prepared to act. The military had become increasingly politicized since their involvement in the world conflict, where they had come into contact with Anglo-US views on democracy and commerce. Having contributed to the defeat of totalitarian regimes in Europe they were now faced with the paradox of an authoritarian dictatorship at home. The *Estado Novo* could no longer survive in a post-war climate where democracy had triumphed over totalitarianism. Gois, as Minister of War, publicly promised to guarantee presidential elections, then resigned from his post, put military commands throughout Brazil on standby alert and made himself supreme commander of the Air Force and Navy. When Vargas refused to negotiate with the generals, Oswaldo Cordeiro de Farias, commander in the Brazilian expeditionary force, reluctantly took their ultimatum to the President. Vargas was assured that there would be no dramatic military intervention, and he calmly agreed to stand down from the presidency, asking only to be flown to his family home of São Borja, in Rio Grande do Sul.

Popular music could not fail to record the event, albeit in a

light-hearted manner which was, by and large, in keeping with the mood
of the nation. The carnival *marcha* '*Palacete no Catete*' ('Little Palace in
Catete', a mocking allusion to Vargas's official residence in the Rio
district of Catete, usually referred to as the *Palácio do Catete* or Catete
Palace), written in December 1945, hot on the heels of the President's
departure from office, provides a clear illustration of the irreverent attitude
of many musicians towards authority, now that censorship controls were
more relaxed. Furthermore, it highlights the symbiotic nature of the
relationship between politics and popular song throughout the era that had
just come to a close:

'*Palacete no Catete*', December 1945, Herivelto Martins and Ciro de Souza

Existe um palacete no Catete
E consta que foi desocupado
O vizinho do lado estava informado
Que o seu vizinho
Já pensava em se mudar
Este inquilino, apesar dos desenganos
Morou neste palacete ... 15 anos!

Catete, zona preferida
Todo mundo quer
Porque lá é de colher
Bonde na porta
Condução lá é mato
Mas a senhoria
Quer seis anos de contrato

'Little Palace in Catete', December 1945, Herivelto Martins and Ciro de Souza

There's a little palace in Catete
And it says it's been vacated
The next-door neighbour was informed
That his neighbour
Was already thinking of moving
This tenant, in spite of the disappointments
Lived in this little palace ... for 15 years!

Catete, a sought-after area
Everyone wants to live there
Because there it's all on a plate
The tram passes right by
It's great for public transport
But the landlady
Wants a six-year contract

Notes

1. Bourne, R. (1974), p. 92.
2. Quoted in Carone, E. (1977), p. 116.
3. Ibid., p. 120.
4. See Lesser, J. (1994). For a more detailed study of Brazilian anti-semitism between the First World War and the Second World War, see Lesser, J. (1995).
5. See Williams, D. (1994), pp. 45-75. Vargas was also responsible for the creation of the *Museu Imperial* (Imperial Museum) in Petrópolis, the summer retreat of the imperial court. He took a personal interest in taking back there the mortal remains and possessions of the emperors, and as Daryle Williams explains, he clearly wanted to remind Brazilians that their nation had imperial, European origins. When the museum was opened to the public in 1943 a bust of Vargas was positioned next to the entrance, a constant reminder of the President's desire to be associated with Dom Pedro II and the ideals of empire.
6. Bourne, R. (1974), p. 94.
7. Carone, E. (1977), p. 167.
8. *Coleção das leis de 1939; atos do poder executivo, decretos-leis de outubro a dezembro* (1939), VII, Imprensa Nacional, Rio de Janeiro, pp. 590-7. Quoted in Goulart, S. (1990), p. 62.
9. Goulart, S. (1990), p. 20.
10. Tota, A. P. (1980), p. 47.
11. Goulart, S. (1990), p. 116.
12. Ibid., p. 55.
13. The DIP's *Divisão do Rádio* created other official broadcasts for overseas audiences, and under its guidance *Radio El Mundo* in Buenos Aires transmitted the *Hora do Brasil* twice a week. Programmes in English or Spanish, which aimed to promote the different regions of Brazil and regional folklore, as well as to boost tourism and trade, were transmitted in the USA and Spanish America respectively.
14. Goulart, S. (1990), p. 28.
15. Cabral, S. (1975), p. 40.
16. Ibid., p. 68.
17. *Nosso século 1930/1945: a era de Vargas* (1982), p. 196.
18. Tota, A. P. (1980), p. 46.
19. Goulart, S. (1990), p. 27. In spite of the appropriation of 'national' culture on the part of the state, Antonio Candido says that after the revolution of 1930 there was a greater awareness among intellectuals and artists of the contradictions inherent in Brazilian society. For the first time intellectuals/artists were perceived as opponents of the conservative, authoritarian regime, yet paradoxically they were intensely coopted by that same regime. For this reason tensions could be noted in their work, and even when they were working on behalf of the government they did not necessarily identify with the latter's ideology. He shows how even apparently coopted writers and artists could develop objective antagonisms in their work in relation to the established order. Antonio Candido (1987), pp. 181-98.
20. Cabral, S. (1975), p. 40.
21. Ibid., p. 39.
22. Ibid., p. 41.
23. In Ataúlfo Alves's samba '*Nós das Américas*' ('We of the Americas') of 1942, the call for democratization belies the superficial patriotic sentiment; see p. 72.
24. Severiano, J. (1983), p. 26.

CHAPTER THREE

Samba and the Nascent Music Industry

The identity of samba's musical ancestors continues to give rise to theory and counter-theory. Many argue that the *lundu*, first performed in Brazil by African slaves in the eighteenth century, was samba's true musical forefather, whilst others claim that the genre's essential elements were taken to Rio de Janeiro from the northeastern state of Bahia by Afro-Brazilians towards the end of the nineteenth century. Nevertheless, no one is in any doubt that samba emerged as an autonomous musical form in the city of Rio in the early twentieth century. The community of former slaves and their descendants that established itself in the city brought with it African and Afro-Brazilian percussion-based *batucadas* and dances, both usually referred to under the umbrella term of *batuque*. The talented instrumentalists who met up at the home of the Bahian matriarch Tia Ciata, namely Pixinguinha (Alfredo da Rocha Vianna Jr, 1898-1973), Donga (Ernesto Joaquim Maria dos Santos, 1891-1974), João da Baiana (João Machado Guedes, 1887-1974), Heitor dos Prazeres (1898-1966) and Sinhô (José Barbosa da Silva, 1888-1930), played *lundus*, *marchas*, *choros*, *maxixes* and *batuques* in jam sessions, as well as discussing music and writing songs. It was here that they also began to mould and perfect the musical features that would define the *carioca* samba from then on.[1] In the words of Chris McGowan and Ricardo Pessanha:

> The emerging style gained influences from polka, habanera, and the lively genres of marcha and maxixe. From this rich matrix emerged samba, a vibrant musical form, distinguished by its responsorial singing and percussive interplay and a less formal sound than either maxixe or marcha. Technically, samba has a 2/4 meter, an emphasis on the second beat, a stanza-and-refrain structure, and many interlocking, syncopated lines in the melody and accompaniment. The main rhythm and abundant cross-rhythms can be carried by handclapping or in the percussion (the batucada), which may include more than a dozen different drums and percussion instruments. Samba is commonly accompanied by instruments such as the guitar and four-string cavaquinho and - less frequently - brass.[2]

In the second decade of the twentieth century the musical distinctions between samba, *maxixe* and *marcha* were not yet entirely manifest, and there was even some suggestion that '*Pelo telefone*', the first officially designated samba, fell within the generic boundaries of the *maxixe*. Even today certain musicologists refer to this composition as a *samba-maxixe*. The musicians who congregated at Tia Ciata's house each brought with them a particular skill; Donga was a gifted player of the guitar and the *cavaquinho* (a small, four-string guitar of European origin, akin to the ukelele), João da Baiana is thought to have introduced the *pandeiro* (tambourine) as a samba instrument, and Pixinguinha was a talented arranger who enriched the harmonies of samba. Together with the accomplished dance hall pianist Sinhô, and Heitor dos Prazeres, who was also adept with the *cavaquinho*, these three musicians began to elaborate the genre's musical structure.[3]

The Rio *bairro* of Estácio de Sá was home to another band of popular composers and musicians who would go on to play a major role in the development of samba and would become legendary *sambistas* in their own right. By the 1920s Estácio was an enclave of samba and dangerous *malandros,* many of whom were pimps for prostitutes in the nearby red-light district of Mangue. This community was composed of blacks, whites and mulattos, all of them impoverished and surplus to the requirements of industrialization, and within it samba represented the only artistic manifestation of interest and prestige. Four black musicians, in particular, who were involved in the creation of the first *escola de samba* called 'Deixa Falar' ('Let Them Speak') in 1928, were instrumental in leading the emergent musical genre in a new direction, adapting the rhythm to provide accompaniment for the first carnival processions. These semi-literate composers, with no formal musical training or knowledge, who were sometimes referred to disparagingly as '*maestros de assobio*' ('maestros of whistling'), were Ismael Silva (1905-78), noted for his inventive melodies and modulations, Bide (Alcebíades Barcellos, 1902-75), Armando Marçal (1902-47), and Nilton Bastos (who was born in the late nineteenth century and died in 1932). They accentuated the samba rhythm, adapting it for percussion instruments, and in doing so appealed more to the tastes of the popular masses. They were the creators of carnival samba and responsible for establishing the rhythm that would characterize this brand of music until the present day.

The impact of these *sambistas* from Estácio on samba's self-definition, and on the communicative power of the genre as a mouthpiece for the marginalized poor, is undeniable. McGowan and Pessanha assess the influence of these uneducated, black songwriters as follows:

> They took the fledgling samba genre and clearly differentiated it from maxixe and marcha, introducing longer notes and two-bar phrasing, and making the tempo slower, in contrast to the maxixe-like sambas composed by Sinhô and Donga. The form they codified became the standard reference of samba, to

which sambistas always return ... The musical language elaborated by the Estácio masters was an important form of expression for the Carioca lower classes in the early twentieth century. Samba became a voice for those who had been silenced by their socio-economic status, and a source of self-affirmation in society.[4]

The compositions of the Estácio songwriters, along with those of other talented popular musicians like Ataúlfo Alves (1909-69), who brought to the samba genre new elements from his native region of Minas Gerais, and Assis Valente (1911-58), were popularized via the radio and the gramophone record by the leading vocalists of the era, such as Francisco Alves (who also recorded under the pseudonym of Chico Viola to enable him to sing for two different record labels, Odeon and Parlophone), Orlando Silva, Carmen Miranda, Araci de Almeida, Marília Baptista, Sílvio Caldas and Mário Reis. The last introduced important changes into the vocal interpretation of samba, putting greater emphasis on clear diction and on the rhythm, and shying away from the exaggerated, operatic style traditionally favoured by male vocalists.

In order to participate in the new urban social order, Rio's poor adapted their musical traditions, deriving benefit from the transformations in society at large while continuing to make their own voice heard. Black composers would often collaborate with their white counterparts, usually in a very informal way, and for non-commercial *sambistas*, such as those who wrote primarily for the carnival samba schools, selling their songs was common. Such false *parceria* (partnership) is referred to by the *sambista* Ismael Silva in a newspaper interview from 1964. He explains how one day, when he was ill in hospital, the singer Francisco Alves, who had heard some of Ismael's sambas, sent Alcebíades Barcellos to visit him and to ask if he would sell him a particular samba that Alves had heard. Ismael agreed to sell him '*Me faz carinho*' ('Show Me Affection') and later accepted one hundred *mil-réis* for another song entitled '*O amor de malandro*' ('The Love of the Spiv'). When the samba was recorded Ismael's name did not appear on the record label. Thus was born one of the most successful business partnerships of the era. Francisco Alves started to visit the Rio district of Estácio on a regular basis, and he and Ismael Silva struck a deal by which the white singer would record all of the *malandro sambista*'s compositions, on the condition that both of their names would appear on the record label and sheet music as the songwriters. Ismael imposed a further condition, namely that Nilton Bastos, another of the Estácio *sambistas*, be included in the *parceria*, an arrangement which continued until Bastos's premature death in 1932. Promoted by Alves, known as the '*Rei da Voz*' ('King of the Voice'), Ismael Silva was soon to gain fame as the '*Rei do Estácio*' ('King of

Estácio'), and the two worked in tandem until 1935. Francisco Alves actively sought out other poor anonymous songwriters, in the knowledge that the music they produced held mass appeal in the lowest echelons of society, as well as among many middle-class radio fans who would buy his records.

Noel Rosa also spoke of his personal experience of people purchasing sambas and admitted that he sold many which were subsequently credited to other people. The *sambista* Sinhô's famous phrase: 'Samba é como passarinho, é de quem pegar' ('Samba is like a little bird, it belongs to whoever catches it') sums up the relaxed attitude to the issue of authorship, and the underhand dealings that were often involved.[5] In the interview mentioned above, Ismael Silva also explains the casual way in which he and Noel came to co-write the samba *'Para me livrar do mal'* ('To Free Myself of the Pain'): 'Um dia, no Café Nice, mostrei uma prim-eira parte de uma música ao Noel e ele foi pedindo: 'Deixa eu fazer a segunda?' ('One day in the Café Nice, I showed the first section of a piece of music to Noel, and he asked: Will you let me do the second part?').[6] By all accounts the Café Nice, which was the meeting place for all those connected with Rio's popular music scene in this era and until it closed in 1954, was also the market place for dealing in sambas. It was there that musicians would help their less educated counterparts by writing down the music that the latter had composed by ear, but it was also where so-called *'comprositores'* (a pun in Portuguese on the word composer and the verb to buy) would purchase the right to call a samba their own, some of them criminals who wanted to conceal their true activities.[7]

As samba became more respectable and found a wider audience among the middle-class, record-buying public and radio listeners, a new strand or sub-genre developed which emphasized melody over rhythm, and later came to be known as *samba-canção*, or *samba-de-meio-de-ano* (literally 'mid-year samba' as opposed to carnival samba, written at the start of the year). Many of the songs written by the up-and-coming white *sambistas* of the age, such as Noel Rosa and Ari Barroso, which were simply classified as sambas at the time, would ultimately fall into this more melodious sub-division of the genre. Such compositions '... added more complex harmonies, and had more sophisticated lyrics - usually tied to sentimental themes. It was a kind of cool, softened samba ... and it popularized the genre with the middle class.'[8] Many of the songs analysed in Chapters Four, Five and Six would, in fact, now be considered examples of *samba-canção*, particularly those which deal with affairs of the heart. In 1939 Luiz Heitor wrote in the *Revista Brasileira de Música* (*Brazilian Music Review*):

No caminho em que vamos, dentro de alguns anos, toda espécie de música, no Brasil, receberá a designação de 'samba'; 'samba' será, então, verdadeiro sinônimo de 'música' ... Há sambas arrastados e melancólicos como um 'blue' ('Camisa Amarela' de Ari Barroso, cantado por Araci de Almeida, disco Victor); outros há que se movimentam com energia, quase marcialmente ... e o Rei Jazz, finalmente, que é o soberano mais imperialista do nosso tempo, enfeuda outros tantos, como 'E não me esqueço de você', que Francisco Alves canta, em disco Odeon. A movimentação instrumental, contraponteada, bordando a linha alongada do canto, é, nesse samba, puro efeito de 'Jazz' (The way we are going, within a few years all types of music, in Brazil, will be called 'samba'; 'samba' will be, then, a true synonym for 'music' ... There are slow, melancholy sambas like 'blues' ('Yellow Shirt' by Ari Barroso, sung by Araci de Almeida, on Victor records); there are others that move along with energy, almost marching ... and King Jazz, finally, who is the most imperialistic sovereign of our times, feudalizes many more, like 'And I Don't Forget You', that Francisco Alves sings, on Odeon records. The contrapuntal instrumental accompaniment, which enhances the extended vocal line, is, in that samba, a pure Jazz effect).[9]

Various off-shoots and hybrids of samba, such as the *samba-choro* and the *samba-tango*, appeared as the genre evolved and widened its audience. The *samba-de-breque* (break samba), created by the singer Moreira da Silva (born 1902), was characterized, as its name suggests, by the inclusion of pauses or breaks in the performance of a song to allow the singer to make a comment, often ironic or humorous, on the situation described in the lyrics. These spoken asides were made in the so-called *conversa macia* or snappy street vernacular of the *malandro* hustler. Moreira da Silva's 1938 recording of the samba '*Acertei no Milhar*' ('I've Won the Lottery'), written by Wilson Baptista and Geraldo Pereira, came to epitomize this vocal style.[10] The *samba-exaltação*, perfected by Ari Barroso in the late 1930s and early 1940s, set hyperbolic lyrics, which extolled the virtues of the Brazilian nation, to the harmonious melodies of *samba-canção*, and both genres were heavily influenced by the orchestration of North American music. The *samba-de-morro*, as created by the musicians of Estácio, remained virtually untainted, and its relative isolation in the hillside shantytowns allowed this more traditional samba to retain its original features, such as its use of instruments like the *cavaquinho*, the *pandeiro*, and the *tamborim* (a small, cymbal-less tambourine, struck with a stick), and lyrics which centred on the everyday experiences of the poor, marginalized community of the *morros*. When in its almost purely percussive form, the *samba-de-morro* is sometimes referred to as the *samba-de-batucada*.[11]

In his book *Música Popular Brasileira* (*Brazilian Popular Music*) the musicologist Oneyda Alvarenga identifies three main categories of samba which co-existed in the 1930s. The first is the *maxixe*-inspired samba, such as '*Pelo telefone*' and the works of Sinhô, the rhythm and melody of which varied greatly, and which was heavily influenced by the particular performing style of the singer or musician concerned. The semi-literate composers of this type of samba were unable to write down the complicated rhythms that they invented, and thus when committed to paper their creations were impaired by a rudimentary, rhythmic schematization. Secondly, Alvarenga cites the *samba-de-morro*, as established by the popular composers of Estácio and developed as an accompaniment for the carnival processions of the 'Deixa Falar' *escola de samba*. This samba consisted of a single verse, sung by a solo voice and frequently improvised, which was taken up again in the chorus by a group of singers. The entrance of the chorus was often preceded by an instrumental introduction, played by two guitars, a *cavaquinho* and a tambourine. The singing was accompanied by percussion instruments, namely a *pandeiro*, a *tamborim*, a *tambor surdo* (bass drum) and a *cuíca* (friction drum). This structure of an improvised solo verse followed by a fixed choral refrain, together with the rhythms and melodies which typified this type of samba, owed much to African musical traditions, and to the music of Brazil's rural plantations prior to the abolition of slavery. In his samba '*Quem dá mais?*' ('Who'll Give Me More?') of 1930, Noel Rosa refers to this type of samba: '... um samba feito nas regras da arte/Sem introdução e sem segunda parte ...' ('... a samba written within the rules of the art/Without an introduction or a second part ...'). The third and final category referred to is the *samba de salão* or dance hall samba, generally composed of a verse and chorus, both preceded by a brief instrumental introduction. This samba was either accompanied by guitars and percussion, or by the bands that had traditionally played *choros* during the genre's golden age at the turn of the century. This was the type of samba disseminated by the radio and the gramophone record, and which was influenced by a variety of imported musical genres, such as the tango and the rumba. All three categories were essentially dance music, unlike *samba-canção*, with its slower tempo, and more lyrical, elaborate melodic line.[12]

The birth of the music industry

The 1880s saw the abolition of slavery in Brazil and the appearance of the so-called *máquinas falantes* (talking machines), early cylinder phonographs, which allowed *lundus* and *batuques* to be captured for posterity. 1904 signalled the beginnings of the mass production of gramophone records, and a watershed for popular music. Overnight all genres of music became fodder for industrial production, to cater for the expanding market. Popular composers were easily exploited by the industry at the start of the century, and found it difficult to carve out a decent living from their trade. From 1913 onwards advertisements for *vitrolas* (gramophones) targeted the well off. Those who could not afford the luxury of the latest vogue were, nevertheless, able to listen to records in bars and later in cinema halls. There followed a pitched battle between North American and European recording companies, which took the form of large-scale advertising campaigns and a race to see who could come up with the most impressive technical advances. Fred and Gustavo Figner's Casa Edison offered competitive prices and advanced know-how, and dominated the market until 1924, the year in which engineers from the Victor Talking Machine in the USA began a new era in recording and sound production. In 1927 the electric system replaced the mechanical recording of music, thus ensuring greater fidelity, and from then on record companies developed a keen interest in the music of the *morros* and the poor *bairros* of Rio.[13] So-called *'orquestradores'* or orchestrators were employed by record companies to polish up melodies and to embellish lyrics, especially those of the sentimental *samba-canção*, in preparation for recording.

According to José Ramos Tinhorão, companies like the pioneering Casa Edison and Odeon considered Brazilian popular music to be 'picturesque' and ideal for wider consumption. Foreign record companies, such as the US Brunswick label and RCA Victor, both of which set up a local branch in Rio in 1929, began to market samba and other forms of regional music.[14] However, the continuing middle-class fashion for hosting musical evenings at home for friends and neighbours meant that sales of sheet music or *partituras* far outstripped those of gramophone records at the beginning of the 1930s. In spite of technical improvements within the recording industry, relatively few records were produced in these early years. A major carnival hit, for example, would warrant the production of only 5000 copies.[15] By the early '30s the market was monopolized by three names, Victor, Columbia, and Edison, and the old Brazilian companies had virtually disappeared.

The record industry was given a major boost by the rapid rise of the radio. Originally a preserve of erudite culture and educational material, the radio was to be transformed during the 1930s into a source of popular entertainment, largely thanks to the introduction of commercial advertisements. The economic pressure exerted by the advertisers led radio stations to opt for mass appeal, and popular music held the key to winning over new audiences. Consequently, musical genres like samba, once considered unsuitable for the radio, were performed by a growing number of stars on shows such as the *Programa Casé*, the brainchild of a young man from the northeastern state of Pernambuco, Ademar Casé. First broadcast on Radio Philips in 1932, the *Programa Casé* went on to launch the careers of Noel Rosa, Lamartine Babo, Marília Baptista, Carmen Miranda and many more. It was the prototype variety show, recorded before a live audience seated behind a glass screen, and which lasted from three to four hours. The show moved to various radio stations throughout the 1930s and 1940s, from Radio Philips to Radio Transmissora, then to Radio Sociedade, and on to Radio Mayrink, where its popularity peaked. The final recording of the show was made at Radio Tupi in 1951.[16] This winning formula was copied repeatedly by the many radio stations that sprang up in the 1930s, some of which built luxurious studios for the benefit of the audiences in order to compete for popularity. Radio studios were regularly besieged by fans, and became important meeting places for the public, notably for courting couples. Record companies set up their own radio stations, such as Radio Transmissora in Rio, owned by RCA Victor, and saw their profits soar as the public, who now enjoyed greater economic power, began to buy records by their favourite radio stars. From the mid-1930s onwards the impact of the radio on the Brazilian public was much greater than that of the television 30 years later. Commercial radio established a link between the individual and the collective, and the urban middle class, who constituted the principal listening public, saw their tastes, beliefs and values standardized by the pervasiveness of the airwaves. It was chiefly thanks to the radio and the record industry that samba reached the other main urban centres of Brazil and was consecrated as the most important form of urban popular music by the end of the 1930s. The radio, in particular, was responsible for bringing about vast improvements in artistic professionalism and the quality of recordings. In addition, radio advertisers started to use popular music as a marketing ploy, commissioning songs to promote their products. Conversely, the lyrics of samba and other types of popular song then began to include indirect references to consumer goods and brand names. It is said that one night in 1935, in a cabaret bar in the city of Vitória in the state of Espírito Santo, Noel Rosa improvised the following lines, in which he pays homage to a young woman, and to a famous make of cigarettes of the same name made by the Souza Cruz tobacco company:

> É você a que comanda
> E o meu coração conduz
> Salve a dona Yolanda
> Rainha da Souza Cruz

> You are the one that is in control
> And leads my heart
> Three cheers for lady Yolanda
> Queen of Souza Cruz

Educated young men, such as Noel Rosa and Ari Barroso, were attracted to writing and performing samba, in particular, and this period of great creativity was centred on the commercialization of the genre. These white musicians transformed the samba in order to appeal to a more middle-class audience, making its rhythm less syncopated, and its lyrics and melody more sophisticated and more easily performed by dance hall bands. Many black *sambistas*, such as Wilson Baptista, who had initially scorned the first radio professionals, soon realized that by modifying the musical features of their sambas and by complying with the ideals of the Vargas regime in their lyrics, they could gain access to the new vehicles of the radio and the record industry, and ascend the social hierarchy. Thus a new breed of professional composers, made up of blacks and whites who were independent of their respective communities, created songs for a heterogeneous, mass audience, for financial gain. In his article 'O negro e a comercialização da música popular brasileira' ('Blacks and the Commercialization of Brazilian Popular Music'), João Baptista Borges Pereira shows how samba was coopted to become a national form of popular music, and explains how the growing respectability of this black cultural product and its commercialization, within a wider process of urbanization and industrialization in Rio, increased the professional opportunities open to blacks, especially within the radio and record industries. Similarly, their music gained kudos as white composers, and performers like the popular singer Mário Reis, many from well-to-do backgrounds, carved out successful careers on their own. Consequently, jobs that had been stigmatized, such as teaching the guitar, an instrument associated with the lower classes, became respectable occupations. Borges Pereira concludes that blacks were further assisted in their careers linked to the new entertainment media because they were so closely associated with their music that the latter's sudden rise in prestige affected their social standing. Their musical skills were seen by whites as having racial foundations.[17] It is not surprising, therefore, that black musicians were able to gain access to the new media in order to disseminate their increasingly commercial work. With such an incentive it was natural that even the most bohemian composer should try to market his goods accordingly.

Prior to the rise of the radio and the record industry, popular music was only heard in live performances, and its audience was restricted to members of the lower classes in a given local area of a city. Consequently, the various creative forces at work were kept relatively isolated from external influences. After the emergence of these new media in the late 1920s and early '30s, samba gradually ceased to be the collective property of the black inhabitants of the shantytowns of Rio, lost its intrinsic associations with dance, and became a commodity destined for mass consumption.[18] The changes in the nature of samba's performance and reception, and in the degree of intimacy between the performer/creator and the audience, over the course of the 1930s and 1940s, naturally led to modifications in the genre's musical aspects and in the choice of instrumentation, as did the inevitable exposure to imported genres. The single voice and simple guitar accompaniment of compositions written by Noel Rosa and Ataúlfo Alves in the late 1920s and early 1930s, for example, were ideally suited to the atmosphere of greater intimacy afforded by the live performances and primitive recordings. In this respect these performances, particularly those of Noel Rosa, paved the way for the easy, informal recording style of early bossa nova, discussed in more detail below. In contrast, Ari Barroso's use of often quite elaborate orchestration in his sambas from the late 1930s onwards is a telling reflection of the greater distance between him as a singer-songwriter and the more heterogeneous, anonymous audience of radio listeners and record buyers.

After 1930, Brazilian culture as a whole, but particularly literature, became more democratic and less élitist, but within popular music this same process of democratization operated in reverse. The 1930s witnessed a surge of interest in all things Brazilian, which allowed popular music to break down social barriers for the first time. This, according to Antonio Candido, was to pave the way for the huge influence of popular music in the 1960s and its interpenetration with erudite poetry.[19] As an illustration of this growing interest in popular music among the intelligentsia, Ismael Silva recounted how a group of intellectuals, including the poet Manuel Bandeira and the Modernist writer Mário de Andrade, used to gather in a certain café in the centre of Rio to hear him play, and how on Sundays he used to go to the house of the writer Aníbal Machado, where, on his arrival, the literature would stop and samba would take over. He would sing for the intellectuals who met there and would repeat his songs over and over again for their benefit.[20] Likewise, the *gafieiras*, or dance halls, which represented the first attempt at upward mobility by the poorest, predominantly black inhabitants of the city of Rio, an imitation of the *bailes* or balls frequented by whites, aroused the interest of the latter in the 1930s. The musical accompaniment at these dances was usually provided by a pianist who played waltzes, polkas, *maxixes*, and later sambas and foxtrots. In the 1940s sociologists began to study the phenomenon of the *gafieira*, focusing, in particular, on the ease with which whites gained access to what was essentially a black stronghold. In the 1960s these dance halls were rediscovered by university students and members of the middle class, in the context of the renewed interest in the *samba-de-morro*, considered in more detail below.

The arrival of the talking cinema and the *chanchadas carnavalescas*, full-length films made in Brazil that featured contemporary carnival music, was also responsible for publicizing samba to a wider audience. The musical entitled '*Coisas nossas*' ('Our Things'), which premiered in 1931, is often cited as the first Brazilian 'talkie'. Produced by an American, Wallace Downey, this film heralded a tradition of musicals that each premiered a week before carnival and featured the forthcoming hits of the annual celebration. Films such as '*Voz do Carnaval*' ('Voice of Carnival') of 1933, '*Alô, alô, Brasil*' ('Hello, Hello, Brazil') of 1935 and '*Alô, alô, Carnaval*' ('Hello, Hello, Carnival') of 1936 were the Brazilian cinema industry's response to the onslaught of Hollywood musicals. The historian Nicolau Sevcenko has called 1920 a dividing line in Brazilian history, in recognition of the pervasive impact of the 'Hollywood Effect' on street fashions and Brazil's self-image.[21] Brazilian women began to emulate the dress and hair styles of actresses like Greta Garbo and Jean Harlow, whereas the likes of Ronald Colman and Douglas Fairbanks became male idols and role-models. The *chanchadas* tapped into this fascination with Hollywood glamour, and the Rio-based Cinédia studios, in particular, realized that films which featured songs destined for the annual carnival celebrations and competitions had mass appeal and offered huge commercial potential. The inhabitants of the big cities, who already crowded into radio studios to watch live performances and talent contests being recorded, provided a ready-made viewing public for Brazilian musicals. Cinédia's '*Alô, alô, Brasil*' set the trend for using radio artists in front of the cameras to perform the most popular songs of the moment in the run-up to *carnaval*. These home-spun replicas of the tremendously popular North American originals lacked technical sophistication, and the loosely constructed plots were largely dependent on the songs that were chosen to feature in the films. However, they played a fundamental role in popularizing the samba and the *marcha carnavalesca*, and in turning popular musicians and performers, like the sisters Carmen and Aurora Miranda, into household names and media celebrities.

Samba, bossa nova and MPB

In the 1940s samba increasingly felt the effects of the influence of North American music, especially jazz and bebop, which began to undermine its intrinsic features. By the 1950s the commercially popular *samba-canção*, in particular, had become tainted by imported musical genres, such as the foxtrot and the bolero, and was performed by a host of crooners. Towards the end of the decade students and intellectuals from Rio's affluent *Zona Sul* (literally 'South Zone', the collective title given to the wealthy, beach-side districts of the city, such as Copacabana and Ipanema), tired of the absence of musical innovation, began to experiment with the samba rhythm, simplifying it in an effort to make it more universal, and thus the seeds of the bossa nova or 'new fashion' were sown. This experimentation coincided with a renewed interest in the traditional *samba-de-morro*, and ageing *sambistas*, most of whom still lived in the hillside shantytowns, such as Zé Keti, Nelson Cavaquinho, Clementina de Jesus and Cartola, and who had continued to write songs and perform to live audiences in relative obscurity, were brought down from the hills, and their music was disseminated to the whole nation. These traditional musicians had a great influence on the young, white, middle-class creators of the fledgling bossa nova. In the early 1960s the restaurant Zicartola, run by the black *sambista* Cartola and his wife Zica, became the meeting place for these white musicians from the *Zona Sul* and the black *samba-de-morro* artists from the shantytowns and down-market districts of the *Zona Norte* (North Zone).

By the beginning of the 1960s the *samba-de-morro* had been adopted and modified by the *escolas de samba*, which were now vast institutions in their own right. 'They gave *samba-de-morro* a stronger and more elaborate rhythmic force and presented it in a new, grandiose form, with thousands of singers and dancers, and hundreds of drummers and percussionists.'[22] The *samba-de-morro* gave rise to the *samba-de-enredo*, which today provides the music for the extravagant *desfiles* or carnival processions that are broadcast all over the world. Samba has proved to be the most popular and enduring musical accompaniment to carnival.[23] Songs written by popular composers from the 1930s and 1940s, such as Ari Barroso, Lamartine Babo, Wilson Baptista and Noel Rosa, are still sung at carnival time and are recorded by contemporary artists. The so-called 'Golden Age' of popular music, which virtually coincided with the Vargas era, and which hinged on the commercialization and democratization of the samba, bequeathed a valuable legacy to subsequent musical styles. Nowhere is this more apparent than within the bossa nova movement. The minimalist, intimate, almost conversational vocal delivery, exemplified by João Gilberto's performances of the first examples of the genre, owes much to the singing style of Noel Rosa, in particular. In the words of Renato Murce:

> O que podemos dizer, sem medo de contestação, é que o verdadeiro criador da bossa nova no Brasil foi Noel Rosa. Lançou, com sucesso que todos conhecem, um estilo de música. Completamente diferente de tudo o que se

conhecia no gênero (embora também produzindo muito do que já existia de tradicional). 'Conversa de botequim', 'Com que roupa?', 'Gago apaixonado', 'Três apitos' e outros, são autênticos representantes do movimento bossa nova (What we can say, without fear of being challenged, is that the real creator of bossa nova in Brazil was Noel Rosa. He launched, with the success that everyone is aware of, a style of music. Completely different from everything that had characterized the genre (although he also produced a lot of the traditional type). 'Bar Talk', 'In What Clothes?', 'Smitten Stammerer', 'Three Whistles' and others, are authentic examples of the bossa nova movement).[24]

José Ramos Tinhorão draws many parallels between Noel and the pioneers of bossa nova. They shared a precocious talent for capturing the nuances of modernization and the resulting shifting demographic structure of the societies they lived in, and for creating lyrics and melodies that appealed to the new social groups that these changes gave rise to.[25] In his biography of Wilson Baptista, Bruno Ferreira Gomes recounts how the *sambista* sometimes met up with João Gilberto in later life. The father of bossa nova showed great appreciation for Wilson's compositions, and those of Ataúlfo Alves and Geraldo Pereira, and went on to record several of them himself.[26] Bossa nova was essentially a new type of samba, with a simplified rhythm. It owed much to the *samba-canção* tunes written by the likes of Noel Rosa and Ari Barroso, in particular. Many Brazilian music critics have dismissed bossa nova as a mixture of samba and jazz, but as McGowan and Pessanha say: 'Jazz certainly influenced most bossa musicians, but the genre's greatest songwriter, Jobim, was most heavily influenced by *samba-canção* and classical music. In any event, it is clear that bossa nova put together many musical elements in an original way and was something definitely Brazilian.'[27] Antonio Carlos (Tom) Jobim and Vinícius de Moraes became the most influential songwriting partnership of the bossa nova movement, and composed many of the classics of the genre, such as *'Garota de Ipanema'* ('The Girl from Ipanema') and *'Chega de Saudade'* ('No More Blues'), the English versions of which took the US market by storm. The influence of Brazilian music on North American trends was not, however, confined to the bossa nova. In 1958 John Coltrane recorded a jazz version of Ari Barroso's samba 'Bahia' of 1937 (known in Brazil as *'Na Baixa do Sapateiro'*).

MPB, an acronym for *música popular brasileira* (Brazilian popular music) is the term used to refer to the eclectic movement which emerged in the late 1960s and early 1970s, the leading lights of which included Chico Buarque de Holanda, Caetano Veloso, Milton Nascimento, Gal Costa and Maria Bethânia. This umbrella term covers a variety of musical styles, which draw on various traditions and genres, such as samba, bossa nova, rock and roll and regional folk music. Chico Buarque has become

Brazil's foremost contemporary singer-songwriter, and the linguistic dexterity displayed in his lyrics bears a striking resemblance to some of Noel Rosa's sambas. Prevented from recording his own material by the censors of the post-1964 dictatorship, Chico tacitly acknowledged his debt of gratitude to Noel by recording a cover version of one of his songs on the 1974 album *Sinal Fechado* (Red Light). Chico and various other stars of MPB, including Caetano Veloso and Gal Costa, went on to perform some of Noel's most famous songs on the double album *Songbook Noel*, recorded in 1991. Likewise, compositions by Ari Barroso and Ataúlfo Alves are often performed by contemporary artists. In 1988, for example, Gal Costa released an album appropriately entitled *Aquarela do Brasil*, consisting of songs composed by Ari.

The commercialized samba of the 1930s and '40s has proved to be a lasting influence on popular music in Brazil, and the warm reception given to the recent series of re-releases on CD by the Revivendo Project confirms the continued popularity of recordings from this era. Even in the 1970s it was difficult to come across original recordings by Noel Rosa and his contemporaries, and up until the end of the 1980s the best source of such material was the collection of LP records called *'História da música popular brasileira'* (*'The History of Brazilian Popular Music'*), issued by Abril Cultural, which nevertheless had to be sought out in second-hand record shops, for the most part. The 'Golden Age' of the 1930s and '40s has enjoyed something of a renaissance among scholars of popular music and journalists in the last ten years or so, with the appearance of several academic and well-researched books on the subject, in particular João Máximo and Carlos Didier's best-selling *Noel Rosa: uma biografia* (*Noel Rosa: a Biography*) of 1990, and Sérgio Cabral's *No Tempo de Ari Barroso* (*In Ari Barroso's Day*) of 1994. These two excellent biographies have proved to be a valuable addition to the extensive written sources on the development of popular music in the Vargas era, which have tended to rely on informal recollections and to lack factual detail and analytical rigour.

In the following chapters the lyrics of sambas composed by Ataúlfo Alves, Noel Rosa and Ari Barroso between 1930 and 1945 are analysed in detail. These three composers were chosen as they represented very different groups within society, in terms of their skin colour and social position, and because all three enjoyed considerable fame and success. They all belonged to the first generation of professional *sambistas* and each one made his mark on the genre. Noel, in particular, was a pioneering lyricist, whose inventive genius was to influence many popular composers in subsequent decades. Like jazz in the USA, which was born among the black creators of spirituals and blues in New Orleans and was commercialized for middle-class consumption by the jazz bands of New York and Chicago, samba's evolution was one of social ascension. By studying these lyrics we can gain a clear picture of samba's shifting status in a period of dynamic change ushered in by the birth of industrialization. Although music and lyrics do not exist in isolation, a study of lyrics permits a greater understanding of the social context in which songs are written. The lyrics studied in the following chapters therefore provide us with a unique insight into the experiences and aspirations of three of the founding fathers of popular music in Brazil, and tell us much about the changing identity of both the samba genre and the Brazilian people in the Vargas era.

Notes

1. McGowan, C. and Pessanha, R. (1998), p. 23.
2. Ibid., p. 23.
3. Ibid., pp. 24-5.
4. Ibid., pp. 25-7.
5. Rangel, L. (1962), p. 56.
6. Bloch, P. (1964), pp. 88-91.
7. Holanda, N. de (1970), pp. 51, 56, 121-2.
8. McGowan, C. and Pessanha, R. (1998), p. 28.
9. Heitor, L. (1939), p. 134.
10. McGowan, C. and Pessanha, R. (1998), p. 27.
11. Ibid., pp. 21, 33.
12. Alvarenga, O. (1982), pp. 337-44.
13. Tinhorão (1981), pp. 14, 23, 38.
14. Tinhorão, J. R. (1990), pp. 232-3. Unfortunately, there is very little information available on the history of the recording industry in Brazil, and thus it is virtually impossible to assess and evaluate notions of 'popularity' statistically.
15. *Nosso Século 1930/1945: A era de Vargas* (1982), p. 62.
16. Moreira, S. V. and Saroldi, L. C. (1984), p. 18.
17. Pereira, J. B. B. (1970), pp. 7-15.
18. Matos, C. (1982), pp. 107-27.
19. Souza, A. C. de M. e (1987), pp. 181-98.
20. Bloch, P. (1964), pp. 88-91.
21. Sevcenko, N. (1995).
22. McGowan, C. and Pessanha, R. (1998), p. 34.
23. For more information on carnival in Brazil, the history of the *escolas de samba*, the percussion instruments used in the celebration, and contemporary samba, see McGowan, C. and Pessanha, R. (1998), pp. 35-53.
24. Murce, R. (1976), p. 149.
25. Tinhorão, J. R. (*Música popular: um tema em debate*, [n.d.]), pp. 42-5.
26. Gomes, B. F. (1985), pp. 84-5.
27. McGowan, C. and Pessanha, R. (1998), p. 66.

CHAPTER FOUR

The Sambas of Ataúlfo Alves
(1909-69)

Carioca by default, Ataúlfo Alves de Sousa was born in the small town of Miraí in Minas Gerais, 500 kilometres from the state capital, Belo Horizonte, on 2 May 1909, one of seven children born to Dona Matilde Alves de Sousa and her husband Severino, who passed on many of his musical skills to his son Ataúlfo. Ataúlfo's father was a well-known musician all over the region, who played the *viola* (a type of guitar) and performed as a *repentista* (improviser). At eight years of age Ataúlfo improvised lyrics with his father, but he was only ten when his father died. He was then obliged to help his mother support the family, which he did by working as a milkboy and a porter at the railway station, amongst other jobs. As a result of financial difficulties he was only to complete some most basic schooling. When he was 18 he set off for Rio, accompanied by a doctor friend of his father, Afrânio Moreira de Rezende, for whom he was to work in his establishment at number 34 Rua da Assembléia. Eventually, when he could no longer tolerate having to do the doctor's housework and being constantly watched over by him, he applied for another job. He had taught himself to decipher prescriptions and make them up and thus managed to be taken on as a pharmacist's assistant in the Farmácia do Povo, Rua São José, and despite the fact that he never obtained a licence he was recommended by many Rio doctors.

It was thanks to this job that he first came into contact with the young Carmen Miranda, a friend of the owner's two daughters, to whom he sometimes had to take messages and errands. By the end of the 1920s Ataúlfo had joined a group which performed samba and in which he played the *violão* (six-string guitar), the *cavaquinho* and the *bandolinzinho* (a kind of mandolin). In 1928, at the age of 19, he married Judite and the first of their four children was born the following year. With a family to support, commercial success in carnival became all the more important. However, acclaim was not far off, and the black popular composer Alcebíades Barcellos, better known as Bide, is credited with having 'discovered' Ataúlfo. Familiar with his compositions, Bide introduced him to the RCA Victor record company in 1933. As luck would have it, Carmen Miranda herself was called on to pass opinion on his work.

Recognizing him immediately, she chose his song *'Tempo perdido'* ('Wasted Time'), which she recorded shortly after in 1934. This and *'Sexta-feira'* ('Friday'), a samba performed by the singer-songwriter Almirante, were the first two of his compositions to be recorded.

Ataúlfo's first hit was to come the following year, entitled *'Saudades do meu barracão'* ('Longing for My Shack'). On arrival in Rio he had lived in the Rio Comprido area of the city, near the *bairro* of Estácio and thus a very important part of samba territory. He began to establish himself as a *sambista* in the Morro do Querosene hillside shantytown, where in 1930 he became director of harmony in the 'Fale Quem Quiser' ('Let Anyone Speak') samba *bloco* or carnival group. His first sambas were written alongside the other *bambas* or musicians of the *bloco* and performed by the group. The big names of samba at that time, including Lamartine Babo, Ismael Silva, Ari Barroso and João de Barros, used to congregate in the Café Papagaio, in Rua Gonçalves Dias. On the next rung down were the *sambistas* of the Café Belas-Artes, followed by those of the Café Opera in Praça Tiradentes. In no time at all Ataúlfo progressed from the Opera to the Belas-Artes.

Once given a taste of life as a professional *sambista* he obtained even greater success in the 1930s, and in the carnivals of 1940 and 1941 with his sambas *'A mulher do seu Oscar'* ('Oscar's Woman') and *'O bonde São Januário'* ('The São Januário Tram'), the latter epitomizing the new work ethic of the dutiful *operário* (factory worker) helping to build a better Brazil. Both of these songs were written in *parceria* with Cabo Wilson, better known as Wilson Baptista, whereas in the 1930s it had been Bide who had collaborated with Ataúlfo in various sambas. Throughout his career he worked with many different *parceiros*, attracting more as he became more famous. He had most successes when writing with Wilson Baptista but equally composed excellent sambas on his own. Despite his obvious talents for songwriting, many singers refused to record his material because they did not think it was stylistically suited to their voices. As a result of this Ataúlfo began to record them himself, and in 1941 he experimented with *'Leva meu samba'* ('Take My Samba'), which proved to be a hit. Since his voice lacked power he needed to find a backing group. His famous *Pastoras* (Shepherdesses) was thus formed, a group of very stylish female singers, originally Olga, Marilu and Alda, although the members changed many times during his career. Ataúlfo too was to adopt a very sophisticated image. He was known for his confident swagger or *'andar amalandrado'* and in samba circles his nickname was *'o Urubu Malandro'* ('the Spiv Vulture'), a reference perhaps to his dark skin as well as to his distinctive gait.[1] However, he sought to distance himself in his lyrics from the marginal ethos of *malandragem* and to gain respectability. Not only was he one of the greatest writers and performers of samba, but he was also its elegant ambassador throughout the world, representing Brazil in the first International Festival of Black Art in Dakar in 1966. He even featured in Brazil's 'Best Dressed' list compiled by Ibrahim Sued, and was regularly referred to as the most dapper *sambista*. Despite having no formal education he was, by all accounts, a refined gentleman, always jovial and courteous, eloquent and communicative. Along with his *Pastoras* he adopted a sharp image that appealed to a more middle-class audience in particular. Darwin Brandão said of him: 'Elegante, bem falante, pronunciando certo as palavras, cuidando sempre da concordância, o negro Ataúlfo é toda uma organização' ('Elegant, well-spoken, pronouncing words correctly, taking care to always make the grammatical agreements, the negro Ataúlfo is impeccably organized).[2]

Although Ataúlfo became director of harmony for the carnival *bloco* 'Fale Quem Quiser', he played no major role in the creation of the 'Deixa Falar' samba school, unlike Bide and Ismael Silva. His independent spirit and the unique quality of his compositions are attributed in part to his childhood in Minas Gerais, which fused with his adoptive yet totally convincing *carioca* spirit. In the words of the musicologist João Máximo:

> ... em matéria de estilo e temperamento artístico, Ataúlfo sempre foi ind-ependente. Ouviu o que os sambistas do Estácio faziam, mas não os copiou. Entrou para o rádio, passou a conviver muito de perto com os compositores brancos dos anos 30 e 40, mas não foi influenciado por eles. Suas composições são inconfundíveis. Pelo menos as mais representativas não podiam ter sido feitas por ninguém mais. Há nelas o sabor tipicamente carioca ... mas também um tempero interiorano, uma mineirice que lhe confere um caráter único, puro Ataúlfo (... in terms of style and artistic temperament, Ataúlfo was always independent. He listened to what the *sambistas* of Estácio were doing, but did not copy them. He went into radio, and worked alongside the white composers of the 1930s and 40s, but he was not influenced by them. His compositions are unmistakable. At least the most representative ones could not have been written by anyone else. They contain a typically *carioca* flavour ... but also seasoning from the interior, a touch of Minas Gerais which gives them a unique character, pure Ataúlfo).[3]

McGowan and Pessanha refer to his marrying of lyrical laments with long, slow musical phrases, and suggest that his songwriting style may have been influenced by his youth in slow-paced, rural Minas Gerais.[4] According to Darwin Brandão, however, Ataúlfo was a *carioca* in spirit: 'Ataúlfo é o próprio sambista carioca com sua ginga malandra, sua bossa de morro' ('Ataúlfo is the *carioca sambista par excellence* with his *malandro* swagger, his *morro* style').[5]

Ataúlfo resisted foreign influences in his work, shying away from the trend for anglicisms in lyrics and the encroachment of North American music fashions, especially prevalent in the 1940s, '50s and '60s. His songs often have a strong emotional intensity, sentimental content and poetic quality when focused on the theme of women and love. With the samba '*Ai, que saudades da Amélia*' ('Oh, How I Miss Amélia'), written in 1941, he reached the zenith of his popularity, capturing the essence of samba in his treatment of the *cotidiano* with simplicity and humour, striking a chord in the *carioca* soul. Amélia was, in fact, the real-life washerwoman of the singer Araci de Almeida, and Araci's brother joked about her and her domestic skills with the *sambistas* who used to gather in the Café Nice. And so the samba was born which portrayed in a comic fashion the dedicated, subservient housewife, the ideal woman of the macho man of the people. The lyrics were, in fact, first written by Mário Lago but Ataúlfo changed them so considerably as he composed the accompanying music that they were barely recognizable, which displeased Lago. Ataúlfo said of this samba: 'Em casa meti os peitos no samba. Mudei então alguns versos. Não o sentido. Uma ou outra palavra, trocando de lugar uma frase para melhor adaptar minha música' ('At home I put my heart into this samba. I then changed some lines. Not the meaning. A word or two, moving a phrase around to adapt it to suit my music').[6]

Ataúlfo Alves died on 20 April 1969 after an operation for a duodenal ulcer, leaving a priceless legacy of songs, many of which remain virtually unknown, overshadowed by his 'classics'. One of the aims of this study is to bring greater exposure to the extensive, varied and enlightening output of this great *sambista*. He was one of the best known and most commercially successful of his kind in the 1930s and '40s, yet in spite of his popularity and prolific output (according to his son Ataulfinho he composed more than 1000 songs), no attempt has been made to produce a detailed, extensive examination of his work.[7] In a newspaper article written to commemorate the fifteenth anniversary of his death, the musicologist João Máximo wrote: 'Sambista da estatura de um Cartola, um Ismael Silva, um Nelson Cavaquinho, parece não disfrutar hoje, sobretudo entre os estudiosos da música popular, do mesmo prestígio daqueles três' ('A *sambista* of the stature of a Cartola, an Ismael Silva, a Nelson Cavaquinho, yet he does not appear to enjoy today, especially among scholars of popular music, the same prestige as the other three').[8]

In this chapter the key features of the lyrics that Ataúlfo composed between 1930 and 1945 will be outlined, in an attempt to suggest how they developed to remain in tune with the evolution of samba as it was transformed from the essence of black popular culture, with a strong oppositional stance *vis-à-vis* the hegemony of the dominant classes, into a coopted symbol of national identity. The corpus of 80 sambas chosen for this study was taken from a total of 185 sambas and *marchas*. The songs analysed include all those found in sheet music form which were written between 1930 and 1945. The precise number of sambas written by Ataúlfo in this period is impossible to ascertain, since many would never have been recorded or set down on sheet music, especially during his early career. The figure of over 1000 suggested by his son, although feasible, is not backed up by any further concrete evidence. In the sheet music archive in the *Ministério de Educação e Cultura* (Ministry of Education and Culture) in Rio de Janeiro there were over 350 entries for Ataúlfo, and although this collection is not exhaustive it does give some indication of his prolific output.

The discourse of the samba lyrics of Ataúlfo Alves

Of the 80 sambas studied here, the vast majority fall within the category of what is termed *lírico-amoroso* (lyrical-romantic) discourse, concentrating on the trials and tribulations of relationships with the opposite sex, most frequently the abandonment of a heartbroken man by a heartless, often unfaithful, woman. Ataúlfo's depiction of women is highly conventional, and he portrays all three of the stock types identified by Manoel Tosta Berlinck: the *malandra*, the idealized fantasy woman, and the domestic drudge.[9] The latter became synonymous with the character Amélia from his ultra-famous samba *'Ai, que saudades da Amélia'*:

'Ai, que saudades da Amélia', 1941, Ataúlfo Alves and Mário Lago

Nunca vi fazer tanta exigência
Nem fazer o que você me faz
Você não sabe o que é consciência
Não vê que eu sou um pobre rapaz?
Você só pensa em luxo e riqueza
Tudo que você vê você quer
Ai, meu Deus! Que saudade da Amélia
Aquilo, sim, é que era mulher

Às vezes passava fome ao meu lado
E achava bonito não ter que comer
Quando me via contrariado
Dizia: meu filho, o que se há de fazer?
Amélia não tinha a menor vaidade
Amélia é que era mulher de verdade

'Oh, How I Miss Amélia', 1941, Ataúlfo Alves and Mário Lago

I never saw anyone demand so much
Nor do what you do to me
You don't know what a conscience is
Can't you see I'm only a poor boy?
You only think about luxuries and riches
Everything you see you want

Oh, my God! How I miss Amélia
She was a real woman

Sometimes she went hungry at my side
She thought it was sweet having nothing to eat
When she saw I was angry
She would say: my dear, what can you do?
Amélia wasn't vain in the slightest
Amélia was a real woman

This masterpiece of explicitness and simplicity so captured the imagination of the people that the name Amélia is still used in colloquial speech to refer to a long-suffering wife or girlfriend. The thematic and stylistic immediacy, the latter captured by the natural, uncontrived speech forms, and the comical devotion of the poor woman in question, conspire to create an affectionate caricature which earned a place in popular consciousness in Brazil. This samba is something of an anomaly in Ataúlfo's work for the unaffected naturalness of its discourse. The sense of immediacy captured by the straightforward language and the way he directly addresses his new lover, is, however, a hallmark of his songs. They often begin abruptly, addressing an imaginary interlocutor. One such example is the samba 'Mal agradecida' ('Ungrateful Woman') written in 1940 by Ataúlfo in parceria with Jardel Noronha, in which a slighted lover launches a bitter verbal attack on his errant malandra partner, and which begins with a brusque command in the opening line:

Vai, vai fingida
Mal agradecida
Que não reconhece
O bem que eu lhe fiz

Go away deceitful one
Ungrateful one
That doesn't recognize
All I've done for her

Often the opening lines of his songs convey movement and action, such as in the samba 'Antes só do que mal acompanhado' ('Better Off Alone Than Badly Matched') of 1944, which begins:

Lá vem ela pedindo perdão do que fez

Here she comes asking forgiveness for what she's done

Likewise, the samba 'Não irei lhe buscar' ('I Won't Go and Look For You') of the same year has a startling opening, with the deceitful malandra being kicked out of the house. Once again the immediacy of the event and the emotional reaction of the embittered eu (I) are vividly evoked:

Arrume tudo que é seu, vá embora

Get all your things, go away

Ataúlfo's artistic personality is characterized by an absence of irony and of humour. In 1942, for example, he wrote a samba in defence of his famous creation Amélia entitled *'Represália'* ('Reprisal'), presumably written in response to someone poking fun at this character. In this samba he stresses that Amélia is a symbol of Brazilian women and thus should not be derided:

'Represália', 1942, Ataúlfo Alves

Não, não está direito não
Você não tem
A menor compreensão
Você merece
Receber uma lição
Por dizer que a minha Amélia
Morreu de inanição
Onde eu dizia
Que a coitada não comia
Era pura fantasia
Era força de expressão

Sua intenção foi de menosprezar
Esse amigo seu
Chegando até a afirmar
Que Amélia morreu
Sua ironia foi muito infeliz
Porque Amélia é apenas
Simbolismo
Da mulher do meu país

'Reprisal', 1942, Ataúlfo Alves

No, it's not right
You don't have
The slightest idea
You deserve
To be taught a lesson
For saying that my Amélia
Died of malnutrition
When I said
That the poor thing didn't eat
It was pure fiction
Force of expression

Your intention was to undermine
Your friend
By even stating
That Amélia died
Your irony was very unfortunate

Because Amélia is only
Symbolism
For the women of my country

Here Ataúlfo presents Amélia in a straightforward, ingenuous way. He
seems to have taken the witty criticisms of his song at face value and fails
to respond in a similarly light-hearted manner. Instead, in this naïve,
apologetic defence, he simply states the obvious, and makes his
symbolism explicit.

Ataúlfo avoids the theme of *malandragem* and rarely portrays the more
mundane aspects of daily life, concentrating instead on the acceptable
subject matter of women and love. He steers clear of the *malandro* both as
a source of inspiration and as an artistic persona, rejecting the witty,
ambivalent discourse that characterized the *samba malandro*, favoured by
the likes of Geraldo Pereira and Noel Rosa. In total contrast to Noel,
Ataúlfo is concerned with simple language as a fact of life and everyday
expression, on the whole. The use that each of these two *sambistas* makes
of rhyme in their lyrics is particularly telling. Ataúlfo's work is defined by
run-of-the-mill, predictable rhyme schemes or bland non-rhymes. Unlike
Noel, whose sambas displayed extraordinary linguistic dexterity, and who
thrived on comic, off-beat rhymes, Ataúlfo's rhymes are, by and large,
uninspired, repetitive and dull. In the samba '*Fale mal, mas fale de mim*'
('Speak Ill, but Speak of Me'), written circa 1944, for example, little
thought seems to have been spared for the easy rhymes, especially in the
first verse:

'*Fale mal, mas fale de mim*', circa 1940, Ataúlfo Alves and Marino Pinto

Fale mal
Mas fale de mim
Não faz mal
Quero mesmo assim
Você faz cartaz pra mim
O despeito seu
Me põe no apogeu

'Speak Ill, but Speak of Me', circa 1940, Ataúlfo Alves and Marino Pinto

Speak ill
But speak of me
It doesn't matter
That's how I want it
You're a walking billboard for me
Your spite
Puts me in my apogee

The obvious attempt at sophistication in the final line of this verse, with
the sudden introduction of the pseudo-literary *apogeu* (apogee), which
contrasts sharply with the banalities and relaxed, conversational tone of

the rest of the verse, and in particular with the 'Brazilianized' positioning of the direct object pronoun before the verb (*me põe*), is a significant reflection of Ataúlfo's creative aspirations, which are commented on in more detail later in this chapter.

Although Ataúlfo's lyrics are distinguished by their overwhelming simplicity and transparency, pseudo-poetic leanings can be seen when he deals with the theme of romantic love in particular. Such flowery discourse is a fitting accompaniment to this theme, and formed part of the convention itself. His efforts to embellish lyrics by drawing on techniques from erudite literature can be seen in the following samba:

'*Diz o teu nome*', 1941, Ataúlfo Alves and José Gonçalves

Diz o teu nome
Que eu desejo saber
Pela primeira vez
Que os meus olhos te viram
Tenho imenso prazer em conhecer

Tens quando quiseres
Tudo que é meu
O meu sobrenome
Depois do teu nome
Dar-te-ei um lar, minha flor
Pra fazer nosso ninho de amor

'Tell Me Your Name', 1941, Ataúlfo Alves and José Gonçalves

Tell me your name
I want to know it
Since the first time
That my eyes saw you
I've been delighted to know you

You can have when you want it
All that is mine
My surname
After your name
To you I will give a home, my flower
To make our love nest

Here the use of the grammatically complex future tense form with an epenthetic object pronoun (*Dar-te-ei*), rarely used in speech even among the highly educated, as well as clichéd motifs (*minha flor*, my flower; *ninho de amor*, love nest), bear witness to Ataúlfo's desire to gain credibility as a professional *sambista,* vying for the middle-class audience alongside educated whites like Ari Barroso and Noel Rosa. In the same way, in the following samba, in which we see his clear anti-*malandro* stance, Ataúlfo incorporates snippets of poetic discourse (*Oh! sultão*, Oh! sultan; *Na ilusão dos beijos viciosos/E dos carinhos pecaminosos*, In the illusion of vicious kisses/And of sinful caresses) in stark contrast to the snappy vernacular associated with the *samba malandro*:

'*Boêmio*', 1937, Ataúlfo Alves and J. Pereira

Boêmio
Nos cabarés da cidade
Buscas a felicidade
Na tua própria ilusão
Boêmio
A boemia resume
O vinho, o amor e o ciúme
Perfume, desilusão
Boêmio
Oh! sultão, porque é que queres
Amar a tantas mulheres
Se tens um só coração?
Boêmio
Pensa na vida um instante
E vê que o amor inconstante
Só traz por fim solidão
Boêmio, que fica na rua
Em noite de lua
Insone, a cantar
Na ilusão dos beijos viciosos
E dos carinhos pecaminosos
Boêmio, tu vives sonhando
Com a felicidade
Mas não és feliz
Vives, boêmio, sorrindo e cantando
Mas o teu sofrer, o teu riso não diz

'Bohemian', 1937, Ataúlfo Alves and J. Pereira

Bohemian
In the city's cabarets
You look for happiness
In your own illusion
Bohemian
Bohemia encompasses
Wine, love and jealousy
Perfume, disillusionment
Bohemian
Oh! sultan, why do you need
To love so many women
If you have only one heart?
Bohemian
Think about life for a minute
And you'll see that fickle love
Only brings loneliness in the end
Bohemian, who stays out
In the moonlight

Insomniac, singing
In the illusion of vicious kisses
And of sinful caresses
Bohemian, you live dreaming
Of happiness
But you aren't happy
You live, bohemian, smiling and singing
But your suffering your laughter belies

Ataúlfo's quest for commercial success led him to dodge the thorny issue of *malandragem*. Although the *malandro* very rarely features in his work, his reformed counterpart, the *malandro regenerado,* dutifully makes his presence felt from 1940 onwards, particularly between 1940 and 1941, reflecting Vargas's new work ethic and the quest to give the proletariat a positive, dignified self-image. This character is epitomized by the prot-agonist of the hit samba '*O bonde São Januário*' ('The São Januário Tram'):

'*O bonde São Januário*', 1940, Ataúlfo Alves and Wilson Baptista

Quem trabalha é quem tem razão
Eu digo, e não tenho medo de errar
O bonde São Januário
Leva mais um operário
Sou eu que vou trabalhar

Antigamente eu não tinha juízo
Mas resolvi garantir meu futuro
Vejam vocês
Sou feliz vivo muito bem
A boemia não dá camisa a ninguém
E digo bem

'The São Januário Tram', 1940, Ataúlfo Alves and Wilson Baptista

He who works is right
That's what I say and I know I'm right
The São Januário tram
Takes one more factory worker
It's me on my way to work

Before I had no sense
But I decided to secure my future
Just look
I'm happy and live very well
Bohemia doesn't put a shirt on anyone's back
And I say so

It would seem that Ataúlfo was swayed by the censorship constraints imposed by the DIP, and was eager to toe the official line. He wrote a spate of nationalistic, propagandist compositions, which extolled the virtues of the Brazilian nation, between 1940 and 1942. The highly patriotic *'Terra boa'* ('Good Land'), written circa 1940, which praises Vargas without naming him in the final lines, is typical of this trend:[10]

'Terra boa', circa 1940, Ataúlfo Alves and Wilson Baptista

Que terra boa
Para se ganhar o pão
Tem batucada
Tem luar e violão
Terra da liberdade
Onde o verso é um esporte
Ai, por essa terra
Dou o meu peito à própria morte

Terra que tem ferro e aço
Pra viver a eternidade
Canta a ave no espaço
O hino da liberdade
Tem lourinhas, tem morenas
Desde o sul até o norte
Ai, por essa terra
Dou o meu peito à própria morte

Terra de Santos Dumont
Carlos Gomes, Rui Barbosa
Grande Duque de Caxias
Castro Alves, Noel Rosa
Tem ainda um grande homem
Destemido e braço forte
Ai, por essa terra
Dou o meu peito à própria morte

'Good Land', circa 1940, Ataúlfo Alves and Wilson Baptista

What a good land
To earn your bread
It's got *batucada*
Moonlight and guitars
Land of liberty
Where writing poetry is a sport
Oh, that land
For it I'd give my life

Land that has iron and steel
To live for eternity
The bird sings in space
The hymn of liberty
It has blondes and brunettes
From the south to the north
Oh, that land
For it I'd give my life

Land of Santos Dumont
Carlos Gomes, Rui Barbosa

The great Duke of Caxias
Castro Alves, Noel Rosa
It has another great man
Fearless and strong
Oh, that land
For it I'd give my life

This samba gives value to rather clichéd aspects of life in Brazil, such as its moonlight, and the blondes and brunettes from all over the nation. Ataúlfo also venerates the country's mineral wealth,[11] as well as its popular musical production and famous sons from various fields: the aviator Alberto dos Santos Dumont (1873-1932), the classical composer Antônio Carlos Gomes (1836-95), the Bahian statesman and one of the founders of the Republic Rui Barbosa (1849-1923), Luís Alves de Lima e Silva (1803-80), decorated as the Duke of Caxias for his leadership of the Brazilian armed forces, and the great poet and champion of the slaves Antônio de Castro Alves (1847-71). The hackneyed allusions to *batucada*, *luar e violão* (moonlight and guitars) and *morenas* (brunettes and/or dark-skinned women) are typical of this kind of stirringly nationalistic song, with its innocent language, intended to strike a chord with the uneducated masses, and conventional appeal to national unity. In the lines *Canta a ave no espaço/O hino da liberdade* (The bird sings in space/The hymn of liberty) there are echoes of Brazil's most famous poem, which has come to symbolize the nation's past and identity, '*Canção do Exílio*' ('Song of Exile') by the Romantic poet Antônio Gonçalves Dias (1823-64).[12] Ataúlfo's 'quoting', however, is very vague, and it is doubtful that this is a conscious use of this well-worn image since he rarely includes learned references in his lyrics. This process of simplification and banalization is one of the trademarks of his work, both in terms of its linguistic and its thematic content. Motifs and expressions which for Ataúlfo were common currency, with no deeper significance, create a view of life that has an ingenuous simplicity, and is also politically obliging.

It seems odd that the Duke of Caxias, patron of the Brazilian armed forces and detested by blacks for his conscription of former slaves to fight in the brutal Paraguayan war (1865-70), should be revered in this song. However, the Paraguayan war and the figure of Caxias himself constituted a popular theme in the carnival celebrations under the *Estado Novo*, as the musicologist José Ramos Tinhorão shows.[13] The heroism and the memory of the blacks who perished during this conflict would presumably have been the justification for such a theme. The fact that, in this song, this list of supposed great national figures should end with the penniless, popular composer Noel Rosa himself, by now deceased, creates a rather kitsch effect. There was a series of songs written about Noel after the famous *sambista*'s death in 1937, and he earned a place in popular consciousness alongside establishment figures like those included above. For Ataúlfo there would have been no incongruity in bringing these varied celebrities together in his samba. The ostensible praise of Getúlio's fearlessness and strength in the closing lines could be interpreted as a reference to his resistance to relaxing the authoritarian control of his regime and to its repressive mechanisms. But it seems more likely that this song and others written in the same vein were the result of indirect cooption by the state.

Nevertheless, by 1942 the ambiguities of these apparently nationalistic songs were even more apparent, as we can see in Ataúlfo's samba '*Nós das Américas*' ('We of the Americas'), written in that year. Here it is possible to perceive an allusion to Vargas and a call for democratization in the final lines:

Há um gigante
Neste continente
Que tem um chefe
Que mora no coração do seu povo
E o mundo novo
Há de saber
Que esse gigante
Sabe cumprir seu dever

There is a giant
In this continent
That has a leader
Who lives in the heart of his people
And the new world
Will know
That this giant
Knows how to fulfil his duty

As the regime became more authoritarian the discourse of samba became more patriotic, and hyperbole was increasingly employed. Sérgio Augusto, in his article 'Getúlio Vargas em versos e trovas' ('Getúlio Vargas in Verses and Songs'), comments on the abundance of sambas of a highly nationalistic nature composed during the years of the New State, and he singles out the samba '*É negócio casar*', written by Ataúlfo and Felisberto Martins in 1941:

'*É negócio casar*', 1941, Ataúlfo Alves and Felisberto Martins

Veja só
A minha vida como está mudada
Não sou mais aquele
Que entrava em casa alta madrugada
Faça o que eu fiz
Porque a vida é do trabalhador
Tenho um doce lar
E sou feliz com meu amor

O Estado Novo
Veio para nos orientar
No Brasil não falta nada
Mas precisa trabalhar
Tem café, petróleo e ouro
Ninguém pode duvidar
E quem for pai de quatro filhos
O Presidente manda premiar

'The Thing To Do is To Marry', 1941, Ataúlfo Alves and Felisberto Martins

Just look
At how my life has changed
I'm no longer that person
Who used to come home in the early hours
Do what I did
Because life belongs to the worker
I've got a home sweet home
And I'm happy with my love

The New State
Came to lead us
In Brazil we want for nothing
But we must work
We have coffee, oil and gold
Nobody can doubt it
And the father of four children
Gets a prize from the President

Sérgio Augusto states that this song '... pertence à colheita adubada ... pelo ufanismo em alta durante a ditadura estadonovista' ('... belongs to the harvest fertilized ... by the chauvinism that peaked during the New State dictatorship'). He calls Ataúlfo an opportunist for apparently toeing the line in 1941 and yet, only four years later, in 1945, with the demise of the Vargas regime, criticizing its failings and making fresh demands in the samba *'Isto é o que nós queremos'* ('This Is What We want') ('... leite, carne, pão, açúcar ... escolas, liberdade e progresso', '... milk, meat, bread, sugar ... schools, freedom and progress').[14] Obviously Ataúlfo was not alone in seemingly spouting pro-establishment propaganda in his songs when it suited his career to do so. It is in this context that his use of simplistic exaggeration must be considered.

It is no coincidence that most of these propagandist songs were written after Brazil had declared war on the Axis powers on 21 August 1942, when rousing anthems were naturally most sought after by the DIP. In *'Salve a Bahia'* ('Viva Bahia'), written in 1943, Ataúlfo reproduces a string of platitudes to convey his appreciation of the city of Salvador in the northeastern state of Bahia. As in the previous example, overstated regal qualities are attributed to the object of the eulogy; in this case the city itself is crowned queen of both pilgrimage and poetry:

'*Salve a Bahia*', 1943, Ataúlfo Alves

Bahia terra que tem candomblé
Bahia de preta do acarajé
Bahia tradicional do meu Senhor
Bahia terra que só dá doutor

Cidade rainha da romaria
Cidade do batuque de Sinhá
Cidade rainha da poesia
(Ai Bahia)
Castro Alves nasceu lá
Bahia foi quem primeiro rezou
A missa que batizou meu país
Bahia terra que Rui consagrou
(Ai Bahia)
Ser baiano é ser feliz

'Viva Bahia', 1943, Ataúlfo Alves

Bahia the land of *candomblé*
Land of the black girl selling *acarajé*[15]
Traditional Bahia of our Lord
Bahia the land that only gives us scholars

The city of pilgrimage
The city of the *batuque* of *Sinhá*
The city of poetry
(Oh Bahia)
Castro Alves was born there
Bahia was where the first mass
That baptized my country took place
Bahia the land that Rui glorified
(Oh Bahia)
To be from Bahia is to be happy

Allusions to the state of Bahia and, indeed, to Rui Barbosa can be found in the songs of many other popular composers, such as Sinhô, who wrote the samba '*Fala meu louro*' ('Speak My Parrot') in 1920, poking fun at the Bahian senator, whom he refers to as a *papagaio louro* (blond parrot). Rui Barbosa had been, at the beginning of the 1920s, '... o comentário de todos os dias, a notícia permanente, a caricatura infalível nas admiráveis revistas de sátira política do tempo' ('... daily commentary, permanent news, the infallible caricature in the admirable political satire magazines of the era'), in the words of Edigar de Alencar.[16] Given that negative views were expressed about Rui Barbosa in song lyrics and in the press, Ataúlfo's veneration of him here is all the more conventional. This allusion to *Rui* is a good illustration of Ataúlfo's attempts to incorporate learned references into his lyrics to add a touch of refinement. The reference is brought down to earth, however, by the familiar use of his first name only. Ataúlfo takes the idea of bringing in an erudite allusion, but true to form he simplifies the device itself, thus making it more in keeping with the rest of his discourse.

In spite of the intrinsically casual nature of his style, Ataúlfo took care to ensure that elements of a semi-poetic nature were woven into his songs, often along with more natural features of lower-class vernacular. The music scholar Fernando Sales cites an interview in the course of which Ataúlfo showed a journalist examples of his lyrics in their original version, and later, modified versions of the same songs. Sales states that these revised sambas contained 'modificações para melhor, dando assim uma perfeita idéia de como trabalha' ('modifications to improve them, thus giving a perfect idea of how he works'). There can be no doubt that he tried to refine his lyrics in order to give them a more elegant, literary style, and Sales illustrates this by comparing an original and a modified version of the first part of a particular samba:[17]

Original version:

Ela foi embora
Antes do baile acabar
E a minha vida agora
É noite e dia procurar
O pé que tem a medida
Da sandália colorida

She went away
Before the dance ended
And I spend my life now
Night and day searching
For the foot that fits
The coloured sandal

Amended version:

Procuro a dona da sandália colorida
Que ficou na minha vida
Que ficou no meu olhar
Sei que ela está nessa louca multidão
Mas eu hei de encontrar
Para alegrar meu coração

I search for the owner of the coloured sandal
That remained in my life
That remained in my mind
I know that she is out there in that mad multitude
But I will find her
To cheer up my heart

The use of the pseudo-literary future tense form (*hei de*) in the revised version is especially interesting since it would rarely be used in speech, even amongst the educated, and would certainly be totally incongruous in colloquial language.

Ataúlfo uses a variety of techniques in order to elevate his discourse, to give it greater finesse. A selection of popular sayings and set phrases can be found in his lyrics, for example, and they often provide the inspiration for a song, such as the 1944 samba '*Antes só do que mal acompanhado*' ('Better Off Alone Than Badly Matched'):[18]

'*Antes só do que mal acompanhado*', 1944, Ataúlfo Alves and Benedicto Lacerda

Lá vem ela pedindo perdão do que fez
Mas não posso lhe perdoar outra vez
Ela foi para mim
Tudo quanto sonhei
Mas foi também
Um golpe errado que eu dei

Vou descansar um pouco
Trabalhei como um louco
Sem nenhuma compensação
O meu lar está vazio
Mas eu lanço um desafio
A quem mudar minha opinião
Diz um velho ditado
Antes só do que mal acompanhado

'Better Off Alone Than Badly Matched', 1944, Ataúlfo Alves and Benedicto Lacerda

Here she comes asking forgiveness for what she did
But I can't forgive her again
For me she was
Everything I'd dreamed of
But she was also
A mistake that I made

I'm going to rest a little
I've worked like a madman
For no reward
My home is empty
But I'll challenge anyone
To change my opinion
As the old saying goes
Better off alone than badly matched

Here he proudly acknowledges his use of a common proverb, in the penultimate line of the song. A similar use of ready-made sayings can be seen in the title and lyrics of the sambas '*Aconteça o que acontecer*' ('Come What May') and '*A mulher faz o homem*' ('Woman Maketh Man'), both of 1940. In the latter song Ataúlfo again explicitly points to his source of inspiration:

A mulher faz o homem
É o ditado quem diz

Woman maketh man
As the saying goes

He is more than willing to reveal the origin of such material, virtually boasting about his use of well-known sayings. The recourse to these set phrases reflects his efforts to make his lyrics more cultured, however banal the raw material. In the samba '*Só me falta uma mulher*' ('The Only Thing I'm Missing is a Woman') of 1942, he 'quotes' a popular poet, and his choice of the term *poeta* is a reflection of the status he attached to these proverbial phrases:

Eu já ouvi um poeta
Popular dizer
Que um homem sem mulher
Não vale nada

I've heard a popular
Poet say
That a man without a woman
Is worth nothing

One of the most obvious illustrations of Ataúlfo's appropriation of learned discourse is his use of literary devices. Again the majority of these aspiring erudite techniques are found in sambas of the *lírico-amoroso* type, dating right through from 1935 to 1944. Various examples of imagery in his work are worthy of mention. In the samba '*Laura*' ('Laura') of 1944 the abandoned *otário* begs Laura to return and, in an effort to convey the extent of his emotional distress, calls on a poetic metaphor in the following lines:

Sem ela sou uma ave ferida
Caída, sem força para voar

Without her I am an injured bird
Fallen, without the strength to fly

In '*Foi covardia o que eu fiz*' ('What I Did Was Cowardly') of 1943, the reformed *malandro* protagonist of this song is full of remorse at having abandoned his perfect mate. He first draws on a religious metaphor, quite common in *samba-canção* in particular, in order to stress his love for her. However, he then switches metaphors and enters the world of the judiciary:

'*Foi covardia o que eu fiz*', 1943, Ataúlfo Alves

Foi covardia o que eu fiz
Abandonando
Aquela pobre infeliz

Deus lhe ajude
Dê-lhe vida, pão e luz
Enquanto eu vivo
Carregando a minha cruz

Fui culpado de tudo que aconteceu
Sou um réu-confesso
Pois o erro é todo meu
Quando ela era sincera e leal
Não sei porque, me portei assim tão mal

Mas não me canso
De falar a vida inteira
Aquilo, sim
É que era companheira

'What I Did Was Cowardly', 1943, Ataúlfo Alves

What I did was cowardly
Abandoning
That poor unfortunate girl

God help her
Give her life, bread and light
Whilst I'm living
Carrying my cross

I was guilty of everything that happened
I'm a defendant that pleads guilty
Because the fault is all mine
When she was sincere and loyal
I don't know why, I behaved so badly

But I never tire
Of saying every day of my life
That that woman
Was a real companion

The combination of these two divergent metaphors in close proximity gives the song a rather kitsch quality but fully serves Ataúlfo's purpose. The *eu* is desperate to convey the intensity and sincerity of his regret and penitence, and therefore calls on the highest authority in both the spiritual and secular worlds. By aligning himself with the two pillars of justice and thus implicitly with the values of law-abiding bourgeois society, he seeks to give credence to his emotional outpourings.

At times Ataúlfo's use of extended metaphors is highly complex and skilful. In *'Errei, erramos'* ('I Made a Mistake, We Made a Mistake'), of 1938, the legal terminology is interwoven into the entire song. Again the *eu* of the samba wants to beg forgiveness for the failed love affair and chooses to use this elaborate, extended metaphor to say what is said so simply in others of Ataúlfo's songs. As suggested above, the choice of such imagery, the gravity of its associations and the sobriety of the language used, combine to substantiate the strength of his emotions. His ex-partner would find it hard to remain unimpressed by such eloquent, convincing manipulation of this baffling 'legalese' jargon:

'Errei, erramos', 1938, Ataúlfo Alves

Eu na verdade
Indiretamente sou culpado
Da tua infelicidade
Mas, se eu for condenado
A tua consciência
Será meu advogado
Mas
Evidentemente
Eu devia ser encarcerado
Nas grades do teu coração
Porque se sou um criminoso
És também nota bem
Que estás na mesma infração
Venho ao tribunal da minha consciência
Como réu-confesso
Pedir clemência
O meu erro é bem humano
É um crime que não evitamos
Este princípio alguém jamais destrói
Errei, erramos

'I Made a Mistake, We Made a Mistake', 1938, Ataúlfo Alves

I in truth
Am indirectly guilty
Of your unhappiness
But, if I'm condemned
Your conscience
Will be my lawyer
But
Obviously
I must be imprisoned
Behind the bars of your heart
Because if I'm a criminal
You are too, take note
You have committed the same offence
I come to the court of my conscience
As a defendant who pleads guilty
To ask for clemency
My mistake is very human
It's a crime we cannot avoid
This principle no one ever destroys
I made a mistake, we made a mistake

Likewise, personification is used in various compositions, particularly those of the sentimental, lyrical type. In *'Saudade dela'* ('Longing For

Her', date of composition unknown) Ataúlfo personifies his *saudade* (longing or nostalgia) for a former lover and begins by giving it a direct command to go away. This song is entirely constructed around the *saudade*, the inference being that his longing is so heartfelt and painful that it is physically palpable, and has come to life. Here he gives his longing such human qualities that it becomes a woman itself and ironically takes the place in his life left vacant by his ex-girlfriend:

> Vai, vai saudade
> À casa daquela ingrata
> Que deixou você pra mim
> Você vai dizer a ela
> Que eu agora sou feliz
> Que você está no lugar
> Da mulher que não me quis

> Go away, longing
> Go to that ungrateful woman's house
> The one who left you for me
> Go and tell her
> That now I'm happy
> That you've taken the place
> Of the woman who didn't want me

Sometimes simplicity of style is synonymous with immediacy and clarity in Ataúlfo's work, and the language he uses appeals to everyday experience. At other times, however, his solution to the problem of credibility is precisely the opposite, as he uses linguistic complexity and literary devices in order to convey the intensity of emotion, more in the manner of a *samba-canção*.

Self-referential elements in his work, although few in number, clearly illustrate the intellectual leanings of samba discourse in the 1930s and 1940s, as they hint at an aspiration towards a kind of metalanguage within the lyrics. '*Assunto velho*' ('That Old Theme') of 1940 is based on an explicit reference to the predictable nature of samba lyrics themselves, and in a tongue-in-cheek way Ataúlfo pokes fun at their obsession with the theme of women and love, in doing so paradoxically falling into this trap himself. Here he seems unable to escape the pull of the trite and the familiar, and admits that he is still bound to produce it in order to abide by the tacit conventions of the genre. It seems that the art of composition itself is beyond his control, since he begins with good intentions of writing something original but cannot escape the attraction of this well-worn subject:

> '*Assunto velho*', 1940, Ataúlfo Alves

> Eu que procurava um assunto novo
> Pra fazer um verso do povo

Sem falar no nosso amor
Que castigo
Falei num assunto antigo
Sem querer, eu rimei com a minha dor
Nosso amor

Minha dor é o sinônimo de uma saudade
Saudade vem de amizade
E não é original
E um assunto novo
Que eu queria escrever pro povo
Sem eu querer, terminei banal

Era minha intenção
Dizer nesta canção
Tudo aquilo que o meu pobre peito não diz
Mesmo não sendo verdade
Dizia, embora mentindo
Que passo a vida sorrindo
Que vivo alegre e feliz

Eu que pensava somente dizer novidade
Mas contra a minha vontade
A mulher veio à cena
Eu, que nem pensava nisso
Parece até que há feitiço
No papel, na tinta, e na minha pena

'That Old Theme', 1940, Ataúlfo Alves

I, who was looking for a new theme
To write some verses for the people
Without mentioning our love
What torture
Mentioned an old theme
Unintentionally I rhymed with my pain
Our love

My love is the synonym of longing
Longing comes from friendship
And isn't original
And a new theme
That I wanted to write for the people
Without intending to, I made banal

It was my intention
To say in this song
All that my poor heart can't say
Even not being true
I'd say, although lying
That I spend my life smiling
That I'm happy and cheerful

I only planned to write something new
But against my will

A woman came to mind
I wasn't even thinking about that
It's as if a spell has been cast
On the paper, the ink and my pen

The final two lines of the first verse are particularly clever. Here at the same time as mocking the unimaginative nature of the rhymes used in this type of samba, he creates one himself, the self-parody producing an ironic effect. This samba can be seen as a summing up of Ataúlfo Alves's whole ethos of samba writing. It constitutes a candid and humorous admission of his own creative limitations and holds a vital key to his artistic personality. Here he is recognizing that he is bound by convention to tackle the topic of love. He is also obliged to follow certain stylistic norms, such as predictable, tried-and-trusted rhymes and phrases, that are not original, as he confesses in this song. He is writing for the people, an audience which subconsciously understands these rules. He acknowledges that in the process he has created something banal. He wants to express emotion so he calls on hackneyed, formulaic lexis (*dor*, pain; *amor*, love; *saudade*, longing), with the odd touch of pseudo-erudition (*sinônimo*, synonym).

In his endeavours to make his lyrics more sophisticated Ataúlfo not surprisingly sometimes comes unstuck. When attempts at elegance and erudition come into sharp conflict with his natural plain talking, the result is an intermingling of different styles and registers of language. Such juxtapositions are telling reflections of his aspirations to appeal to a wider audience by moulding his lyrics to the tastes of the educated classes. This is a true *malandro* response to the challenge and opportunities offered by the commercialization of popular music in the 1930s and '40s, in that he is drawing on learned discourse for his own ends. In the sambas examined for this study, this clash of linguistic registers is most evident in those categorized as the *lírico-amoroso* type, which were written between 1937 and 1944 in general, as well as in those dealing with the figure of the reformed *malandro* composed between 1940 and 1943. To quote one example, in '*Por amor ao meu amor*' ('Out of Love for My Love') a heartbroken man, forced to leave his lover, but vowing to return, spouts everyday turns of phrase (*Se Deus quiser*, God willing) and speech forms (*Vou ver se faço*, I'll see if I can do), along with outpourings of a pseudo-literary type (*Embora o pranto/Inundasse os olhos meus*, Although my weeping/Flooded these eyes of mine), complete with the marked positioning of the possessive pronoun after the noun for poetic effect:

'*Por amor ao meu amor*', 1937, Ataúlfo Alves

Chorei porque
Tive que me despedir

Chorei de dor
Por amor ao meu amor
Se Deus quiser
E a sorte me ajudar
Você mulher
Breve venho lhe buscar

Vou ver se faço
Tudo para o nosso bem
Depois então
Levarei você também
Embora o pranto
Inundasse os olhos meus
Como sei que vou voltar
Não lhe digo adeus

'Out of Love for My Love', 1937, Ataúlfo Alves

I cried because
I had to say goodbye
I cried with pain
Out of love for my love
God willing
And if luck helps me
You woman
I'll come and look for you soon

I'll see if I can do
Everything for our good
So then
I'll take you away as well
Although my weeping
Flooded these eyes of mine
Since I know I'm going to return
I won't say goodbye to you

On occasion, these stylistic incongruities are more marked, as in *'Vem, amor!'* ('Come, love!') of 1939, which begins quite conventionally, but in the fourth line the tone is changed brusquely:

'Vem, amor!', 1939, Ataúlfo Alves and Raúl Longras

Vem amor
Reviver o nosso antigo lar
Vem amor
Que a saudade é um horror
É de amargar
Vem amor
Deixe o povo falar mal
Não faz mal
Eu, de novo, acabar nossa união
Não
Isso não

Duas lágrimas
Rolaram dos olhos meus
Quando ouvi você dizer
Passe bem, adeus

'Come, love!', 1939, Ataúlfo Alves and Raúl Longras

Come love
And bring our old home back to life
Come love
Longing is awful
It's murder
Come love
Let people speak ill
It's all right
Me, break up our marriage again
No
That no

Two tears
Rolled from these eyes of mine
When I heard you say
Take care, goodbye

By rhyming the nouns *amor* (love) and *lar* (home) with the colloquial expressions *é um horror* (is awful) and *É de amargar* (It's murder) respectively, Ataúlfo puts his personal stamp on this song. He brings the lyrics down to earth abruptly, and the obvious question that poses itself here is whether the bathos that results from these rhyming pairs is intentional or just inadvertent, a half-baked attempt at literary sophistication. Similarly, the informal expression *Não faz mal* (It's all right) and the repetitions of casual speech (*Não/Isso não*, No/That no) contrast with the pseudo-poetic motif of the tears and the marked, literary positioning of the possessive pronoun in the following two lines (*Duas lágrimas/Rolaram dos olhos meus*, Two tears/Rolled from these eyes of mine).[19]

It would be a grave mistake, however, to criticize this unorthodox marrying of apparently conflicting styles. Far from being a weakness of such lyrics, it is an innovative and unique characteristic of samba, highly appropriate for the ambiguous status enjoyed by this genre in the 1930s. Caught somewhere between a form of grass-roots popular culture and commercially viable commodity, it is not surprising that its discourse should be pulled in two opposing directions. Rather than contributing to the impoverishment of the genre, it is this very tension that is so intrinsic to the complex significance of these lyrics.

There are various instances of grammatical inaccuracies and inconsistencies in Ataúlfo's work. They are a reflection of the essentially oral process of composition that he used, which was naturally vulnerable to the slips and deviances common in speech, even among the educated. In various sambas from this corpus there are errors of Portuguese in the lyrics. It is of course impossible to determine whether these were typographical slips made when producing the sheet music. One example of this kind of mistake can be seen in the samba *'Pra esquecer uma mulher'* ('In Order to Forget a Woman') of 1940. The sheet music analysed confuses the words *mas* (but) and *mais* (more), a common type of spelling error, stemming from the phonetic identity between these two words in *carioca* Portuguese. The fact that similar kinds of mistakes occur relatively frequently would seem to suggest that many were made by Ataúlfo himself at the time of writing, in spite of his conscious efforts to be correct and learned, both in his work and in his personal demeanour.

It would seem that the subject pronouns *tu* and *você*, both meaning 'you', and their corresponding verb forms were a particular source of confusion for many *sambistas*. In his book of recollections of the Café Nice in this era, the journalist Nestor de Holanda refers to an incident when Jorge Veiga, the head of a recording studio, had to correct the grammar of a set of samba lyrics which mixed together these two forms. However, during the recording of the song the singer failed to remember the changes and sang the grammatically incorrect *você foste* (which roughly translates as 'you has gone') to which Veiga shouted *'O verbo é tu'* ('The verb is you')![20]

At times Ataúlfo can appear pedantic, striving to produce grammatically perfect constructions that a purist grammarian would be proud of, frequently creating very verbose lyrics in the process.[21] Bia Borges suggests that lower-class *sambistas* actually used tautology, redundant expression, repetition and verbosity in order to ensure that their language had the desired results and that their message was conveyed with as much clarity as possible.[22] Redundancy and pleonastic structures are other common features of Ataúlfo's work, and often simply take the form of direct repetition of a lexical item, such as the adverb *novamente* (again) in *'Covardia'* ('Cowardice') of 1938:

> Tenho medo francamente
> De te encontrar novamente
> E novamente te amar
>
> I am scared frankly
> Of meeting you again
> And of again loving you

and the verb *destruir* (to destroy) in the samba *'Continúa'* ('It Continues') of 1940:

> Pra que procurar me destruir
> Se eu luto noite e dia pra viver

Se você o faz pra me destruir
Deve desistir e me deixar em paz

Why try to destroy me
If I fight night and day to live
If you do it to destroy me
You must stop and leave me in peace

Reiteration of words and ideas is especially common in sambas of the *lírico-amoroso* type, where sentimental, clichéd nouns and verbs such as *saudade* (longing), *chorar* (to cry), *rir* (to laugh), *amor* (love), *esquecer* (to forget), *lembrar* (to remember), *dor* (pain), *sofrer* (to suffer or suffering), *pranto* (weeping) and *zombar* (to mock) are repeated from song to song and often within the same composition, for example in '*Mas, que prazer!*' ('But, What Pleasure!') of 1941:

'*Mas, que prazer!*', 1941, Ataúlfo Alves and Felisberto Martins

Que prazer
Tem você em zombar?
Quando vê meu pranto rolar
Você ri porque não sabe
A razão da minha dor
Quanto mais o tempo passa
Mais eu sinto
Saudades do meu primeiro amor

Quem teve um amor
A quem sincero se entregou
Há de compreender
O meu sofrer
E você
Vive sempre zombando de mim
Quer me ver sofrendo
Constantemente assim

'But, What Pleasure!', 1941, Ataúlfo Alves and Felisberto Martins

What pleasure
Do you have in mocking me?
When you see my weeping
You laugh because you don't know
The reason for my pain
The more time that passes
The more I feel
Longing for my first love

Whoever had a love
To whom he sincerely gave himself
Will understand
My suffering
And you
Are always mocking me
You want to see me suffering
Constantly like this

It would seem that Ataúlfo intends to reinforce his emotions via the constant repetition of their verbal labels like *dor* (pain), *saudade* (longing) and *sofrer* (to suffer or suffering), in order to convince his audience of his sincerity. Thus what appear to be negative, defective features of such songs do, in fact, have a positive function, whether intentional or not. Pleonasms become devices in themselves, which conspire to emphasize emotion.

In conclusion, Ataúlfo's artistic personality is full of contradiction and contrast. On the one hand, his linguistic style is natural and uncomplicated, and his choice of vocabulary and grammatical structures is undeniably banal. Irony and parody rarely feature in his work, the exception that proves the rule being the self-parodic samba '*Assunto velho*' ('That Old Theme') of 1940. In most cases his trite turns of phrase and naïve sentiments are what they seem. However, at times we also see Ataúlfo the aspiring poet and pseudo-intellectual, drawing on elements of learned, bourgeois discourse in an effort to glamorize the content of these songs and to gain wider commercial acceptance and success among the middle-class record-buying public and radio listeners. The ambiguities and paradoxes of register seen in many of his sambas provide a very telling reflection of broader socio-cultural phenomena at play during the 1930-45 period. A unique discourse emerges, which combines raw, uneducated speech forms, hackneyed expressions and even grammatical inaccuracies, with elements of literary tradition, such as poetic imagery and artistic devices. The flagrant stylistic juxtapositions that result from such combinations are charged with socio-cultural significance. It is essential when evaluating Ataúlfo's work, and any other form of popular production, to be constantly aware of our own education in erudite culture, and the specific criteria for evaluating such cultural forms that we have assimilated. When examining his work and that of other *sambistas* we must adjust our perspective accordingly. It is imperative to understand the social origins of both the artist and his audience, and never let value judgements distort our view of the artistic production in question.

The wider implications of Ataúlfo's lyrics are linked to the cultural issue intrinsic to the dubious, unstable nature of popular culture as a whole, and more specifically to samba in the 1930s and first half of the 1940s. With the rise of the culture industry, particularly the new media of the radio and gramophone record, and the appropriation of this genre by educated white musicians, samba was no longer the pure, untainted preserve of poor Afro-Brazilians, but neither was it an entirely democratized commodity for mass consumption. Black *sambistas* like Ataúlfo thus began to adopt many of the stylistic techniques of their social superiors, incorporating them into their own characteristic discourse. The resulting clash of styles, whether deliberate or not, is a direct reflection of the socio-cultural gap between these two strata of Rio society, and of the efforts made by the poor to bridge this gap by climbing the professional ladder of the *sambista*. Ataúlfo, and other black samba composers, drew on the literary style of the middle classes, but they never abandoned their own discourse and the traditional themes of samba. Far from being restricted by this innovative adoption of apparently alien techniques and language, they used them imaginatively, intermingling them with those of their own creation, and thus opening up many new artistic options.

Like any form of popular culture, *carioca* samba is inextricably linked to its social context. The dramatic shifts in social hierarchy and class structure that were taking place in Rio in the 1930s and early '40s are reflected in the ambiguities and antagonisms so intrinsic to Ataúlfo's discourse. Furthermore, unlike an example of erudite, literate culture, where we naturally expect to find a single, easily identifiable personality at work, it serves no purpose to search for absolutes and constants in Ataúlfo's work. It is his inconsistent, erratic style itself which is enlightening, since it gives us invaluable information concerning the social context in which he was writing, his own artistic and commercial aspirations, and, finally, the ambivalent, ever-changing role and status of samba itself in this era.

Notes

1. Holanda, N. de (1970), p. 118.
2. Brandão, D. (1956), pp. 46-9.
3. Máximo, J. (1984), 'Um mestre que mereceu bem mais', p. 1.
4. McGowan, C. and Pessanha, R. (1998), p. 27.
5. Brandão, D. (1956), p. 46.
6. Ibid., p. 49.
7. Aragão, D. (1984), p. 1.
8. Máximo, J. (1984), 'Um mestre que mereceu bem mais', p. 1.
9. Berlinck, M. T. (1976), pp. 101-2.
10. See also '*É negócio casar*' of 1941, written by Ataúlfo Alves and Felisberto Martins, pp. 72-3.
11. The reference to Brazil's mineral wealth should be seen in the context of the loan of 20 million dollars granted to Brazil by the US Export-Import Bank in September 1940, which financed the construction of the huge Volta Redonda steelworks in the state of Rio de Janeiro, and was an important foreign policy coup for the Vargas administration.
12. 'Minha terra tem palmeiras/Onde canta o sabiá/As aves que aqui gorjeiam/Não gorjeiam como lá ...' ('My homeland has palm trees/Where the thrush sings/The birds that chirp here/Do not chirp like they do there ...'). It is interesting to compare and contrast this 'quoting' of Brazil's unofficial 'national poem' with that of Noel

Rosa in the samba '*O orvalho vem caindo*', pp. 126-7, and with the echoes of it in Ari Barroso's '*Aquarela do Brasil*', pp. 169-71.
13. Tinhorão, J. R. [n.d.], *Música popular: um tema em debate*, p. 84.
14. Augusto, S. (1983), p. 68.
15. An Afro-Brazilian dish typical of Salvador, made from beans fried in palm oil.
16. Alencar, E. de (1981), pp. 33, 53.
17. Sales, F. (1984), pp. 31-2.
18. Bia Borges notes that this is also a common feature of *samba-canção*. She suggests that these set expressions in *samba-canção* form a contrasting diction with more spontaneous, frank outbursts, what she terms a '*quebra lingüística*' ('linguistic break or rupture'). Borges, B. (1982), pp. 75, 89.
19. A further example of this intermingling of divergent styles and registers of language in sambas on the topic of love can be found in '*Já sei sorrir*' ('I Know How To Smile'), written by Ataúlfo Alves in 1939 in *parceria* with Claudionor Cruz. An unusual song in that it deals with romantic love from a positive point of view, the errant lover having returned, it includes banal, almost comic elements (*Hoje vivo a gargalhar*, Today I spend my life guffawing) and examples of everyday vernacular (*Graças a Deus*, Thank God), alongside sophisticated literary devices, such as the romantic metaphor in the final lines (*Porque tenho duas luas/A iluminar os sonhos meus/Que são os lindos olhos seus*, Because I have two moons/Illuminating these dreams of mine/That are those beautiful eyes of yours), complete with marked positioning of the possessive pronouns, which creates a highly sentimental effect.
20. Holanda, N. de (1970), p. 190.
21. In the samba '*Diz o teu nome*' ('Tell Me Your Name') of 1941, p. 67, for example, Ataúlfo painstakingly reproduces the elaborate, purist future indicative tense form (*Dar-te-ei*, I will give you).
22. Borges, B. (1982), p. 68.

CHAPTER FIVE

The Sambas of Noel Rosa
(1910-37)

Noel de Medeiros Rosa was born on 11 December 1910. From an early age he showed an interest in music, stealing the keys to the family's piano and playing it in secret. He would confess to this and seek forgiveness by leaving messages for his family in the form of short poems. He was born into a middle-class family of changing fortunes, which experienced wealth in the coffee boom but also poverty: Noel's father, Manoel, became bankrupt on more than one occasion. Noel thus learned to consider money as a necessary evil and deplored avarice. However, his childhood was not an unhappy one, in spite of his physical defect, caused by the use of forceps during his birth, which earned him the nickname of '*O Queixinho*' ('Little Chin'). His love of pranks and dare-devil antics soon ensured that none of the other local children mocked him. Unlike his younger brother Hélio, who was considered to be a child prodigy by his family, Noel preferred the outside world to books. He loved the street and his *bairro* of Vila Isabel. He was a very observant child, and was interested in people from all walks of life, a trait of character that would provide him with much raw material for his songs in later life.

Few *bairros* of Rio de Janeiro have such a diverse population as Vila Isabel had in the first 40 years of the twentieth century. It was a place where varied social classes and races mixed together in the bars and streets. It was perhaps such an eclectic population because of the area's proximity to other *bairros* of very diverse types, such as affluent Tijuca, Andaraí, a working-class area where various factories were located, Engenho Novo, with its provincial air, Maracanã, the home of conservative families, and the *morros* of Mangueira and of Macacos. Vila Isabel was, consequently, a mixture of all these districts, and its inhabitants ranged from respectable professionals to marginals. It also attracted occasional visitors, like travelling salesmen and loan sharks, the latter mostly European immigrants, but collectively known as *judeus* (Jews) or *turcos* (literally Turks, but in reality Syrio-Lebanese Christians who were subjects of the Turkish Empire, in most cases), and some Portuguese.[1] Noel sensed the whole community's dependence on and fear of these immigrants. His own father resorted to borrowing from them in order to pay off his loans, and prejudice against them was widespread. In his sambas Noel drew heavily on his experiences in Vila Isabel, creating microcosms of life there. The villain of the piece is often the loan shark or *prestamista*.

At the age of 13 Noel moved from a small day school in Vila Isabel, where he had been taught by family friends, to the Benedictine monastery of São Bento - a very solemn and austere school with military-style discipline and high academic demands. Noel, however, was unwilling to adapt and give up his free-and-easy childhood. He was reared in a home where poetry readings and family sing-songs provided the evening entertainment, and his mother taught him to play the mandolin. In the poorer suburbs of Rio, and in the shantytowns, especially where there was a black or *mestiço* (mixed race) population, the upper-class interest in *estrangeirismos* (foreign fashions and styles), such as French and English poetry, and European and North American dances, like the waltz, the polka and the charleston, was unknown. Instead, in these communities samba ruled, and in the working-class *Zona Norte* Brazilian poets took precedence. Vila Isabel fell between these two camps, between the simplicity of the poorer areas, and the snobbery of the upper-class districts. Noel was therefore exposed to all kinds of music and grew to love this variety. After learning to play the mandolin, he was given his first guitar lesson by his father. He gradually abandoned the mandolin and taught himself to play the guitar, which gave him a great sense of importance.

He was a rebellious pupil, forever playing tricks on and mimicking his teachers, and had no interest in his education. By the age of 14 he was already smoking and drinking beer in the bars that he frequented. He was, nevertheless, a bright and creative teenager, and set up and ran a clandestine alternative school newspaper - *O Mamão* - a name with the kind of *risqué double entendre* that he loved, and which he incorporated into his songs in later life.[2] Noel was already mixing in varied circles, playing football on the *morros*, befriending tram drivers, and becoming a regular at the bar O Cavaquinho de Ouro, in Rua da Alfândega, where famous popular musicians like Sinhô and João Pernambuco met and played.

Noel's gift for writing poetry was evident from an early age. When asked by a teacher to write all that he knew about the chemical bromide in a 40-minute test, he produced a correct answer written in perfect rhyming verse. As Máximo and Didier say: 'Métrica e rimas perfeitas, prosaíco bromo transformado em poema' ('Perfect rhyme and metre, prosaic bromide transformed into a poem').[3] This was a foretaste of his ability to transform the most banal of subjects into samba lyrics.

Noel's interest in women began at a precocious age. He was intrigued by prostitutes when a young boy and had his first sexual encounter at the age of 12 or 13. By his fifteenth birthday he was visiting brothels on a regular basis, a practice that continued throughout his life, and he claimed to feel at home among this marginal community. He befriended young prostitutes from the red-light district of Mangue, but when he was in his late teens, he met Clara, who had recently arrived in Vila Isabel with her family. From childhood sweetheart, she was to become perhaps his only true love.

From about the age of 17 Noel began to show a fascination for the *malandro* character, and although he did not live entirely by the rules of *malandragem* himself, he accepted them and vaunted this lifestyle in his songs. He counted several *malandros* among his friends, and he thus became very familiar with their world and gained a greater understanding of how it operated. In many ways Noel was the protagonist of his samba 'Malandro medroso' ('Fearful *Malandro*') of 1930, in that he believed in the ethos of *malandragem* but was also somewhat afraid of its repercussions.[4]

Vila Isabel was a hive of musical activity in the 1920s and '30s, and Noel's home soon became the meeting place for middle-class musicians, such as Vicente Gagliano and the pianist Nonô, as well as poor *sambistas* from the surrounding shantytowns. Together they would take part in serenades. The local *botequins* (bars) and street corners brought people together, and music constituted an effective leveller of social classes. The bar De Carvalho is thought to have been where Noel wrote many of his songs.[5] Carvalho, the owner, acted as a kind of agent for Noel, informing him of who wanted him to perform where and when. Although there was a contrast in Vila Isabel between the less well-off, long-standing inhabitants, and the wealthier new arrivals, the Boulevard or main street, where most of the bars were located, was a neutral zone. All classes and races mingled freely there. Like other amateur musicians, Noel would compose and perform in these bars, receiving payment in the form of beer and food bought by the customers. By the age of 18 he was well known in Vila Isabel as a guitarist and was frequently called upon to accompany singers. As well as producing its own musicians and performers, Vila Isabel attracted others from outside, such as Lamartine Babo and Francisco Alves.

By 1929 there were five record companies in Brazil. All were eager to sign up new artists and approached amateur groups like Flor do Tempo (Flower of Time), whose members were middle-class young men, who asked Noel to join them. In 1929 he joined up with four of them - Almirante, João de Barros, Álvaro Miranda and Henrique Britto - to form the Bando de Tangarás (Band of Manakins).[6] All were from respectable, bourgeois families and gave themselves pseudonyms to conceal their identities, on the advice of Carlos Alberto Ferreira Braga, better known as João de Barros, the son of an industrialist. They decided to preserve their amateur status since it was still frowned upon to earn a living from music, although the radio and the record industries were beginning to open up great opportunities for educated, young musicians. The Bando de Tangarás signed a recording contract with Parlophone and in 1930 launched their first hit entitled *'Na Pavuna'* ('In Pavuna'), which brought together string instruments like the guitar and *cavaquinho*, and the percussion instruments used by the carnival groups or *blocos*, such as the small *tamborim* and the *bumbo* or *bombo*, a larger drum, which were used to mark the rhythm of the processions in the Praça Onze by the first samba schools. Despite the misgivings of friends who believed that these percussion instruments were unsuitable for the medium of the gramophone record, this combination was a success.[7]

Unlike the other members of the group, who attended up-town parties, Noel preferred to socialize with *malandros*, gamblers, factory workers and bohemians. He dressed eccentrically, in the style of the spiv, in his white suit, black shirt, pale tie and two-tone shoes. He did not care what people thought of him, and would wear whatever he felt like wearing, regardless of the occasion. This disregard for convention and his eccentricity were also to manifest themselves in his lyrics. It was at this stage in his life that he began to take songwriting seriously. Although the Bando de Tangarás had originally concentrated on northeastern music, which was very fashionable among similar groups at that time, Noel did not remain faithful to these regional styles, and he started to experiment with other popular musicians, such as Renato Murce. Noel began to establish his individuality as a songwriter, while still fluctuating between different genres and between his commitments to the band and his solo career. He found that the samba was the genre best suited to expressing both his own feelings as a fervent *carioca* and the everyday life of the city of Rio. He adopted the type of samba that originated in the Estácio de Sá district of the city, and had been disregarded by record companies for many years because of its associations with marginality, both in its lyrics and as a result of the social status of its poor, black creators. Like Francisco Alves, Noel frequented these areas and recognized the talents of *sambistas* such as Ismael Silva and Nilton Bastos. Noel's first solo hit, the samba *'Com que roupa?'* ('In What Clothes?') of 1929, was revolutionary in that it was based formally on the sambas of Estácio and signified a break with convention by a middle-class musician. Sérgio Cabral says that Noel symbolized a new breed of educated composers of popular music, who looked to the poor people for inspiration. He brought together in his lyrics information acquired from school and from his readings, and the values of the masses.[8] Fifteen thousand copies of the record *'Com que roupa?'* were sold, a figure rarely attained by Noel's contemporaries. A friend distributed copies of the sheet music in the streets, singing the samba to publicize it, and the song took over the city. It was also the first of his sambas to be used in the theatre, in a show called *'Deixa essa mulher chorar'* ('Let That Woman Cry') starring Araci Cortes. After this huge success Noel was pursued by famous singers and those in the world of radio.

After completing his senior schooling, thanks only to decree 19.404 of 14 November 1930, by which all students automatically passed on to the next stage of their education without sitting the relevant examinations, Noel narrowly passed the entrance examination for medical school. It was hoped that he would follow in the footsteps of his uncle, grandfather and great-grandfather, who were all doctors. But Noel soon decided that he could not study medicine and write sambas at the same time, and he abandoned his university studies during the first year.

At this time Noel's romantic interests became increasingly complicated. He continued to court Clara, but also maintained a long-standing relationship with Josefina Teles Nunes, better known as Fina, a factory worker from Vila Isabel and the inspiration for his samba *'Três apitos'* ('Three Whistles'), written in 1933. The third woman in his life was Julinha, a worldly night club artist some ten years older than Noel. He managed to keep all three romances alive, yet his mother continued to prepare a modest *trousseau* for Clara, who still believed that she would be his bride. However, Noel was eventually forced into marrying a 16-year-old girl called Lindaura, who worked in a laundry in Vila Isabel, and whose mother had reported Noel to the police for kidnapping her daughter when she found out that they had spent the night together in a hotel. But Noel's womanizing was not tamed by matrimony, and he continued a liaison with Ceci (Juraci Correia de Morais), a beautiful night club hostess, who inspired his samba *'Dama do cabaré'* ('Lady of the Cabaret') of 1936.

Noel collaborated extensively with other *sambistas* and consciously sought out *parceiros* in the black community. Unlike the singer Francisco Alves, who bought false *parcerias* in business transactions, Noel became integrated into this group and forged many friendships with Afro-Brazilian musicians. He became close friends with Cartola and adored life in the shantytown of Mangueira, where he watched the rehearsals of the samba school. He also wrote many sambas in partnership with Ismael Silva, some of which were sold to Francisco Alves to help pay off a debt for a

Chevrolet car that Noel had bought from him. It was not unusual for Noel to sell lyrics that he had scribbled down on the back of a cigarette packet.[9]

By 1932 Noel's work was reaping considerable profits for the publishers of his sheet music. By 1933 the Bando de Tangarás had virtually disintegrated, with Almirante pursuing a varied radio career. Noel recorded many of his own songs himself, since the electric recording system allowed even singers with the weakest voices to do so. His singing technique has been referred to as *meia voz* or half voice, a semi-spoken style, which suited the melodies of many of his satirical sambas and the slower, more sombre *samba-canção*.[10] He was also performing constantly in cinemas, theatres, and on the radio, as well as in the recording studio. He became the star of the Programa Casé on Radio Transmissora, owned by RCA Victor, but he had no exclusive contract with any radio station, and was able to work on various shows. In his work for Parlophone he corrected the lyrics of other composers and even improved those of famous musicians. Many people wanted to be his musical *parceiro* and in 1933 he replaced the ill Lamartine Babo on a tour of southern Brazil with Francisco Alves and the Ases do Samba (Aces of Samba). No other popular musician of this period was as well known as Noel Rosa.

In 1933 he produced about 40 songs. This same year he fell ill and the first signs of tuberculosis appeared when he fainted during a show. He was subsequently coerced into marrying Lindaura and, at the beginning of 1935, they went to stay with his aunt in Belo Horizonte, the state capital of Minas Gerais. But Noel refused to rest there, and wrote lyrics into the early hours of the morning. On his return to Rio he continued to live intensely and rented a love-nest for himself and Ceci. On 3 May 1935 his father committed suicide in hospital, after treatment for depression. Throughout that year Noel continued his frenetic work schedule, in spite of his failing health, and performed on four of the 14 radio stations in Rio, as well as giving many live performances. He wrote parodies for Almirante's radio show and two comic operas which he never heard broadcast, entitled '*O barbeiro de Niterói*' ('The Barber of Niteroi') and '*A noiva do condutor*' ('The Tram Driver's Fiancée'). He was also the first musician to write to order for the Brazilian cinema. '*Alô, alô, carnaval*' ('Hello, Hello, Carnival'), which premiered on 20 January 1936, was the first film to include his songs. In the carnival of that year Noel was the big name, and predominated in both the quantity and quality of his work, although not all his songs were newly written. He was still involved with the Programa Casé on the radio, but in 1936 he wrote very little new material, apart from songs for the film '*Cidade mulher*' ('Woman City'), set in Rio.

By now he had begun seriously to neglect his health and appearance.

Despite the threat of tuberculosis recurring he refused to eat properly or rest, and persisted in spending his nights in the local bars. He also discovered that his wife was expecting a child, which she later lost in an accident. Progressively his lyrics became more melancholy. Ceci had started dating Mário Lago, a well-known musician, and Noel had stopped frequenting his old haunts in the bohemian district of Lapa, preferring to wander around the bars of Vila Isabel alone. As if he sensed death approaching, he sorted out his possessions, giving some to his friends, and collecting together his own press cuttings and theatre programmes.

For the carnival of 1937 Noel composed no new songs, and the sambas that he wrote in this final stage of his life are marked by bitterness and self-pity, such as '*Só você*' ('Only You') and '*Eu sei sofrer*' ('I Know How To Suffer'). After two brief periods of rest outside Rio, in Nova Friburgo and Piraí, Noel was confined to his room in his mother's house in Vila Isabel, where he died, aged 26, on 4 May 1937.

Noel Rosa played a decisive role in creating a new kind of popular music in Brazil. His sambas were written in a climate of great social, political and economic ferment, when there was no tradition of consumer music, and the radio and gramophone record were only just taking root. He wrote over 200 melodies and/or sets of lyrics between the ages of 16 and 26, and undoubtedly sold many others just to hear them recorded or to earn a fast buck. Many of these false *parcerias* never acknowledged his contribution. In most cases he wrote both the music and the lyrics, and only about 40 per cent of his output was written in collaboration with other musicians.[11] In his lifetime he had 56 *parceiros*, which was more than any other composer in a comparable period of time. The samba was his favourite genre, and over 70 per cent of his compositions, whether solely of his authorship or written in *parceria*, were classified as sambas. However, many of these are difficult to categorize. Luiz Antônio Afonso Giani examines a sample of 20 recordings of his work, most dating from before his death and some sung by Noel himself, and discovers that only eight can be categorized by the generic samba rhythm, with an emphasis on percussion and syncopation, and have the traditional humorous or satirical lyrics. The majority, Giani believes, would now be termed *samba-de-meio-de-ano* or *samba-canção,* and 12 of the sample have an average or slow tempo, more akin to this sub-genre of samba. Among these he cites '*O orvalho vem caindo*' ('The Dew is Falling') of 1933, and '*Dama do cabaré*' ('Lady of the Cabaret') of 1936. But Noel called them all simply 'sambas'. Giani underlines the rich melodies and harmonies that Noel created, which are often overshadowed by his lyrics. He adds that the quality of his music is comparable with that of Ari Barroso or Lamartine Babo, who each produced little more than Noel in 35 years.

Women and love affairs constitute a major thematic strand in Noel's sambas, and he reproduces this convention with authenticity. He also draws on his own chequered and largely unhappy experiences of relationships with the opposite sex as a source of inspiration. He is, thus, overwhelmingly pessimistic in his portrayal of love and very critical in his representation of women. Máximo and Didier say that he did not believe that he could be loved and, therefore, saw love as deceit, lies, trickery and pretence. They calculate that less than half a dozen of all his songs deal with romantic love in a positive way.[12] His lyrics explore various aspects of romance, predominantly the deceitful nature of the opposite sex, domestic strife, often resulting from the latter and, ultimately, the painful breakdown of a partnership, usually occasioned by a faithless woman's abandonment of her mate. The thematic emphasis of Noel's love sambas is placed on the disintegration of romantic unions and the resulting heartache caused to the male *eu* of these songs. There is, without doubt, a heavy autobiographical content in many of his melancholy compositions, and the prevalence of pain and despondency, particularly in the sambas written in the final years of his life, mirrors closely his own frustrated attempts at finding true, long-lasting love. Moments of optimism and carefree expressions of his love are virtually non-existent. According to Okky de Souza, Noel was probably Brazil's most brilliant popular composer of all time, and translated the soul of Rio with the perceptiveness of a sociologist and the simplicity of a barstool philosopher. Noel, he says, revolutionized the lyrics of samba, which were formerly of little importance.[13] He was given the title of '*O Filósofo do Samba*' ('The Philosopher of Samba') by César Ladeira, a radio presenter, and, as a temporary member of the group Gente do Morro (Shantytown People), Noel was introduced on stage as the Bernard Shaw of samba. The former title was to remain with him for ever.

The discourse of the samba lyrics of Noel Rosa

Noel Rosa was a consummate wordsmith, whose song lyrics display a wit and linguistic ingenuity unrivalled by his contemporaries. He earned the title of '*Filósofo do Samba*' for the realism and universal truths that served as inspiration for many of his sambas, but he was essentially a barstool thinker whose short life was largely spent in the cheap bars of Rio's more humble northern districts, or the night spots of bohemian Lapa, the then capital's red-light district. Noel was influenced by the characters who inhabited Rio's poorer quarters, and had a particular fascination with the *malandros* that he encountered in the socially mixed *bairro* of Vila Isabel, where he grew up, and elsewhere. He was the first *sambista* to draw attention to the lyrics of popular song, and any study of his work must focus on his linguistic approach to the conventional themes of samba. His attitude to life itself is reflected in the style of his language, and the theme and form of his songs are inextricably linked. Furthermore, his acclaim as the 'Philosopher of Samba' was closely connected to the uncon-ventionality of his style and his foregrounding of language itself. It seems fitting to begin this study of Noel's work in the *botequim* - the street-corner bar, where Noel wrote many of his sambas and found much of his inspiration and personal enjoyment. The samba '*Conversa de botequim*' ('Bar Talk') of 1935 exemplifies Noel's inimitable treatment of the well-worn theme of *malandragem* and his interest in the minutiae of everyday existence:

'*Conversa de botequim*', 1935, Noel Rosa

Seu garçom, faça o favor
De me trazer depressa
Uma boa média que não seja requentada
Um pão bem quente com manteiga à beça
Um guardanapo
E um copo d'água bem gelada
Fecha a porta da direita
Com muito cuidado
Que não estou disposto
A ficar exposto ao sol
Vá perguntar ao seu freguês do lado
Qual foi o resultado do futebol

Se você ficar limpando a mesa
Não me levanto nem pago a despesa
Vá pedir ao seu patrão
Uma caneta, um tinteiro
Um envelope e um cartão
Não se esqueça de me dar palitos
E um cigarro pra espantar mosquitos
Vá dizer ao charuteiro
Que me empreste umas revistas
Um isqueiro e um cinzeiro

Telefone ao menos uma vez
Para 34-4333
E ordene ao seu Osório
Que me mande um guarda-chuva
Aqui pro nosso escritório
Seu garçom me empreste algum dinheiro
Que eu deixei o meu com o bicheiro
Vá dizer ao seu gerente
Que pendure essa despesa
No cabide ali em frente

'Bar Talk', 1935, Noel Rosa

Waiter, kindly
Bring me quickly
A large white coffee, not reheated
A warm roll with heaps of butter
A napkin
And a nice cold glass of water
Shut the door on the right
Carefully
I don't feel like
Being exposed to the sun
Go and ask that customer there
The football score

If you carry on wiping the table
I won't get up or pay the bill
Go and ask your boss
For a pen, an inkwell
An envelope and a card
Don't forget the toothpicks
And a cigarette to keep away the mosquitoes
Go and tell the cigar seller
To lend me some magazines
A lighter and an ashtray

Phone at least once
Number 34-4333
And tell Osório
To send me an umbrella
Here to our office
Waiter, lend me some money
I left mine with the bookie
Go and tell your boss
To hang this bill
On the hook over there

Adopting the persona of the *malandro* here, Noel introduces innovations into the typical treatment of the theme by incorporating elements of everyday discourse and mundane aspects of daily life into the lyrics. He establishes himself as a silver-tongued spiv in the opening line, with the polite form of address to the lowly waiter, and with his choice of the respectful third-person command forms throughout. The immediacy is captured in this use of direct address, the colloquial speech form *à beça* (heaps of), the banal nature of the objects requested (such as butter, a napkin, toothpicks) and the inspired inclusion of the telephone number, which neatly fits into the rhyme scheme. Noel has a keen eye for the absurdities and the inherent tragi-comedy of life. Here the penniless *malandro*, who admits, euphemistically, to having left all his money with the *bicheiro* or clandestine bookie, is demanding impeccable service from a down-market, mosquito-ridden bar, which he ironically terms his office. Noel gives status to the commonplaces of *carioca* life, such as football, the illegal gambling game known as the *jogo do bicho*, and the figure of the *malandro* himself, which are all unofficial national institutions, albeit associated primarily with the poor, and controversial and marginalized in the case of the latter two. This samba epitomizes Noel's iconoclastic approach to the lyrics of popular song, and clearly illustrates his unique portrayal of the *cotidiano*, which combined attention to realistic but quirky details and street vernacular.

Noel: the 'cronista do cotidiano'

Noel's genius can be attributed, in part, to the fact that he gave poetic status to the *vida cotidiana* (daily life), and he has often been referred to as a chronicler of everyday life. Máximo and Didier say that by 1931 almost all Noel's songs had the quality of a *crônica* or newspaper column. In their words: 'Cantar o seu bairro, a sua cidade, o seu país. Retratar os personagens que trafegam por aí, focalizar os episódios que testemunha, captar o espírito de tudo isso, eis o destino de Noel Rosa, poeta e cronista' ('Singing about his district, his city, his country. Portraying the characters that pass by, homing in on the episodes that he witnesses, capturing the spirit of all this, this is all the destiny of Noel Rosa, the poet and chronicler').[14] The literary critic Antonio Candido, in his article 'A vida ao rés-do-chão' ('Life on the Bottom Floor'), examines the tradition of newspaper *crônicas* in Brazil. He defines this as a characteristically Brazilian genre, which was adopted by a growing number of writers and journalists, such as Mário de Andrade, Manuel Bandeira and Carlos Drummond de Andrade in the 1930s.[15] He summarizes the genre as follows: '... pega o miúdo e mostra nele uma grandeza, uma beleza ou uma singularidade insuspeitadas' ('... it takes the minute detail and reveals the unsuspected greatness, beauty or unique quality within it'), and he says that it combines humour, everyday life, simple, even colloquial language, and, when properly executed, covert social criticism.[16] Although he was not, of course, directly inspired by the newspaper *crônica*, Noel's lyrics served a similar function within the realm of popular music, and he unconsciously abided by many of the literary genre's conventions.

Noel's love of Rio's low life and the apparently trivial is exemplified in his famous samba '*São coisas nossas*' ('They are Our Things') of 1932, inspired by the first Brazilian 'talkie' entitled '*Coisas nossas*' ('Our Things'), which premiered in 1931. In this song, the poverty and shabbiness of life are evoked by the references to the *palhoça* (shantytown shack) and the hunger of the *malandro*, to parasitic loan sharks and conmen, who rub shoulders with newspaper sellers and tram drivers, and finally to ubiquitous skirt chasers:

'*São coisas nossas*', 1932, Noel Rosa

Queria ser pandeiro
Pra sentir o dia inteiro
A tua mão na minha pele a batucar
Saudade do violão e da palhoça
Coisa nossa, coisa nossa

O samba, a prontidão e outras bossas
São nossas coisas, são coisas nossas

Malandro que não bebe
Que não come, que não abandona o samba
Pois o samba mata a fome
Morena bem bonita lá da roça
Coisa nossa, coisa nossa

Baleiro, jornaleiro
Motorneiro, condutor e passageiro
Prestamista e vigarista
E o bonde que parece uma carroça
Coisa nossa, muito nossa

Menina que namora
Na esquina e no portão
Rapaz casado com dez filhos, sem tostão
Se o pai descobre o truque dá uma coça
Coisa nossa, muito nossa

'They are Our Things', 1932, Noel Rosa

I would like to be a tambourine
To feel all day long
Your hand beating on my skin
Longing for the guitar and the shack
Our things, our things

Samba, pennilessness and other fashions
They are our things, they are our things

The spiv who does not drink
Who does not eat, who does not quit the samba
Since samba kills his hunger
The pretty dark girl from the country
They are our things, they are our things

Street traders, newspaper vendors
Tram drivers and passengers
Loan sharks and conmen
And the tram that looks like a cart
Our things, very much ours

The girl courting
On the street corner and in a doorway
A married man with ten children and no money
If her father finds out he'll use his fists
Our things, very much ours

Noel does not embellish reality, but portrays the seedier side of life with genuine fondness. Here, for example, the tram is lovingly mocked for being clapped out.[17] In this one line (*E o bonde que parece uma carroça*/And the tram that looks like a cart) the dualities inherent in *carioca* life are captured. The electrified tram, introduced into Brazil in 1892, was still the vehicle for physical mobility and supposed social advancement in the 1930s, since it transported Brazil's new urban workforce to their places of employment. In total contrast, the cart (*carroça*) is a vestige of colonial, agrarian Brazil, yet is still very much in evidence. For the inhabitants of the *favelas* and working-class suburbs of Rio, the first-world trappings of the city have only a superficial effect on existence. Their tram is not gleaming and sprightly, but a rickety, old wreck.[18]

As we see in the samba '*São coisas nossas*', the dusky-skinned mulatto girl is an intrinsic facet of lower-class life, a rare thing of beauty among the squalor and the mundane. She is a metaphor for the *morro*, with her dark colouring and lascivious good looks, and the blonde ice-maiden embodies the artificial *cidade* or middle-class city, tainted with foreign influences. In the samba '*Leite com café*' ('Milk with Coffee') the *mulata* is portrayed as the pride of the Afro-Brazilian community. Even for white-skinned Noel she is the ideal woman, and the insipid, would-be Hollywood blonde just makes him feel ill. The blonde tries to lure him away from his origins, just as bourgeois tastes try to impinge on authentic Brazilian music and dance forms. Here Noel alludes directly to the mulattos of Brazil (*a nossa grande raça*) who are portrayed as being the true Brazilians:

'*Leite com café*', 1935, Noel Rosa and Hervé Cordovil

A morena lá do morro
Cheia de beleza e graça
Simboliza a nossa grande raça
É cor de leite com café
E a loura da cidade
Nunca foi nem é meu tipo
Perto dela eu sempre me constipo
De tão gelada que ela é

A lourinha sobe o morro e desce
Implorando sempre o meu amor
E, pensando em mim, se esquece

Que a mulher que se oferece
Perde todo o seu valor

Foi no samba que encontrei socorro
Para a minha sorte tão mesquinha
Eu prefiro ser cachorro
Da morena lá do morro
Do que dono da lourinha

'Milk with Coffee', 1935, Noel Rosa and Hervé Cordovil

The dark girl from up there on the hill
Full of beauty and charm
Symbolizes our great race
She's the colour of milk with coffee
And the blonde girl from the city
Was never my type
When I'm near her I catch a cold
Because she's so icy

Blondie goes up the hill and down again
Always begging for my love
And, thinking about me, she forgets
That a woman on a plate
Loses her appeal

It was in the samba that I found help
For my meagre life
I'd rather be a dog
Belonging to the dark girl from the hill
Than the owner of the blondie

In his sambas, Noel's home *bairro* of Vila Isabel, rather than the Brazilian nation as a whole, is revered with patriotic vigour. *'Na Pavuna'* ('In Pavuna'), written in 1929 by Almirante and Homero Dornellas, started this trend for songs which praised the different districts of the city. Pedro Bloch says of Noel's veneration of his home suburb of Vila Isabel:

> Querendo cantar um bairro, Noel logrou cantar a cidade, o Brasil, o mundo. Vila Isabel é o nome simbólico do bairro de cada ser humano sobre a face da Terra. É o encantamento da infância, da pedra do chão, da goiabeira ou de uma árvore de qualquer latitude. Sendo brasileiríssimo, Noel consegue empolgar todos os corações (Wanting to sing about his home district, Noel managed to sing about the whole city, Brazil, the world. Vila Isabel is the symbolic name of the home district of every human being on the face of the earth. It is the charm of childhood, of the stone on the ground, of the guava-tree or a tree found in gardens of any latitude. By being dyed-in-the-wool Brazilian, he manages to capture everyone's heart).[19]

In this same article, Bloch cites Noel himself: 'A idéia mais original é sempre expressa por gestos e palavras comuns' ('The most original idea is always expressed through common words and gestures'). João Antônio says, in his article 'Noel Rosa: um poeta do povo' ('Noel Rosa: a poet of the people'), that Noel knew how to capture the essence of the city of Rio and was also able to give his work a universal appeal, creating 'poetry' that was far richer than the rather primitive and empirically based lyrics of most of his contemporaries. He was 'capaz de ridicularizar o formal, o sacrossanto e o vigente' ('able to ridicule the formal, the sacrosanct and the powers that be') but likewise 'de se enternecer diante do feio, do burlesco' ('to be moved by the ugly, the burlesque').[20] The singer Araci de Almeida knew best how to capture the cadence of his songs and the bitterness and drama that are often beneath the surface of his lyrics. Antônio stresses that Noel had a deep love for the *povo* (ordinary people) but had no socialist leanings or political awareness to speak of. He distinguishes Noel's lyrics from those of even the most respected popular musicians of the day, for the absence of set phrases which others used to achieve an instant aesthetic effect, stating that in Noel's work everything is honest, legitimate and in keeping. His patriotism is tinged with an implicit critique, unlike the *sambas-exaltação* or what Antônio terms the 'nervosismo apatriotado da grossa maioria dos nossos compositores de música popular' ('the pseudo-patriotic nervousness of the vast majority of our popular music composers').[21]

The glorification of the city's poorer quarters forms part of Noel's elevation of the mundane. The *bairro* and the *morro* are presented in direct opposition to the bourgeois *cidade*. The former are associated with authenticity, traditional customs and values, whereas the latter is seen as a fickle, alien community, tainted by foreign cultural influences.[22] Noel fiercely defends the *morro* and its creativity, and criticizes the *cidade* for its affectation, and its love of foreign languages and imported cultural products, as we see in the following samba:

'*Não tem tradução*', 1933, Noel Rosa

O cinema falado
É o grande culpado
Da transformação
Dessa gente que sente
Que um barracão
Prende mais que um xadrez
Lá no morro, se eu fizer uma falseta
A Risoleta
Desiste logo do francês e do inglês

A gíria que o nosso morro criou
Bem cedo a cidade aceitou e usou
Mais tarde o malandro deixou de sambar
Dando pinote
E só querendo dançar o fox-trot

Essa gente hoje em dia
Que tem a mania
Da exibição
Não se lembra que o samba
Não tem tradução
No idioma francês
Tudo aquilo que o malandro pronuncia
Com voz macia
É brasileiro, já passou de português

Amor, lá no morro, é amor pra chuchu
As rimas do samba não são 'I love you'
E esse negócio de 'alô, alô, boy'
'Alô, Johnny'
Só pode ser conversa de telefone

'There's No Translation', 1933, Noel Rosa

The talking cinema
Is the major cause
Of the transformation
Of those people who feel
That a shantytown shack
Holds you more than a prison cell
Up on the hill if I play a dirty trick
Risoleta
Gives up on her French and English

The slang that our shantytowns created
Quickly the city accepted and used
Later the spiv stopped dancing samba
Playing his guitar
And only wanted to dance the foxtrot

Those people today
Who are obsessed
With showing off
Don't remember that samba
Cannot be translated
Into the French language
Everything that the spiv utters
When smooth talking
Is Brazilian, it's no longer Portuguese

Love, up on the hill, there's loads of it
The rhymes of samba are not 'I love you'
And that stuff about 'hello, hello, boy'
'Hello, Johnny'
Can only be telephone talk

Noel comments here on the effects that the introduction of the talking
cinema in Brazil in 1931 had on middle-class habits. In the early 1930s the
talking cinema left its mark on virtually all aspects of life in urban

Brazil, but especially fashion. Record companies like Odeon and Victor released songs from Hollywood films, either in their original form or translated into Portuguese.[23] In a reassertion of Brazilian artistic originality, Noel explicitly praises the *gíria* or slang of the *malandro* and the *morro*, which has now been adopted by the *cidade*. He underlines Brazil's linguistic independence from Portugal, which was achieved, he says, not by the learned *cidade* but by the unschooled *morro*. He also deftly draws on this creative argot himself (*xadrez*, the clink or slammer; *fazer uma falseta*, to do a dirty trick; *voz macia*, the smooth talking of the *malandro*), thus demonstrating its richness and utility. By bringing together typically Brazilian colloquial expressions and anglicisms or code-switches into English in rhyming pairs (*Dando pinote*, literally playing his guitar, but also a slang term for tripping up, and *fox-trot*; *pra chuchu*, loads of, and *I love you*) he ingeniously pokes fun at this incongruous use of the English language in urban Rio. Noel thus mocks the contemporary fashion for singing in English and the use of anglicisms in everyday life, two consequences of the popularity of talking films from the USA. The code-switches into English that appear in the final verse can only be *conversa de telefone* (telephone talk), that is, the speech of the affluent, disloyal city dwellers.[24]

In this samba the uneducated practitioners of samba and *malandragem* confront the learned middle classes, versed in foreign languages. Slang terms borrowed from academic terminology such as *ser bacharel* (literally to be a graduate, but used to refer to someone with a skill or flair, often for creating or performing samba), are often used in Noel's work. Such terms effectively contrast the values held by the down-market, peripheral areas of the city on the one hand, and the wealthier, central districts, on the other. In the former, samba is the most prestigious activity, and is the only vehicle for achieving fame and fortune. Conversely, the middle classes placed paramount importance on formal education, as a means of perpetuating their social and financial well-being. This strategy was in total conflict with the *sambista*'s ethos and lifestyle of *malandragem* and *jeitinho*, the latter being the notion of evading the law and official channels through a crafty, often slightly shady, fiddle or ruse. Use of this imagery can be seen in the opening lines of Noel's samba '*O X do problema*' ('The Crux of the Problem') of 1936:

> Nasci no Estácio
> Eu fui educada na roda de bamba
> E fui diplomada na escola de samba
> Sou independente, conforme se vê
>
> I was born in Estácio
> I was educated in the group of masters

And graduated from the samba school
I'm independent, as you can see

The essence of the discourse of the *malandro* lies in its ambivalence and incongruity. Like the *malandro* himself, it combines elements of both the *morro* and the *cidade* and mixes the vernacular of the lower classes with the erudition of the educated middle classes, thus maintaining the spiv's credibility in his own community and enabling him to save his neck when forced to explain his actions to those in positions of authority, most notably the police. As well as donning the disguise of the layabout hustler, Noel emulates the characteristic eloquence of this figure in these two conflicting registers of language. The *malandro*'s voice is a ubiquitous presence in his work since it was, in reality, so closely bound up and identified with that of Noel himself. The samba '*Filosofia*' ('Philosophy'), written in 1933, can be considered to be a summing up of his whole ethos on life and his view of society, both inextricably linked with those of the *malandro* myth:

Nesta prontidão sem fim
Vou fingindo que sou rico
Pra ninguém zombar de mim ...

... Pois cantando neste mundo
Vivo escravo do meu samba
Muito embora vagabundo

In this endless pennilessness
I pretend I'm rich
So that no one mocks me ...

... Since by singing in this world
I am a slave to my samba
Although I'm a loafer

The real-life *malandros* invented their own lingo, creating a kind of underworld code. Noel is able to juxtapose colloquialisms, slang and even grammatical errors with learned terms and allusions, elegant poeticisms and intellectual word games. Like the *malandro*, he relies on linguistic flexibility and quick wit, and to some extent is also a point of contact between two social classes. Both have the ability to dupe the inhabitants of the *morro*, Noel with his puns and erudite allusions, and yet can equally delude and exploit the wealthy folk of the *cidade* by baffling them with their incomprehensible argot. Noel thrives on puns, word games and learned references, such as in the following lines from the samba '*Contraste*' ('Contrast') of 1933. The biblical allusion to Judas is directed at a deceitful woman and is incorporated into this song in a very simple way.

Tu tens tanta falsidade
Já vendeste tanta gente
Que eu creio ser verdade
Que Judas foi teu parente

You are so dishonest
You have sold so many people
That I believe it's true
That Judas was a relative of yours

Samba's semi-literate creators unintentionally incorporated inaccuracies of grammar and kitsch stylistic inelegances into their songs, as seen in some of the lyrics by Ataúlfo Alves examined in Chapter Four. Noel elevates these features to the status of a poetic tradition in themselves, and deliberately brings them into his lyrics. As a result of his background and formal education these slips are not perceived as having been unwittingly committed, and he therefore has free rein to employ them as a creative element in his work. He exploits the malleability of both the thematic and formal constants of samba lyrics in order to produce something more innovative, and to capture an added dimension of everyday life. In certain sambas he reproduces the typical turns of phrase and errors of the *malandro*'s speech with great authenticity. He has a keen ear for the peculiarities of casual, unrefined spoken language and is well versed in popular sayings and the *gíria* of the shantytown. His samba '*Só você*' ('Only You') begins with a proverbial phrase *Quanto mais se vive, mais se sabe* (The older you are, the wiser you become), and many of his songs are full of everyday expressions. The uniqueness of Noel's work stems from his ability to take these normal features of samba to absurd lengths. The following lines from the samba '*Mulata fuzarqueira*' ('Fun-loving Mulatto Girl') of 1931 exemplify how he convincingly reproduces the discourse of the *malandro* but creates something new out of the standard use of such speech forms in samba lyrics:

Mulata vou contar
As minhas mágoa
Meu amô não tem erre
Mas é amô debaixo d'água

Mulatto girl I'm going to tell you
My troubles
My love (amor) hasn't got an 'r' on the end
But it's underwater love

Here he humorously refers to the tendency to chop off the end of words in casual, unrefined speech (*meu amô* instead of the correct *meu amor*). He reproduces this trait himself, but takes it one step further with the comical reference to someone mouthing the word *amor* underwater and thus being unable to convey the final 'r' sound by the movement of lips alone. This ingenious twist to a common feature of everyday speech is indicative of Noel's powers of observation and his love of outlandish approaches to convention.[25]

Noel's imagination was evidently captured by language, especially by its inconsistencies and inherent humour. The rich creative potential offered by rhyme seems to have particularly fascinated him. When he died he left a dictionary of rhymes which was given to the singer Marília Baptista, and in the margin of which Noel had scribbled snippets of lyrics. He delighted in combining rhyming pairs which brought together conflicting types of language. Often he chooses an absurd, nonsensical word in order to comply with the rhyme scheme and then tries to justify it according to the sense of the particular set of lyrics. He obeys the rules of formal suitability but disregards those of stylistic propriety or semantic aptness. The preservation of the rhyme scheme is paramount and meaning is relegated to a position of secondary importance.

Noel plays with the funny similarities and surprises of language and pokes fun at poetic canons. He asserts the freedom of the *sambista* to disregard such constraints and push forward their boundaries. He tugs at the edges of convention in a quest for greater creativity. His use of rhyme evolved during his years as a *sambista*, progressing from a straightforward technique copied from poetic templates in order to respect tradition, to a highly complex system of connotational meanings and comic effects. In one of his earliest known compositions, the elegiac *'Queixumes'* ('Laments') or *'Meu sofrer'* ('My Suffering') of 1930, written in partnership with Henrique Britto, and when Noel was only 19, his rhyme scheme is very much on its best behaviour. This is arguably the only composition of Noel's which clearly falls within the confines of the *lírico-amoroso* (lyrical-romantic) sub-category, and in it there is none of his characteristic off-beat spontaneity. The end-line rhymes are predictable and conspire to create a classic example of this sentimental, melodramatic type of song. The *Queixumes/ciúmes* and *abrolhos/olhos* pairings in this song are well-worn choices, and unlike in many of his later songs there is no underlying ironic intent in these rhymes:

'Queixumes' (*'Meu Sofrer'*), 1930, Noel Rosa and Henrique Britto

Sem estes teus tão lindos olhos
Eu não seria sofredor
Os meus ferinos abrolhos
Nasceram do nosso amor
Eu hoje sou um trovador
E gosto até de assim penar
Vou te dizer os meus queixumes
Ciúmes tenho do seu olhar

Quero sempre te ver bem junto a mim
Por que te esquivas, assim, coração
De uma paixão?
O teu olhar traz alegria
Mas também traz o amargor
Sem ele então não viveria
Vida não há sem dor

'Laments' ('My Suffering'), 1930, Noel Rosa and Henrique Britto

Without these so beautiful eyes of yours
I would not be a sufferer
My stinging thorns
Were born from our love
And today I am a troubador
And I like to grieve like this
I'm going to tell you my laments
Jealousy I feel for your gaze

I always want to see you right next to me
Why do you flee, like that, heart
From a passion?
Your gaze brings joy
But also brings bitterness
Without it I would not live now
There's no life without pain

Just three years later, in the third verse of his archetypal *samba malandro* *'Capricho de rapaz solteiro'* ('The Whim of a Bachelor Boy') of 1933, his love of outrageously inappropriate rhyming pairs is made apparent as he brings in a ridiculous reference to a deep-sea diver's suit (*escafandro*) to rhyme with the omnipresent *malandro*, a noun difficult to find a rhyme for in Portuguese. This strange mismatch of terms creates a perfect rhyme and Noel then attempts to adapt the sense of the lyrics to accommodate it:

Antes de descer ao fundo
Perguntei ao escafandro
Se o mar é mais profundo
Que as idéias do malandro

Before descending to the bottom
I asked the diver's suit
Whether the sea is deeper
Than the ideas of the *malandro*

A particularly innovative feature of Noel's rhymes is his ability to marry terms taken from foreign languages with Portuguese words. As we see in *'Não tem tradução'* of 1933, quoted above, this stylistic technique is sometimes used to underline the absurdity of rejecting Brazilian Portuguese in favour of foreign tongues in songs and other aspects of everyday life, and incongruous code-switches into foreign languages are spouted alongside typical Brazilian vernacular. But often the foreign 'imports' that he uses are already totally assimilated into Brazilian Portuguese. In the opening lines of *'Dama do cabaré'* ('Lady of the Cabaret') of 1936 he includes the French loan words *cabaret, champagne* and *soirée*. The latter is used in Brazilian Portuguese to mean an evening dress, the *chique* connotations reflecting the self-image of the *malandra* cabaret hostess that he is addressing here. The irony lies in the contrast between these loan words and the setting of the song: Lapa, the city's red-light district. The *soirée* is effortlessly rhymed with the pronoun *você* (you):[26]

> Foi num cabaré da Lapa
> Que eu conheci você
> Fumando cigarro
> Entornando champagne no seu soirée
>
> It was in a cabaret in Lapa
> That I met you
> Smoking a cigarette
> Spilling champagne on your evening dress

Noel finds unexpected rhymes that bridge two languages amusing, as is evidenced in the recording that he made of his samba *'Positivismo'* ('Positivism') of 1933 (September 1933, Columbia no. 22240). In this original version, the first time Auguste Comte is mentioned his name is pronounced with a French accent, but the second time Noel exaggerates a typical Brazilianized version of his name to rhyme it with the Brazilian pronunciation of *base* (basis). Comte and his doctrine soon lose prestige and sophistication by becoming Brazilianized in this way.

Noel picks up on the peculiarities of the Portuguese that he hears spoken around him and the traditions of rhyme in samba lyrics are upturned by his imaginative combinations, where a poetic technique is applied to the most prosaic and unsophisticated of subjects, which include a telephone number in the samba *'Conversa de botequim'* ('Bar Talk') of 1935 (*Telefone ao menos uma vez/Para 34-4333* - Phone at least once/Number 34-4333) and the date in the samba *'Cordiais saudações'* ('Cordial Greetings') of 1931 (*Podendo, manda-me algum/Rio, 7 de setembro de 31!* - If you can, send me something/Rio, 7 September 1931!).

Notions of brasilidade

Vila Isabel, a working-class suburb of northern Rio, eager to gain respectability, is venerated in Noel's work, and is particularly praised for being a samba stronghold, where the spirit of *malandragem* thrives. Noel was not alone in his glorification of his home district. The popular composer Euclydes Silveira, often referred to by his nickname of Quidinho, for example, wrote many sambas in praise of the district of Rio where he was raised, Aldeia Campista. In 1930 the two musicians joined forces and geographical allegiances in the samba *'Bom elemento'* ('Good Element'):

'Bom elemento', *batucada*, 1930, Noel Rosa and Euclydes Silveira

Entrei no samba
Os malandros perguntaram
Se eu era bamba
No bater do tamborim
E o batuque
Eles logo improvisaram
Eu dei a cadência assim

Meu bem, o valor dá-se a quem tem
A Vila e a Aldeia não perdem pra ninguém
(O que é que tem?)
Meu bem, o valor dá-se a quem tem
A Vila e a Aldeia não perdem pra ninguém

Com violência
Enfrentei a batucada
A harmonia
Do meu simples instrumento
Fez toda a turma
Ficar muito admirada

'Good Element', *batucada*, 1930, Noel Rosa and Euclydes Silveira

I entered the world of samba
The *malandros* asked me
If I was a master
At beating the drum
And playing percussion
They then improvised
And I provided the rhythm

My love, respect is given to those who earn it
Vila and Aldeia don't lose out to anyone
(So what about it?)
My love, respect is given to those who earn it
Vila and Aldeia don't lose to anyone

Violently
I confronted the percussion
The harmony
Of my simple instrument
Left the whole crowd
Full of admiration

This could not be a more direct response by two white young men to the attacks and doubts of black *sambistas*. Here they stress that both their *bairros* can produce great samba, in this case a percussion-based *batucada*, favoured by the musicians of the *morro*, and a form that neither of them was accustomed to writing. Obviously, this praise for the *bairro* was not unique to Noel, but his exploitation of the theme's full potential sets him aside from his peers. Several of his sambas employ elaborate imagery to give a new twist to this topic. In the rather self-conscious samba *'Meu barracão'* ('My Shack') of 1933 he underlines the strong emotional bond that links the *eu* to his home, in this case the hillside shantytown of Penha, which is an area of Rio that often features in his work, and that of his contemporaries, such as Ari Barroso.[27] The reason for the importance given to this area in popular song was the church situated on top of a rock, which was the destination for many religious pilgrimages. The intensity of the *eu*'s feelings is such that the ramshackle dwelling comes alive. The personified home becomes his lover and in desperation, after his absence for a year in the city, she comes in search of him:

'Meu barracão', 1933, Noel Rosa

Faz hoje quase um ano
Que eu não vou visitar
Meu barracão lá da Penha
Que me faz sofrer
E até mesmo chorar
Por lembrar a alegria
Com que eu sentia
O forte laço
De amor que nos unia

Não há quem tenha
Mais saudades lá da Penha
Do que eu - juro que não
Não há quem possa
Me fazer perder a bossa
Só a saudade do barracão

Mas veio lá da Penha
Hoje uma pessoa
Que me trouxe uma notícia
Do meu barracão
Que não foi nada boa
Já cansado de esperar
Saiu do lugar
Eu desconfio
Que ele foi me procurar

'My Shack', 1933, Noel Rosa

It's almost a year to the day
Since I last visited

My shack up there in Penha
That makes me suffer
And even cry
Remembering the joy
I felt due to
The strong tie
Of love that bound us together

There's no one in the world
Who misses Penha
More than I do - I swear it
There's no one in the world
Who could make me lose my touch
Only the longing I feel for my shack

But there came from Penha
Today a person
Who brought me some news
About my shack
That wasn't good at all
Now tired of waiting
It moved away
And I suspect
That it came to look for me

The *morro* and the *bairro* are portrayed with genuine devotion and respect, at the same time as being described in unflattering detail. As well as allusions to poverty, the violence and persecution suffered in these deprived areas are mentioned. The *malandro* and the *sambista* are targets for harassment on the *morro*, and the life of *malandragem* brings with it frequent spells in a police cell. In contrast, in the *Avenida* (Avenue), where the well-off perform their samba during carnival, similar debauched behaviour to that of the inhabitants of the *morro* is considered acceptable, and even desirable. The *malandro*, who, by nature of his ambivalent status and quick wit, has access to both the *morro* and the *cidade*, ultimately opts for the former as the better place to live. Noel emphasizes the simple aspects of the life of the poor, especially its lack of pretence and affectation. Often he reinforces his message with the use of prosaic language and colloquialisms, and underlines the hypocrisy and superficiality of up-town fashions. The following samba centres on a *malandro* who, realizing the error of his ways, has returned to the lowly suburb after living in the city:

'*Voltaste (pro subúrbio)*', 1934, Noel Rosa

Voltaste novamente pro subúrbio
Vai haver muito distúrbio
Vai fechar o botequim
Voltaste e o despeito te acompanha

E te guia na campanha
Que tu fazes contra mim

O guarda, que apitava ressonando
Anda alerta envergando
O seu capote de lã
Voltaste pra fabricar defunto
Para fornecer assunto
Aos diários da manhã

Voltaste novamente sem dinheiro
Tapeando o açougueiro
Que não tem golpe de vista
Voltaste com um cão muito valente
Que só tiras da corrente
Quando chega o prestamista

Voltaste pra mostrar ao nosso povo
Que não há nada de novo
Lá no centro da cidade
Voltaste demonstrando claramente
Que o subúrbio é ambiente
De completa liberdade

Voltaste, mas falhou o teu projeto
Não te dou o meu afeto
Quando eu quero eu sou ruim
Voltaste confessando sem vaidade
Que a tua liberdade
É viver bem preso a mim

'You Returned (to the Suburb)', 1934, Noel Rosa

You returned to the suburb again
There are going to be ructions
They're going to close the bar
You returned and brought spite with you
Which you use in the campaign
You are launching against me

The night watchman whose whistle echoed around
Is on the alert in his
Woollen overcoat
You returned
To make corpses
To provide copy
For the morning dailies

You returned again with no money
Cheating the butcher
Whose sight is bad
You returned with a very brave dog
That you only let off the lead
When the loan shark calls

You returned to show our people
That there's nothing new
Down there in the city centre
You returned demonstrating clearly
That the suburb is an environment
Of total freedom

You returned, but your project failed
I'm not giving you my affection
When I want I can be bad
You returned confessing without vanity
That your freedom
Is to live locked up with me

The suburb is associated with violence and deprivation, and the *malandro* is exposed as a cowardly bully by the female *eu* of this song. However, in its favour, the suburb is a place of personal freedom and is unpretentious, as reflected in the unglamorous places and people that are mentioned, such as the simple bar, the butcher (butchers were often Portuguese immigrants and the butt of endless jokes based on their legendary stupidity and gullibility), corpses and the loan shark.

Noel's renown as a chronicler of daily life stems, to a large extent, from his ability to capture the trivial social changes that were witnessed by his community and their reactions to them. He exposes the contradictions of the Brazil he saw around him, and focuses on the silly, trifling details of politics to stress how nothing important changed after the revolution of 1930. In 1931 he wrote two sambas that deal with President Vargas's decision of that year to put all the clocks forward in Brazil by one hour - '*O pulo da hora*' ('The Leap of the Hour') and '*Por causa da hora*' ('Because of the Hour'). In both cases the lyrics are little more than humorous gibberish and illogical reasoning, but veiled references are made to Brazil's dire economic difficulties, as we see in an amended version of '*O pulo da hora*', which was not recorded but which Noel noted down in his own notebook of lyrics. Such nonsensical lyrics form part of Noel's insistent mockery and sceptical attitude towards the pompous obscurantism of the ruling élite. In spite of his genuine playfulness in such songs, he was all too aware of the social and political climate. Often such examples of linguistic agility serve to conceal or detract from allusions to topical events, which are quite knowledgeable by samba's standards, and contribute to his unorthodox inventiveness.

'*O pulo da hora*', 1931, Noel Rosa

Que horas são?
Eu venho agora
Saber a hora
Que o ponteiro está marcando
No relógio da senhora

O meu relógio
É de ouro brasileiro
Trabalha bem sem a corda
Sem ter vidro nem ponteiro
Em minha casa
Surgiu hoje uma briga
Meu credor usa a moderna
E eu adoto a hora antiga

O carioca
Perdeu a calma e a paz
A hora pulou pra frente
E a nota pulou pra trás
Mas eu agora
Já gostei desse brinquedo
Para me vingar da hora
Janto três horas mais cedo

'The Leap of the Hour', 1931, Noel Rosa

What time is it?
I've come
To ask the time
That the hands are pointing to
On your watch

My watch
Is made of Brazilian gold
It works well without a spring
Without a glass or hands
At my house
A fight broke out today
My creditor uses the new time
And I use the old one

The citizen of Rio
Has lost his cool
The hour jumped forward
And the banknote jumped back
But now
I enjoy this plaything
To get my revenge on the hour
I have dinner three hours earlier

Verse two opens with an apparent outburst of patriotic pride, but the image of Brazil is soon deflated as we learn that the wristwatch in question is really useless and worthless. Similarly, in the final verse Noel uses an ironic play of contrasts to allude to the nation's high rate of inflation in the lines *A hora pulou pra frente/E a nota pulou pra trás* (The hour jumped forward/And the banknote jumped back). Noel voices a widespread lack of respect for and lack of faith in the new regime. He hints at social inequality but only beneath these tongue-in-cheek, comic attacks on the establishment. Noel himself had a personal disdain for authority and red tape, but this contemptuous attitude is equally an important trait of the character of the *malandro*, the embodiment of the concept of *jeitinho*. The *malandro* realizes that the powers that be will never help him or his social class, but he is content to flout their control by means of his nonconformist lifestyle.[28]

Noel's attitude to the Vargas regime was scathing, but his opinions were always concealed beneath light-hearted ridicule. Noel once said that he wrote the hilarious samba '*Gago apaixonado*' ('Smitten Stammerer'), in which he imitates the stammer of his friend Manuel Barreiros, during one of the nights of civil disturbances that followed Vargas becoming head of the provisional government.[29] This may have been one of his tall stories, but it is indicative of his feigned insouciance *vis-à-vis* politics. According to Máximo and Didier, no one really took an interest in politics in the milieu of popular musicians, and even if they wrote songs vaguely making fun of politicians, very few, with the exceptions of Mário Lago and Alberto Ribeiro, openly discussed politics in a serious manner.[30] Noel certainly wanted to cultivate an image of indifference towards such matters, in keeping with his laid-back *malandro* approach to life. It would seem, however, that this pose was pure pretence and that he was, in fact, acutely aware of society's predicaments. He subtly reveals his contempt for Brazil's political mismanagement through his ostensible lack of interest in it.[31]

Noel's irreverent stance in relation to authority manifested itself early in life. He delighted in parodying the melody of the Brazilian national anthem when he was a teenager, and he set his own lyrics to it.[32] He was obliged to alter the opening melody of his samba '*Com que roupa?*' ('In What Clothes?') of 1929 because of its close similarity to the anthem. The lyrics of this samba deal with poverty, albeit in a humorous fashion, and announce the demise of *malandragem* as a viable alternative lifestyle. Brazil's economic situation had been aggravated by the Wall Street crash of that year, which threatened the economies of the whole world, and left Brazil in a particularly precarious position. Noel was forced to change some of the notes in the opening section in order to dodge the censors. In an interview which appeared in the *Diário de Notícias* on 15 February 1931, Noel tried to deny the existence of any critique behind the lyrics of this samba, claiming '... não tive em mira fazer alusão ao povo, que, apesar de tudo, sei que ainda tem roupa e faço votos que continue a tê-la em profusão ...' ('... I was not aiming to make an allusion to the people, who, in spite of everything, I know still have clothes and I hope that they continue to have them in profusion ...'). But Noel was well known for playing tricks on journalists and for being deliberately obtuse and ironical when interviewed. The political connotations of these lyrics, despite Noel's half-hearted statement to the contrary, were recognized beyond the realms of popular music, and journalists cashed in on the popularity of the samba, publishing articles criticizing the administration and political life in general. Maurício de Lacerda wrote a long article with the same title as the song, in which he adopted the same metaphor to deal with the political uncertainties following the 1930 revolution.[33]

Humour is a typically *carioca* way of responding to and dealing with serious issues, trivializing them until their gravity is attenuated. Thus, for Noel, the Brazilian economic crisis of the early 1930s becomes a source of comedy and an excuse to ridicule authority with the characteristic irreverence of the *malandro*. Noel stated at the end of 1932: 'Antes, a palavra samba tinha um único sinônimo: mulher. Agora já não é assim. Há também o dinheiro, a crise. O nosso pensamento se desvia também para esses gravíssimos temas' ('Before the word samba had only one synonym: women. It is not like that any longer. There is also money, the crisis. Our thoughts also stray to these very serious themes').[34]

Noel's tongue-in-cheek critiques of the ruling élite are not confined to his own lifetime, as we see in his samba '*Quem dá mais?*' ('Who'll Give Me More?') of 1930, also entitled '*Leilão do Brasil*' ('Auction of Brazil'), in which he imitates the speech patterns of an auctioneer. One of the lots to come under the hammer is:

> ... um violão que toca em falsete
> Que só não tem braço, fundo e cavalete
> Pertenceu a dom Pedro, morou no palácio
> Foi posto no prego por José Bonifácio ...

> ... a guitar that plays falsetto
> That just doesn't have a neck, a back or a bridge
> It belonged to emperor Dom Pedro, and lived in the palace
> It was pawned by José Bonifácio ...

Here he gently pokes fun at Brazil's 'heritage' - in this case a useless guitar, which José Bonifácio (1763-1838), the Brazilian statesman and champion of Independence, was said to have been forced to put up for sale. He implies that even in 1822, when Brazil gained its independence from Portugal, the country was in dire financial straits. In an off-the-cuff fashion, Noel acknowledges that Brazil has always been in debt to others, and that the nation inherited a legacy of economic blunders.

Noel's allusions to political events are few and far between and are casually interwoven with more conventional themes, such as *malandragem* or affairs of the heart. In '*Samba da boa vontade*' ('Good-will Samba') of 1931, the title and opening line satirize Vargas's well-known appeals for sacrifices and good-will from his people. Noel begins by seemingly addressing a woman, but these could equally be the words of Vargas himself. In the second verse he includes obvious allusions to money, but still in the context of a personal relationship. In the third verse, however, he refers to Brazil as a nation, and in verse four attacks its adoption of a capitalist system, which Noel considered to be a means for allowing the rich to become richer, whilst the lower classes were being cajoled into going without for the sake of the nation:

'*Samba da boa vontade*', 1931, Noel Rosa and João de Barros

- Campanha da boa vontade!
Viver alegre hoje é preciso
Conserva sempre o teu sorriso
Mesmo que a vida esteja feia
E que vivas na pinimba
Passando a pirão de areia

Gastei o teu dinheiro
Mas não tive compaixão
Porque tenho a certeza
Que ele volta à tua mão
Se ele acaso não voltar
Eu te pago com sorriso
E o recibo hás de passar
(Nesta questão solução sei dar)

Neste Brasil tão grande
Não se deve ser mesquinho
Quem ganha na avareza
Sempre perde no carinho
Não admito ninharia
Pois qualquer economia
Sempre acaba em porcaria
(Minha barriga não está vazia)

Comparo o meu Brasil
A uma criança perdulária
Que anda sem vintém
Mas tem a mãe que é milionária
E que jurou, batendo o pé
Que iremos à Europa
Num aterro de café
(Nisto eu sempre tive fé)

'Good-will Samba', 1931, Noel Rosa and João de Barros

The good-will campaign!
It's necessary to live happily today
Always keep smiling
Even if life is ugly
And you're living in a right state
Making your porridge with sand

I spent your money
But I didn't feel compassion
Because I'm certain
That it will come back to you
If by chance it doesn't
I'll pay you with a smile
And you'll give me a receipt
(In this matter I know how to find solutions)

In this Brazil that's so great
One shouldn't be mean
Those who gain from avarice
Are always losers in love
I won't stand for pettiness
Since any economizing
Always ends in a right mess
(My stomach isn't empty)

I compare my Brazil
To a spendthrift child
Who is penniless
But has a millionairess for a mother
Who swore, stamping her foot
That we will go to Europe
Across a landfill of coffee
(I've always had faith in this)

In the final two lines Noel uses a clever image to deride the decision taken by Vargas, pressurized by Brazil's coffee producers, to either burn or dump in the sea around three million sacks of coffee which they were unable to sell. Literally, the *aterro* (landfill) will supposedly lead to future economic prosperity, like that enjoyed in Europe, but figuratively, this mountain of coffee would bridge the ocean dividing the two continents. Noel's use of slang expressions in this samba (*na pinimba*, an alternative form of the colloquial expression *pinima*, meaning a bad thing or fatal occurrence), contrasting registers in the rhyming pairs (*economia/ porcaria*), sarcastic asides (*Minha barriga não está vazia* - My stomach isn't empty) and simple similes, such as comparing Brazil to a penniless child with a wealthy mother, brings home the reality of the consequences for the uneducated poor of these economic policies. Noel is concerned with political matters only in so far as they infringe on everyday existence. His down-to-earth linguistic treatment of complex issues such as this mirrors his ostensibly uncomplicated, simplified view of politics, which are seen from the standpoint of the underdog, and thus he concentrates on the real-life, concrete effects of political decisions.

The myth of *malandragem* is central to Noel's work, both as an important thematic strand and as a filter through which many of his songs must be viewed. The *malandro*'s attitude to life, like Noel's own, is philosophical at a grass-roots level, and like Noel the spiv jeers at convention, as is fittingly symbolized by his white suit against his black skin. Noel consciously adopted the world-view and typical expressions of the *malandro* in order to give his sambas credibility. As a white, lower-middle-class *sambista* he seeks to make the myth itself more respectable, yet often adopts the guise of the *malandro* himself, to comply with a tacit rule of his trade.[35] His attitude to the ethos of *malandragem* is consequently ambiguous, ranging from whole-hearted approval to overt criticism, and he constantly shifts within the convention, exploring it to its limits. The *malandro* lies at the heart of the tension in Noel's work since he is both mockery incarnate, like Noel himself, and yet is an established motif and typical of the samba genre. In the samba *'Cadê trabalho?'* ('Where's the Work?'), written circa 1932, for example, Noel dons the *malandro* persona, and with this figure's characteristic wit, outlines his aversion to work and his love of gambling, twisting logic to justify his lifestyle and suggesting that society's priorities are at fault for wasting his obvious talents:

'Cadê trabalho', circa 1932, Noel Rosa and Canuto

Você grita que eu não trabalho
Diz que eu sou um vagabundo
Não faça assim, meu bem
Pois eu vivo ativo neste mundo
À espera do trabalho
E o trabalho não vem
Quando eu me sinto bem forte
Vou procurar um baralho
Mas fico fraco e sem sorte
Se vejo ao longe o trabalho
Se conversa adiantasse
Eu seria conselheiro
Se fraseado vingasse
Não andava sem dinheiro

Acordei com pesadelo
Quase que o chão escangalho
Com dores no cotovelo
Por sonhar com o trabalho
Trabalho é meu inimigo
Já quis me fazer de tolo
Marcando encontro comigo
O trabalho deu o bolo

'Where's the Work?', circa 1932, Noel Rosa and Canuto

You shout that I don't work
You say that I'm a layabout
Don't say that, my love
Because I'm active in this world

Waiting for work
But work doesn't come
When I feel really strong
I'll look for a pack of cards
But I feel weak and luckless
If I see work in the distance
If conversation were useful
I would be an adviser
If the gift of the gab were valued
I wouldn't be skint

I woke up from a nightmare
I almost tore up the floor
With pains in my elbows
Through dreaming about work
Work is my enemy
It already tried to make a fool of me
Having made an appointment with me
Work stood me up

The reference to the pains in the *malandro*'s elbows, in the second verse, that result from just dreaming about manual work, is also an example of the character's quick wit: the expression *dor-de-cotovelo* (pain in the elbow) means problems with your love-life.

Noel does, on occasion, condemn outright the *malandro*'s play ethic, and espouses the counter-culture of *regeneração* or moral reform. For example, he wrote the samba '*Fui louco*' ('I was Mad'), with the black *sambista* Bide, which shows the reformed spiv's repentance for his former existence. This, in itself, reveals a political savvy and awareness that Noel tries to conceal. His comments about political events appear to be almost accidental and spur-of-the-moment, yet he was obviously conscious of political constraints on a personal level.

'*Fui louco*', 1933, Noel Rosa and Alcebíades Barcellos (Bide)

Fui louco, resolvi tomar juízo
A idade vem chegando e é preciso
Se eu choro, meu sentimento é profundo
Por ter perdido a mocidade na orgia
Maior desgosto do mundo

Neste mundo ingrato e cruel
Eu já desempenhei meu papel
E da orgia então
Vou pedir minha demissão

Felizmente mudei de pensar
E quero me regenerar
Já estou ficando maduro
E já penso no meu futuro

'I was Mad', 1933, Noel Rosa and Alcebíades Barcellos (Bide)

I was mad, I decided to be sensible
I'm getting older and it's necessary
If I cry, my feelings are heart-felt
For having lost my youth in orgies
The biggest regret in the world

In this ungrateful and cruel world
I've already played my part
And so from orgies
I'm going to resign

Fortunately I've changed my way of thinking
And I want to reform myself
I'm getting more mature
And I'm thinking about my future

Máximo and Didier claim that neither Noel nor Bide really believed in this reaction against *malandragem*, and the tone of these lyrics would seem to be characteristically tongue-in-cheek, given Noel's respect for this ethos elsewhere.[36] However, his approach to the ubiquitous character of the *malandro* is often refreshingly non-conformist, and he gives a new angle on this clichéd subject. He replaces myth with realistic detail, and it is this undercurrent of realism which differentiates him from the vast majority of popular songwriters working in the 1930s.

Noel recreates life in Rio's poorer quarters with affection and honesty, and in various sambas he exposes the truth behind the *malandro*'s seemingly idyllic existence, creating social documents of the squalor and degradation that such a lifestyle entailed, albeit attenuated with heavy irony and comic touches. The *malandro*'s eternal bravado is replaced by candid admissions of his foibles. The following two sambas illustrate this alternative approach to this subject:

'Malandro medroso', 1930, Noel Rosa

Eu devo, não quero negar
Mas te pagarei quando puder
Se o jogo permitir
Se a polícia consentir
E se Deus quiser
Não pensa que eu fui ingrato
Nem que fiz triste papel
Hoje vi que o medo é um fato
E eu não quero um pugilato
Com teu velho coronel

A consciência agora que me doeu
Eu evito a concorrência
Quem gosta de mim sou eu

Neste momento, eu saudoso me retiro
Pois teu velho é ciumento
E pode me dar um tiro

Se um dia ficares no mundo
Sem ter nesta vida mais ninguém
Hei de te dar meu carinho
Onde um tem seu cantinho
Dois vivem também
Tu podes guardar o que eu te digo
Contando com a gratidão
E com o braço habilidoso
De um malandro que é medroso
Mas que tem bom coração

'Fearful *Malandro*', 1930, Noel Rosa

I owe, there's no denying
But I'll pay you when I can
Gambling permitting
The police consenting
And God willing
Don't think that I was ungrateful
Or that I played a sorry part
Today I saw that fear is a fact
And I don't want a punch-up
With your old sugar-daddy

My conscience hurt me
I avoid competition
I look after myself
Now I miss you but I get out of the way
'Cos your old man is the jealous type
And could take a shot at me

If one day you're left in this world
With no one else in your life
I will give you my affection
Where there's room for one
Two can live too
You can remember what I say to you
And count on the gratitude
And the skilful arm
Of a *malandro* who is fearful
But who's got a good heart

Noel's *malandro* is made to appear more human here. True to form he is wily and silver-tongued, prone to clashes with the forces of law and order, and not averse to gambling or to borrowing money to make ends meet. But here his mask slips a little, exposing his fear in the face of his woman's jealous partner. In giving this character more believable qualities which to some extent demythologize him, the spiv is portrayed in a more sympathetic light. He is man enough to admit his failings, and self-preservation is always his priority. Noel does not seek to destroy the myth but rather to underline an important aspect of the hustler's personality, that is, his ability to avoid trouble wherever possible. Noel affectionately mocks the myth itself here and in the following samba:

'*O orvalho vem caindo*', 1933, Noel Rosa and Kid Pepe

O orvalho vem caindo
Vai molhar o meu chapéu
E também vão sumindo
As estrelas lá no céu
Tenho passado tão mal
A minha cama é uma folha de jornal
(Do Diário Oficial)

Meu cortinado é o vasto céu de anil
E o meu despertador é o guarda-civil
(Que o salário ainda não viu!)

A minha terra dá banana e aipim
Meu trabalho é achar quem descasque por mim
(Vivo triste mesmo assim!)

A minha sopa não tem osso nem tem sal
Se um dia passo bem, dois e três passo mal
(Isto é muito natural!)

'The Dew is Falling', 1933, Noel Rosa and Kid Pepe

The dew is falling
It's going to dampen my hat
And also disappearing
Are the stars in the sky
I've been having a bad time
My bed is a sheet of newspaper
(From the *Diário Oficial*)

My curtain is the vast indigo sky
And my alarm clock is the policeman
(Who's still not seen his wage packet!)

My homeland bears bananas and manioc
My job is to find someone to peel them for me
(But even so I'm sad!)

My soup has no bones or salt in it
If I have a good day, I have two or three bad ones
(This is very natural!)

In this samba the *malandro,* the anti-hero of poor black Brazilians, is demythologized. His supposedly bohemian existence on the fringes of society and outside the law is exposed here as squalid and degrading. The final lines of each verse, noted down in parentheses, were known as *breques* or spoken asides, often improvised during a live perfomance, and frequently critical comments on life. The first two examples in this samba are aimed at mocking the authorities, with the implication that the *Diário Oficial*, an establishment broadsheet, has no greater function than to provide a warm cover for the homeless, and that civil servants are not paid on time. An ironic contrast is drawn between officialdom and the grim poverty endured by the idle spiv and the hard-working civil servant alike. Noel's Brazil can only offer manioc and bananas, two cheap staples of the diet of the poor - hence the phrase *a preço de banana* (banana price) or dirt cheap - and this must surely be a comment on the economic plight of the nation in the 1930s. There is a clear echo here of the highly patriotic poem *'Canção do Exílio'* by the Romantic poet Antônio Gonçalves Dias (1823-64), which begins:

A minha terra tem palmeiras
Onde canta o sabiá
My homeland has palm trees
Where the thrush sings

The intertextuality has an ironic intention. On the surface the *malandro* here appears to be boasting about his decadent life, but, beneath the irony and humour, it is obvious that the anti-hero of the *morros* has a meagre existence, and, furthermore, that despite the stirring rhetoric of patriotic literature, the governing élite is totally inept. Noel ingeniously parodies this ultra-famous poem, and undercuts its symbolic value by revealing the reality of life in lower-class Rio in the 1930s. The *malandro* is the incarnation of the concept of *jeitinho*, that most Brazilian informal institution, a way of subverting authority for personal advantage, which is celebrated elsewhere in Noel's work. As Lívia Neves de H. Barbosa says, *jeitinho* is a positive way of interpreting and portraying Brazil's historical and racial legacy, and emphasizes the human and natural aspects of social reality, rather than the political, bureaucratic, official institutional aspects.[37] It is thus the essence of the *brasilidade* depicted in Noel's samba lyrics.

A debunking of national mythology and iconography can be seen in many of Noel's sambas. The so-called *samba epistolar* (epistolary samba) *'Cordiais saudações'* ('Cordial Greetings') of 1931, which takes the form of a letter, written by an impecunious *malandro*, requesting repayment of a loan of ten *mil-réis,* in an effort to fend off a grasping money-lender, again referred to simply as *um judeu* (a Jew), provides a fitting illustration of this facet of his work:

'Cordiais saudações', 1931, Noel Rosa

(Cordiais saudações!)
Estimo que este maltraçado samba

No estilo rude da intimidade
Vá te encontrar gozando saúde
Na mais completa felicidade
(Junto dos teus, confio em Deus)

Em vão te procurei
Notícias tuas não encontrei
Eu hoje sinto saudades
Daqueles 10 mil-réis que eu te emprestei
Beijinhos no cachorrinho
Muitos abraços no passarinho
Um chute na empregada
Porque já se acabou o meu carinho

A vida cá em casa está horrível
Ando empenhado nas mãos de um judeu
O meu coração vive amargurado
Pois minha sogra ainda não morreu
(Tomou veneno e quem pagou fui eu)

Sem mais, para acabar
Um grande abraço queira aceitar
De alguém que está com fome
Atrás de algum convite pra jantar.
Espero que notes bem
Estou agora sem um vintém
Podendo, manda-me algum
Rio, 7 de setembro de 31!
(Responde que eu pago o selo)

'Cordial Greetings', 1931, Noel Rosa

(Cordial greetings!)
I hope that this poorly written samba
In the simple style of intimacy
Finds you in good health
And completely happy
(Alongside your loved ones, I pray to God)

In vain I looked for you
I found no news of you
And today I'm longing for
Those 10 *mil-réis* that I loaned you
Give your pet doggie a kiss from me
And your little birdie a hug
Give the maid a good kick
Because my affection has run out

Life here at home is horrible
I'm pawned to the hilt with a Jew
My heart is full of bitterness
'Cos my mother-in-law hasn't died
(She took some poison and I had to pay for it)

Without further ado, finally
Kindly accept best wishes
From someone who's going hungry
And is after any invitation to dinner
I hope that you take note
That now I'm broke
If you can, send me something
Rio, 7 September 1931!
(Reply and I'll pay for the stamp)

Here Noel, in *malandro* guise, imitates the appropriate register and letter-writing formalities of the educated middle classes, such as the use of the deferent present subjunctive form *queira aceitar* (kindly accept), comic false politeness in his good wishes for the debtor and even his pet animals, the latter referred to in affectionate diminutive terms. But true to form, he combines such elegance with a typical slang expression of the *morro* (*Um chute* - a kick, a term taken from football terminology and thus intimately linked with the poor), and a common saying (*sem um vintém* - broke). The letter ends in a formal manner, with the inclusion of the address and date. The date in question is, significantly, 7 September, the *Dia da Pátria* (Day of the Fatherland), when a military parade is held to commemorate the proclamation of Brazil's Independence, forming part of a week of celebratory activities. The anthropologist Roberto Da Matta draws a distinct dichotomy between this formal, military celebration, and carnival in Brazil. They are the two longest Brazilian rituals in terms of duration and yet one is the antithesis of the other.[38] With this facetious allusion to the *Dia da Pátria*, and all that it represents, within a form of popular culture intrinsically linked to this celebration's antithesis, carnival, Noel derides the pomp and ceremony of the élite's event of the year, in which the military must symbolically express their respect for authority and national emblems like the Brazilian flag and the Republic's arms.

In the samba '*Positivismo*' of 1933, music by Noel and lyrics by Orestes Barbosa (except for the final verse, written by Noel), the Positivist philosophy of the mathematician Auguste Comte (1798-1857), adopted by the Republican regime in Brazil, is the target of ridicule. The Positivist motto of *ordem e progresso* (order and progress), which appears on the Brazilian flag, is transplanted into the realm of affairs of the heart in the third verse. Once more the traditional symbols of the Brazilian nation are exposed as hollow and meaningless, imitations of European traditions which have no relevance in the real Brazil:

O amor vem por princípio, a ordem por base
O progresso é que deve vir por fim
Desprezaste esta lei de Augusto Comte
E foste ser feliz longe de mim

> Love comes on principle, order as a basis
> Progress must come last
> You ignored this law of Augusto Comte
> And went off to be happy far from me

Noel's lyrics are characterized by their total insouciance over whether they comply with or contravene convention. He may often call into question a convention by overstating and banalizing it, as is sometimes true of his depiction of *malandragem*, but this exaggeration, and not the demythologizing of the theme in itself, is his principal goal. Many of his songs that deal with women and love take their lead from the well-established stereotype of the wanton, greedy and faithless *malandra*, and Noel gives ample evidence of his skill in employing this convention and in combining it with his personal experience.[39] At times he simply spouts the image of the treacherous *malandra* in passing, as in the opening lines of '*Quem dá mais?*' ('Who'll Give Me More?') of 1930:

> Quem dá mais
> Por uma mulata que é diplomada
> Em máteria de samba e de batucada
> Com as qualidades de moça formosa
> Fiteira, vaidosa e muito mentirosa?

> Who'll give me more
> For a mulatto girl with a degree
> In samba and *batucada*
> With the qualities of a beautiful young woman
> Showy, vain and very deceitful?

Similarly, in many of his sambas about failed relationships Noel reproduces the habitual association made by *sambistas* between women and financial exploitation, with the heartless *malandra* fleecing the unsuspecting, naïve *otário eu*. But it is Noel's unconventional approach which characterizes the majority of his sambas on the subject of women and love. The representation of this theme in his lyrics relies on a strong undercurrent of realism and departs from the norm of stereotypical depictions of women and flowery, pseudo-poetic discourse. Noel's love songs break with tradition precisely because they are anti-romantic, on the whole. Their lyrics are unpoetic and often take their inspiration from unsophisticated everyday language. An excellent example is his so-called *samba-anatômico* (anatomical samba) '*Coração*' ('Heart') of 1931, in which he brings together details of the physiognomy of the heart with its well-known symbolic connotations as a source of romantic love and passion. The age-old allusion to the heart is given a uniquely comic treatment, with Noel combining references to the organ's functions, in semi-scientific language, and the unexpected inclusion of the unglamorous *casa de correção* or reformatory and the prosaic methylene blue (a mild antiseptic and biological stain), alongside the literary device of personification. Such humour of the incongruous can be found in many of his sambas, as we see here:

'*Coração*', 1931, Noel Rosa

Coração, grande órgão propulsor
Transformador do sangue venoso em arterial
Coração, não és sentimental
Mas entretanto dizem que és o cofre da paixão
Coração, não estás do lado esquerdo
Nem tampouco do direito
Ficas no centro do peito, eis a verdade
Tu és para o bem-estar do nosso sangue
O que a casa de correção
É para o bem da humanidade

Coração de sambista brasileiro
Quando bate no pulmão
Faz a batida do pandeiro
Eu afirmo, sem nenhuma pretensão
Que a paixão faz dor no crânio
Mas não ataca o coração

Conheci um sujeito convencido
Com mania de grandeza e instinto de nobreza
Que por saber que o sangue azul é nobre
Gastou todo o seu cobre sem pensar no seu futuro
Não achando quem lhe arrancasse as veias
Onde corre o sangue impuro
Viajou a procurar de norte a sul
Alguém que conseguisse encher-lhe as veias
Com azul de metileno
Pra ficar com sangue azul

'Heart', 1931, Noel Rosa

Heart, great propelling organ
That transforms venous blood into arterial
Heart, you aren't sentimental
But meanwhile they say you are the strongbox of passion
Heart, you aren't on the left side
Nor on the right
You're in the centre of the chest, that's the truth
You are for our blood
What the reformatory
Is for the good of human kind

The heart of the Brazilian *sambista*
When it beats against the lung
Beats the rhythm on a tambourine
I state, without any pretension

That passion causes pain in the skull
But does not attack the heart

I met a conceited chap
With delusions of grandeur and a liking for nobility
Who, knowing that blue blood is noble
Spent all his coppers without thinking about his future
Since he couldn't find someone to pull out his veins
Where the impure blood flows
He travelled from north to south searching
For someone who could fill his veins
With methylene blue
To give him blue blood

When Noel does deal with the subject of love in a more established, pseudo-literary style, he transforms this conventional approach itself by overplaying it, as can be seen in the samba *'Silêncio de um minuto'* ('A Minute's Silence') of 1935:

'Silêncio de um minuto', 1935, Noel Rosa

Não te vejo nem te escuto
O meu samba está de luto
Eu peço o silêncio de um minuto
Homenagem à história
De um amor cheio de glória
Que me pesa na memória

Nosso amor cheio de glória
De prazer e de ilusão
Foi vencido e a vitória
Cabe à tua ingratidão
Tu cavaste a minha dor
Com a pá do fingimento
E cobriste o nosso amor
Com a cal do esquecimento

Teu silêncio absoluto
Me obrigou a confessar
Que o meu samba está de luto
Meu violão vai soluçar
Luto preto é vaidade
Neste funeral de amor
O meu luto é a saudade
E saudade não tem cor

'A Minute's Silence', 1935, Noel Rosa

I can't see you or hear you
My samba is in mourning
I ask for a minute's silence
A tribute to the story
Of a love full of glory
That weighs heavy on my memory

Our love full of glory
Of pleasure and illusion
Was beaten and the victory
Was down to your ingratitude
You dug my pain
With the spade of deceit
And covered our love
With the lime of oblivion

Your absolute silence
Obliged me to confess
That my samba is in mourning
My guitar is going to sob
Black mourning is vain
In this funeral of love
My mourning is my longing
And longing has no colour

This *tour de force* of extended metaphor, in which Noel constructs his *desabafo* (emotional outpouring) around images of death and funerary tradition, is inspired by the classic analogy between physical and emotional death. The use of religious imagery was very common in samba lyrics written in this era. In addition, the influence of Romantic literature on such sambas was noticeable.[40] However, the potential of this death imagery is fully explored here and becomes more expressive as a result of its over-use; the samba itself and Noel's guitar are the bereaved parties, and the ex-lover is the grave-digger, armed with deceit as her spade. Noel manipulates this poetic device with great skill and yet, as he infers in the final line, his feelings cannot be truly expressed in words, and elaborate images are useless to try to describe such intense emotions. This line encapsulates Noel's attitude to the contrived language traditionally used in sambas of the *lírico-amoroso* type, and he tacitly admits to the limitations of the *sambista* and his art. Noel's way of conveying sentiment is precisely the opposite. He looks to concrete detail and to the mundane, such as banal yet paradoxically imaginative allusions to the act of grave- digging and even to the shovel used for this purpose. Noel uses conventional imagery, but makes it his own. He deliberately takes the conventions of his trade too literally, whether the intention is to undermine the thematic or formal cliché or to explore its artistic possibilities.

Unlike most of his contemporaries Noel rejected exhausted themes and stock portrayals of life and people, in favour of an *avant-garde* discourse and depictions of the world around him which had a more factual base. In his samba *'Três apitos'* ('Three Whistles'), for example, he evokes one of his girlfriends in language which makes her palpably real, and broaches the subject of the new female factory worker:

'*Três apitos*', 1933, Noel Rosa

Quando o apito
Da fábrica de tecidos
Vem ferir os meus ouvidos
Eu me lembro de você
Mas você anda
Sem dúvida bem zangada
E está interessada
Em fingir que não me vê

Você que atende ao apito
De uma chaminé de barro
Porque não atende ao grito tão aflito
Da buzina do meu carro?

Você no inverno
Sem meias vai pro trabalho
Não faz fé com agasalho
Nem no frio você crê
Mas você é mesmo
Artigo que não se imita
Quando a fábrica apita
Faz reclame de você

Sou do sereno
Poeta muito soturno
Vou virar guarda-noturno
E você sabe porquê
Mas você não sabe
Que enquanto você faz pano
Faço junto do piano
Estes versos pra você

Nos meus olhos você lê
Que eu sofro cruelmente
Com ciúmes do gerente impertinente
Que dá ordens a você

'Three Whistles', 1933, Noel Rosa

When the whistle blows
At the textile mill
Hurting my ears
I remember you
But you must be
Very annoyed with me
And are keen
To pretend you haven't seen me

You obey the whistle
From the clay chimney
So why don't you respond
To the anxious toot of my car horn?

In the winter
You go to work with bare legs
You don't trust warm clothing
Or believe in the cold
But you are really
One of a kind
When the factory whistle
Calls for you

I belong to the night
I am a sad poet
So I'll become a night watchman
And you know why
But what you don't know
Is that while you make cloth
I sit at the piano
Writing these lines for you

In my eyes you can see
That I suffer cruelly
From jealousy of your impertinent boss
Who gives you orders

Forever with his finger on the pulse of *carioca* life, Noel rejects the thematic norms used by other *sambistas*, and adopts a refreshingly down-to-earth approach to the subject of women here, in keeping with their shifting status and new roles in society in the 1930s. In this samba, inspired by a girl by the name of Fina (Josefina Teles Nunes), a factory worker in the textile industry in Noel's home suburb of Vila Isabel, and the object of his affections, he begins with the amusing admission that the factory hooter reminds him of her. It could hardly begin with a more unflattering comment, and the tone is set for a very prosaic portrayal of the girl in question. The song is full of references to the commonplace sights and sounds of Rio's industrial districts, such as the factory chimney, the factory whistle, and the sound of his car horn as he tries to attract her attention. She is no romantic heroine but the victim of precarious economic circumstances, who cannot afford to buy stockings to wear on a cold winter's day. But it is not Noel's intention to offend or mock her. Rather he seeks to woo her with this unexpected approach. He rejects the jaded, unconvincing discourse of more traditional love sambas in favour of a warts-and-all evocation of love and romance in the unglamorous context of Vila Isabel. By combining realism with humour and the language of everyday, lower-class life, his sentiments seem far more sincere than the trite eulogies of female stock types favoured by his peers.

Several of Noel's sambas contain references to domestic strife and disturbances, or take the form of one side of a verbal altercation between two partners. In '*Vai haver barulho no chatô*' ('There's Going to be a

Row In-Doors') of 1933, for example, the male *eu*, cheated by his partner, warns of an imminent slanging-match, which may even lead to his arrest. The sophisticated connotations of the slang term *chatô* (home), taken from the French *château*, form an ironic contrast in this song with the banal subject matter, and give the lyrics a comic twist. This theme forms part of Noel's candid evocation of the *cotidiano* of the poor, uneducated masses. Domestic difficulties and the loutish behaviour of the macho *malandro* types were, for Noel, a valid element of this recreation of eveyday life on the *morro*. The battered wife forms part of the myth of the *morro*, as is illustrated by the inclusion of the figure in the stock depiction of the shantytowns and their inhabitants in the samba '*De qualquer maneira*' ('Anyway') written by Noel and Ari Barroso in 1933.[41] We are told by the *malandro eu* that he is going to Penha to pray to his patron saint, another commonplace allusion in samba lyrics from this period. We then learn that, a month earlier, this saint was able to cure a *mulata* who had been assaulted, presumably by her lover.

Nevertheless, Noel did not content himself with reiterating these predictable approaches to the subject of domestic violence, and he pursued all the avenues that the topic had to offer. In the hilarious samba '*Mulher indigesta*' ('Indigestible Woman') of 1932, for example, we are told by the male *eu* that the *malandra* figure in question, who will not fall in love and exploits men financially, *Merece um tijolo na testa* (Deserves a brick on the forehead) and that *O que merece é entrar no açoite* (What she deserves is a good whipping). But the quirky comparison in the second verse (*Ela é mais indigesta do que prato/De salada de pepino à meia-noite*, She is more indigestible than a plate/Of cucumber salad at midnight) totally undercuts the seriousness of the topic. Noel's powers of observation, so central to the *cronista*, are evidenced by the latter image, and form an integral part of his virtuosity:

'*Mulher indigesta*', 1932, Noel Rosa

Mas que mulher indigesta
(Indigesta)
Merece um tijolo na testa

Esta mulher não namora
Também não deixa mais ninguém namorar
É um bom center-half pra marcar
Pois não deixa a linha chutar

E quando se manifesta
O que merece é entrar no açoite
Ela é mais indigesta do que prato
De salada de pepino à meia-noite

Esta mulher é ladina
Toma dinheiro, é até chantagista
Arrancou-me três dentes de platina
E foi logo vender no dentista

'Indigestible Woman', 1932, Noel Rosa

What an indigestible woman
(Indigestible)
She deserves a brick on the forehead

This woman has no love-life
But lets no one else have one either
She's a good centre-half for marking
'Cos she doesn't let forwards shoot

And when she sounds off
What she deserves is a good whipping
She is more indigestible than a plate
Of cucumber salad at midnight

This woman is crafty
She takes money and is even a blackmailer
She pulled out three of my platinum teeth
And went straight to sell them to the dentist

In the true *crônica* spirit, Noel places more emphasis on his formal, linguistic treatment of the tradition of women and romantic love, and of that of *malandragem*, than on the content of the themes themselves. He plays with both of these conventional subjects, and his social class and skin colour distance him sufficiently from the real-life *malandro* to enable him to poke fun at his mythical lifestyle. In any *crônica* the serious events of life are not portrayed as being particularly serious at all, but are merely excuses for the author to explore his creative skills and imagination. In Noel's lyrics it is the language that he uses to deal with a given topic that is paramount. His genius lies in his ability to rework and breathe life into an exhausted theme by drawing on the peculiarities of daily life and of the language of ordinary Brazilians. He delves into the myriad artistic opportunities presented by language, from puns to learned references, from slang and spoken forms to the subtleties of rhyme. By foregrounding the linguistic dimension he draws attention to himself as a lyricist, instead of to the semantic content of his lyrics. The *cronista* is, by nature, an exhibitionist, who is able to create something out of nothing, and Noel takes the most stock topics but transforms them into novel creations.[42]

There can be no doubt that Noel was an exceptionally gifted lyricist and that the complexity of his lyrics diffentiates him from all other *sambistas* of the same era. Although many of his contemporaries dealt with the *dia-a-dia* in their songs, none did so with the panache and comic genius of Noel. His lyrics reveal an attitude to Brazilian life and society that centres on the unorthodox and often on the polemical. It is the same view as that expressed by some of the Modernist poets, to a certain extent, but in Noel's case the contradictions and uniqueness of the nation are seen from below and not above, and they are portrayed with much more wit. The obvious parallels between elements of Noel's work and that of these poets writing in the 1930s reflect the impact of the rapid changes in both politics and social structure that took place in this decade, which brought about a reassessment of what it meant to be Brazilian.

Underpinning Noel's depiction of the *cotidiano* is an assertion of the true Brazil, the flip-side of which is, of necessity, a rejection of the phoney symbols of an imagined Brazilian identity based on European templates. Thus icons and emblems of a mythical national consciousness like the national anthem, the formal military celebrations to commemorate Independence, and the motto on the Brazilian flag, are replaced by authentic cultural products of the humble *povo*, such as the *botequim*, the *jogo do bicho*, football, samba, the ethos of *malandragem* and that of *jeitinho*, the *favela/morro/palhoça/barracão*, the *morena bem bonita,* the absurdities of daily life and of bureaucracy and politics, the peculiarities of Brazilian Portuguese and the speech and vernacular of the uneducated, the insipid diet of the poor, even wife-beating and the factory girl of the industrializing nation. Noel elevates these commonplaces of everyday existence to the status of foci of local pride. He considers the question of national consciousness, but he concentrates on the points of reference and identity markers of the lower-class, black and mixed-race community of Rio's *favelas* and lowly suburbs. He sees the notion of *brasilidade* in alternative, unofficial terms, a kind of anti-identity. In his work the mundane is not glamorized or idealized from a position of social or intellectual distance, but is portrayed with objectivity, and a candid realism, by a man who lived and breathed the low life that he so affectionately captured.

Notes

1. Máximo, J. and Didier, C. (1990), p. 39.
2. The term *mamão* could mean either someone being fed by a *mamadeira* or baby's bottle, or the fruit papaya, and was also a slang term for a homosexual.
3. Máximo, J. and Didier, C. (1990), p. 69.
4. See pp. 124-5.
5. *Diário de Notícias*, 15 February 1931, p. 95.
6. The full English translation of a *tangará* is Azara's long-tailed manakin, a member of the Pipridae family of South American passerine birds, characterized by their

colourful plumage, short bill and elaborate courtship behaviour.

7. Tinhorão, J. R. (1962), p. 5.
8. Cabral, S. (1972), pp. 83-9 (esp. 85).
9. Nasser, D. (1983), p. 315.
10. Giani, L. A. A. (1987), p. 13.
11. Ibid., p. 2.
12. Máximo, J. and Didier, C. (1990), p. 229.
13. Souza, O. de (1991), pp. 90-91.
14. Máximo, J. and Didier, C. (1990), p. 170.
15. The genre itself dates from the mid-nineteenth century, and one of the greatest *cronistas* was the Brazilian novelist Machado de Assis (1839-1908).
16. Souza, A. C. de M. e (1992), pp. 13-22 (esp. 14).
17. The *bonde*, which first appeared in Brazil in the 1860s, was already the butt of jokes in the 1880s and 1890s. See the *crônicas* by Machado de Assis in *A Semana*, 16 October 1892, and *Balas de Estalo*, 4 July 1893. Assis, J. M. M. de (1962), III, pp. 414-6, 550-2. It frequently served as inspiration for sambas written in the 1930s and early 1940s.
18. Oswald de Andrade's poem 'Pobre alimária' ('Poor Brute') (*Pau-Brasil*, 1925) hinges on this same juxtaposition of the modern and the colonial:

> O cavalo e a carroça
> Estavam atravancados no trilho
> E como o motorneiro se impacientasse
> Porque levava os advogados para os escritórios
> Desatravancaram o veículo
> E o animal disparou
> Mas o lesto carroceiro
> Trepou no boléia
> E castigou o fugitivo atrelado
> Com um grandioso chicote

> The horse and the cart
> Were stuck in the tramline
> And as the driver was getting impatient
> Because he was taking the lawyers to their offices
> They extricated the vehicle
> And the animal bolted
> But the light-footed carter
> Jumped onto his seat
> And punished the harnessed fugitive
> With a fearsome whip

In this poem the first-world city is symbolized by the lawyers, their offices and the tram, but the tram is delayed by the horse and cart, vestiges of colonial times, which are stuck in the tram rails. In the words of Roberto Schwarz: 'On the one side, the tram, the lawyers, the tram-driver and the rails; on the other, the horse, the cart and the carter: they are contrasting social classes, times and worlds, placed in opposition to one another.' Schwarz, R. (1992), trans. by John Gledson, p. 112. The similarities with Noel's observation (*E o bonde que parece uma carroça*) are striking. In both cases, this duality inherent in urban Brazil in the 1920s and '30s is viewed with affection and not in a totally negative light. This dichotomy is, in fact, the essence of Brazil. With respect to Oswald's poem, Schwarz says of this juxtaposition:

'Surprisingly, the result is positive: the suspension of the conflict and its transformation into a picturesque contrast, where none of the terms is negative, goes together with this choice as a symbol of Brazil ...'. Ibid., p. 118.

19. Bloch, P. (1965), pp. 114-17.
20. António, J. (1966), pp. 262-77 (esp. 267).
21. Ibid., p. 274.
22. It is interesting to note the similarities with Cândido Portinari's painting *O Morro* of 1933, in which the monochrome skyscrapers of inner-city Rio are depicted in contrast to the shantytown, with its vitality and wealth of earthy shades. The *morro* was also a favourite theme for the Modernist poets in the 1930s. Carlos Drummond de Andrade's 'Morro de Babilônia' ('Babylon Hill'), for example, pays tribute to the life of this humble community:

> À noite, do morro
> descem vozes que criam o terror
> (terror urbano, cinquenta por cento de cinema,
> e o resto que veio de Luanda ou se perdeu na língua geral).
>
> Quando houve revolução, os soldados se espalharam no morro,
> o quartel pegou fogo, eles não voltaram.
> Alguns, chumbados, morreram.
> O morro ficou mais encantado.
>
> Mas as vozes do morro
> não são propriamente lúgubres.
> Há mesmo um cavaquinho bem afinado
> que domina os ruídos da pedra e da folhagem
> e desce até nós, modesto e recreativo,
> como uma gentileza do morro.
>
> At night, from the hill,
> there come down voices that cause terror
> (urban terror, fifty percent from the movies
> and the rest that came from Luanda and got lost in the local speech).
>
> When there was a revolution, the soldiers spread out on the hill,
> the barracks were burnt, they didn't come back.
> Some, gunned down, died.
> The hill got more bewitched.
>
> But the voices from the hill
> are not exactly lugubrious.
> There's even a well-tuned banjo
> that prevails over the sounds of the stone and the foliage
> and comes down to us, modest and recreational
> like a kindness from the hill.

Translation by John Gledson, in Gledson, J. (1994), p. 31.
23. Máximo, J. and Didier, C. (1990), p. 242.
24. *Chuchu* was also a common nickname for Getúlio Vargas. A *chuchu* is literally a pear-shaped, rather tasteless vegetable, often translated into English as a chayote. The nickname was undoubtedly a reference to Vargas's pear-shaped physique, and was an updated and Brazilianized version of one of the most famous caricatures, that of Louis Philippe, the bourgeois monarch, as a pear. Both were small and fat.

The nickname features in many popular songs from the 1930s, such as *'Chuchu'*, *'Monólogo do Chuchu'* ('Chuchu's Monologue') and *'As mágoas do Chuchu'* ('Chuchu's Sorrow'), all of which were recorded by the Eldorado studios for a television programme to commemorate the fiftieth anniversary of the constitutionalist movement. Severiano, J. (1983), p. 16.

25. Noel created various examples of isomorphism or metalanguage, in which the subject matter is the form of the lyrics themselves and vice versa, such as *'Gago apaixonado'* ('Smitten Stammerer') of 1930, in which he imitates the speech impediment of his friend Manuel Barreiros.

26. In the final verse of the samba *'Você é um colosso'* ('You are the Greatest') of 1934, for example, he rhymes *sandwich* with *maxixe*. Similarly, the following lines from his nonsensical *marcha 'Você, por exemplo'* ('You, For Example') of 1933 give proof of his keen ear for the oddities of language: *Quanto barbado que jejua mais que o Gandhi/Você, por exemplo ... Você, por exemplo/Não tem barba grande* (You're so mature [literally bearded] that you fast more than Gandhi/You, for example ... You, for example/Haven't got a big beard). This humorous and irreverent rhyming of the name of the world-famous Indian religious leader with the adjective *grande* is possible in Brazilian Portuguese, but not in European Portuguese. A similar feature can be found in some of Cole Porter's lyrics, for example his song 'You're the Top' in which he rhymes the word 'top' with the line 'You're *de trop'*.

27. See *'De qualquer maneira'* written by Noel and Ari in 1933, pp. 158- 60.

28. Roberto Da Matta says: '... os malandros preferem reter para si sua força de trabalho e suas qualificações. O vadio, assim, é aquele que não entra no sistema com sua força de trabalho, e fica flutuando na estrutura social, podendo nela entrar ou sair ou, ainda, a ela transcender. A astúcia, por seu turno, pode ser vista como um equivalente do jeito (ou do jeitinho) como um modo estruturalmente definido de utilizar as regras vigentes na ordem em proveito próprio, mas sem destruí-las ou colocá-las em causa' ('... the *malandros* prefer to keep for themselves their labour force and qualifications. The layabout, thus, is the one who does not enter the system with his labour force, and hovers around the social structure, being able to enter or leave it, or even transcend it. His craftiness, in turn, can be seen as the equivalent of *jeito* (or *jeitinho*) as a structurally defined way of using the established rules of society for his own benefit, but without destroying them or calling them into question'). Matta, R. Da (1979) p. 226.

29. Máximo, J. and Didier, C. (1990), p. 166.

30. Ibid., p. 431.

31. It is interesting to note the parallel with Machado de Assis, the great Brazilian novelist of the nineteenth century, who began many of his most subversive *crônicas* by claiming to know nothing about politics.

32. Máximo, J. and Didier, C. (1990), p. 84. The lyrics of the national anthem of Brazil were composed by Osório Duque Estrada, the music by Francisco Manuel da Silva.

33. Ibid., p. 158.

34. *O Globo*, 31 December 1932. See Antônio, J. (1982), p. 97.

35. See *'Conversa de botequim'* of 1935, pp. 98-100, for an example of Noel adopting the persona of the wise-cracking spiv.

36. Máximo, J. and Didier, C. (1990), p. 205.

37. See Barbosa, L. N. de H. (1995), pp. 35-48.

38. The *Dia da Pátria* is a day-time ritual centred on a highly ordered and hierarchical military file-past, organized by the establishment and legitimized by laws and decrees. Carnival, on the other hand, is held at night, night and day being

inverted, is organized by private bodies like the *escolas de samba* who do not parade in an orderly fashion, the order of appearance being dictated by a *sorteio público* or draw, and thus hierarchy is overturned by free competition on equal terms. The former outwardly expresses bourgeois individuality and social distance whereas the latter symbolizes intimacy and the collectivity of the poor masses. Matta, R. da (1979), pp. 41-9.

39.   See '*Dama do cabaré*' of 1936, p. 111, for an illustration of the *malandra* type. In this case Noel models the protagonist on his real-life lover Ceci.

40.   Matos, C. (1982), pp. 131-4.

41.   See pp. 158-60.

42.   Machado de Assis, in a *crônica* in the newspaper *A Semana*, 10 July 1892, encapsulated his craft as follows: 'Eu, quando vejo um ou dois assuntos puxarem para si todo o cobertor da atenção pública, deixando os outros ao relento, dá-me vontade de os meter nos bastidores, trazendo à cena tão-somente a arraia-miúda, os pobres ocorrências de nada, a velha anedota, o sopapo casual, o furto, a facada anônima, a estatística mortuária, as tentativas de suicídio, o cocheiro que foge, o noticiário, em suma. É que eu sou justo, e não posso ver o fraco esmagado pelo forte. Além disso, nasci com certo orgulho que já agora há de morrer comigo. Não gosto que os fatos nem os homens se me imponham por si mesmos. Tenho horror a toda superioridade. Eu é que os hei de enfeitar com dois ou três adjetivos, uma reminiscência clássica, e os mais galões de estilo. Os fatos, eu é que os hei de declarar transcendentes; os homens, eu é que os hei de aclamar extraordinários' ('When I see one or two subjects grabbing all the public's attention, leaving others out in the cold, I get an urge to relegate them to the wings, and to bring on centre stage only the trivial, the poor non-events, the old anecdote, the casual off-the-cuff remark, the theft, the anonymous stabbing, mortality rates, suicide attempts, the escaped tram-driver, the news, in a word. I am a fair man, and for this reason I cannot see the weak crushed by the strong. Furthermore, I was born with a certain pride that I will take to my death-bed. I do not like facts or people to impose themselves on me. I have a horror of any kind of superiority. I am the one who will adorn them with two or three adjectives, a classical allusion, and all the other flourishes of style. The facts, I am the one who will declare them to be transendent; people, I am the one who will acclaim them as extraordinary'). He adds 'Daí o meu amor às chamadas chapas ...' ('From this stems my love of commonplaces ...').

CHAPTER SIX

The Sambas of Ari Barroso
(1903-64)

Ari Evangelista de Rezende Barroso was born into a highly respectable, white, middle-class family in the town of Ubá, in the state of Minas Gerais, on 7 November 1903. The son of João Evangelista Barroso, a trained lawyer and local politician, and Angelina de Rezende Barroso, he was orphaned in 1911. His mother died at the age of 22, and his father, a bohemian who enjoyed playing the guitar and singing *modinhas* (a type of popular song) in his youth in the city of Belo Horizonte, died just two months later. Ari was then raised by his maternal grandmother, who wanted her grandson to become a priest and encouraged him to become a sacristan, and his aunt, whose influence on him was the greater since she taught him how to play the piano. When he was 12 he began to help his aunt Ritinha give piano lessons. He would also take it in turns with her to accompany the silent movies at the local cinema, for which he was paid five *mil-réis* per night. Even before his fourteenth birthday Ari was performing works by Chopin, Beethoven, Wagner and other classics.

Ari was, by his own admission, a tiresome child. He had a particular fascination for the circus, creating his own shows for his family. He was equally keen on football, playing in defence for a local team with success, despite his short-sightedness, which forced him to wear glasses from an early age. He had many friends but did not neglect his studies in favour of boyhood antics. He attended the Externato Mineiro of Cícero Galindo day school, where he completed his primary education, and later the *ginásios* (secondary schools) of São José and Rio Branco. He was expelled from the latter for escaping from the boarders' dormitory to go to a dance. He was only 13 years old at the time yet decided to take a break from his studies. He went to work as a shop assistant, but returned to his studies after just six months. He then enrolled in the *ginásio* of Viçosa, where he sat four examinations, and he spent a year in the town. He did not return to that school the following year, however, and started at the *ginásio* in the town of Leopoldina instead. After only four days he was expelled, on this occasion for getting drunk with a classmate.

In 1920 Ari set off for the city of Rio, at the age of 17. A broken engagement led him to pack his bags and move away from Ubá. On the advice of an old friend of his father's, he sat the entrance examination to study law at university in Rio, and went to live in a string of guest houses. Despite having arrived in the capital with a considerable amount of money from an inheritance, Ari soon spent it on bohemian night life and fashionable clothes. To earn a living he decided to play the piano in the cinemas of the city, accompanying the silent films as he had done back home, and combined this with studying law. He played in the Cinema Íris from midday to six pm, and then in the Odeon, on the corner of the Rua Sete de Setembro, from eight pm until ten pm. In the entrance to the Odeon, the well-known popular musician Pixinguinha also played the piano, and it was there that Ari first performed many of his own compositions. He also found a job playing in the entrance to the Carlos Gomes Theatre in 1923.

It is thought that the first song that Ari ever wrote was 'De longe' ('By Far'), a cateretê (traditionally the accompaniment to a rural dance form of African origin) written in 1918 and later adapted into a samba and recorded by Carmen Miranda in 1932 under the title 'Nosso amô veio dum sonho' ('Our Love Came From a Dream'). His early lyrics were inspired by everyday life and events, such as the samba 'Dá uma folga' ('Take a Rest'), which he wrote in the spare pages of his driving licence in 1924, and which comments directly on the fashion of women dressing like men. In the 1920s he became recognized as one of the best jazz pianists in Rio, and was a fan of the top international pianists of this genre whom he listened to on record. He travelled to other parts of the country as a member of various dance bands, and in Vitória, the capital of the state of Espírito Santo, he met Noel Rosa, whose work he greatly admired. The two joined forces with the singer Sílvio Caldas and put on shows in the local cinemas. Sílvio Caldas was to become Ari's favoured male singer and recorded many of his compositions.

Ari finally resumed his law studies and graduated on 31 January 1930, in the same group of students as Mário Reis, who was to become one of the most famous singers of popular music in the 1930s and 1940s. Ari never practised law, preferring to pursue a career in the music business and the radio. As a university student Ari supported Getúlio Vargas's political party, the Aliança Liberal (Liberal Alliance). He took part in de-monstrations in the run-up to the presidential elections of 1930, and helped lead a meeting in the Fênix Theatre as a member of the Comitê Central dos Universitários Liberais (Central Committee of Liberal University Students), attended by members of parliament. Ari was elected general secretary of the group's campaign committee, and when Vargas came to power Ari was nominated to form part of the reception committee. He also contributed to the music of a theatre revue written to celebrate Vargas's victory entitled '*O Barbado*' ('The Man with the Beard', a reference to the deposed Washington Luís). He composed songs for another pro-revolution theatre production called '*Brasil maior*' ('A Greater Brazil') of 1930.

Ari's links with the theatre began in 1927, when he started to write music for shows. Luís Peixoto chose two of his compositions, '*Vamos deixar de intimidade*' ('Let's Forget Intimacy') and '*Vou à Penha*' ('I'm Going to Penha'), to feature in one of his productions, and was drawn to Ari's unorthodox style, noted for its rhythmic quality and the way it captured the sounds of various instruments on the piano, so different from that of Sinhô, the most famous songwriter and pianist of that era. Luís Peixoto went on to commission many pieces of music from Ari, who spent five years writing music for the Recreio Theatre. These included some of his most famous works, such as '*No tabuleiro da baiana*' ('On The Baiana's Tray'). Ari wrote the song '*Bahia*' ('Bahia') to feature in a show by Afonso de Carvalho. He also participated in the shows themselves, as a comedian who, with a group of others, was in charge of entertaining the audience before the show proper began. Ari wrote music for 26 *revues* and one operetta called '*Malandragem*'. He was also leader and conductor of the orchestra of the Alhambra Theatre company, which visited the north of Brazil and Buenos Aires. In May 1931 he became a member of the SBAT, the *Sociedade Brasileira de Autores Teatrais* (Brazilian Society of Theatre Writers).

Ari's relationship with his future wife Ivone began in 1925 when she was just 13 years old. Her middle-class family disapproved of her 22-year-old boyfriend, largely because of the age difference and his determination to pursue a career in popular music. Their courtship lasted for about three years, and they were devoted to each other throughout that period. Ari was, by all accounts, jealous and possessive, and when he was travelling he would miss her terribly, becoming angered by the lack of letters that he received from her. The ups and downs in his love life evidently provided inspiration for many of his compositions, such as the samba '*O correio já chegou*' ('The Post Has Arrived') and the melancholy '*Por tua causa*' ('Because of You'), and his rather conservative attitude towards women can be seen in his lyrics. There were rumours linking Ari to other women, some of them famous, throughout his married life, and the song '*Risque*' ('Erase') was allegedly composed after one of his mistresses left him for another man. Nevertheless, he cultivated the image of a respectable family man.[1]

In 1930 Ari won a competition organized by the Casa Edison record company with his *marcha* '*Dá nela*' ('Beat Her'), and this was to mark a turning point in his musical career, as well as earning him enough money to marry Ivone later that year. He greatly admired the syncopated rhythms of the *samba-de-morro*, especially the work of Geraldo Pereira and Ataúlfo Alves, and spoke out against the encroaching influence of North American styles and instruments on Brazilian music. He was perhaps the first Brazilian popular musician to treat music as a true profession. When the general climate was bohemian and largely scornful of professionalization, Ari worked extremely hard to survive and to guarantee fair copyright payments for composers. In 1932 his musical career took off, and in December of that year alone, three of his songs were recorded by the Victor label, and in the *Diário Carioca* newspaper of 14 January 1933 an interview with him was published, in which he was referred to as 'o compositor que impressiona o Rio, no momento' ('the composer who is currently impressing the city of Rio'). He remained in close contact with his fellow composers and popular singers, generally in the bars and cafés which they frequented, the recording studios and the Urca casino. Ari wrote in *parceria* with Almirante, Lamartine Babo, and with Noel Rosa on three occasions, as well as with Luís Peixoto.

It was Renato Murce who introduced Ari to the radio in 1932. They met at the Casa Edison record company and Murce invited him to present the programme '*Horas do outro mundo*' ('Hours from the Other World') on Radio Philips, and to accompany the singers on the piano. From there Ari went to Radio Mayrink Veiga, but soon moved on to São Paulo in 1936, where he worked for Radio Kosmos as a comedian. In that same year he entered his *marcha* '*Paulistinha querida*' ('Dear Little Girl from São Paulo') in a carnival music competition. Despite the popularity of this song during the carnival, and the fact that it deliberately dealt with a subject close to the hearts of people from São Paulo, namely the revolution which took place there in 1932, it was awarded only second place. Ari adopted the guise of a Brazilian *malandro* in this new job as comic, and starred in the programme '*Hora H*' ('Hour H'), which attracted large audiences. In 1937 he returned to Rio to work for Radio Cruzeiro do Sul, once again as *humorista* (comic), but his radio career was soon to take a new twist. He took over the management of Cruzeiro do Sul's sports shows and covered all the football matches that he could. He used a harmonica to signal that a goal had been scored, and his fame was such that he was put in charge of providing the commentary for the footage sent back to Brazil from the 1938 World Cup in Italy. In addition, from 15 March 1939 he became head of the sports page in the newspaper *O Jornal*. His football allegiances fluctuated in his early life, but he was to become an ardent supporter of the Rio team Flamengo until his death.

The talent contests or *calouros* directed by Ari first appeared in 1937, on Radio Cruzeiro do Sul. At that time a bell sounded to signify that a contestant had failed and should stop performing, but Ari later became famous for using a gong for the same purpose. This practice began after he took his famous show to Radio Tupi in 1939. Some of the people who passed through the programme went on to gain fame in their own right, such as the singer Ângela Maria, whom Ari advised to study music. His talent shows had a considerable impact on the radio and theatre in Brazil, and turned him into a household name. His attitude to the contestants in the *calouros* was condescending and often rude, and many were angered by his dismissive attitude towards their acts. Luiz Gonzaga, for example, who went on to become a well-known performer of *sertanejo* songs, a genre typical of the interior of Brazil's northeast, was treated dismissively by Ari in one of his shows, a sign perhaps of the latter's limited taste and sense of superiority. On one particular occasion, he was greatly vexed by a contestant who stated that he would perform a *sambinha* (little samba) and proceeded to sing Ari's own '*Aquarela do Brasil*' ('Watercolour of Brazil'), complete with mistakes in the lyrics. Ari's pet hate was the fact that many participants did not know who had written the songs that they chose to perform, often attributing them to the people who sang them on record. He does not appear to have accepted any criticism of his work, and he chose to boycott the Rio carnival music competition in 1941 after failing to be the panel's choice. He believed that his victory was proven by the success and popularity he continued to enjoy among the general public.[2]

Ari had a hectic working schedule, and by all accounts managed to fit his songwriting into the spare moments between his radio broadcasts and sports commentaries. According to Dalila Luciana, he had strange habits when it came to composing, and would sometimes get up in the middle of the night and transform short series of notes into gentle melodies at his piano. She also recounts an anecdote about how he and his favourite *parceiro*, Luís Peixoto, were inspired to write a samba one night while walking through the central Rio district of Cinelândia. They searched for somewhere to be able to compose, and managed to gain access to the attic of a theatre where there was an old piano. It was there that the samba '*Na batucada da vida*' ('In the *Batucada* of Life') was written.[3] Ari was a prolific songwriter and the exact extent of his output is unknown, although it has been estimated that between 1930 and 1945 he wrote well over 200 songs, many of them sambas but also waltzes, foxtrots, *samba-canções* and *marchas,* in addition to the songs that he composed for the theatre.[4]

Ari was criticized by *mineiros* for praising Bahia in the lyrics of his songs and failing to give credit to his homeland of Ubá. There can be no doubt that Ari fell in love with Bahia on his first visit there in January 1929. In his own words: 'Eu é que me descobri na Bahia. Os seus ritmos, os seus candomblés, suas capoeiras, sua gente, em geral, foram uma revelação para mim. Fiquei de tal modo impressionado que o jeito foi exteriorizar a minha admiração através da música' ('I found myself in Bahia. Its rhythms, its *candomblé* and *capoeira*, its people, in general, were a revelation to me. I was so impressed that I expressed my admiration through my music'). On arrival in Salvador he visited the Church of Bonfim and was overwhelmed by the miraculous cures that had supposedly been performed by *Nosso Senhor do Bonfim* (Our Lord of Bonfim). In a letter to Ivone he stated: 'Saí da igreja com o coração alegre, por ter podido cumprir essa obrigação' ('I came out of the church with a joyful heart, for having been able to fulfil my obligation'). The city of Salvador da Bahia provided him with endless inspiration but, as Sérgio Cabral points out, he lacked a thorough knowledge of Bahian folklore which led him, in the samba *'Bahia'*, to wrongly call the region *'terra do jongo'* ('land of the *jongo'*, the latter being a type of dance, accompanied by drums, from the states of Minas Gerais and Espírito Santo).[5] He drew a great deal of inspiration from his visits to Salvador da Bahia, even from the cries of the street vendors that he heard there, and he incorporated many Afro-Brazilian themes and motifs into his song lyrics. However, despite his first-hand experience of the city, Ari still portrayed life there in conventional terms, relying on the stock images with which it was associated in the popular imagination. According to José Ramos Tinhorão, Ari openly admitted that he consulted the works of the folklorist Luís da Câmara Cascudo in order to find information for his songs.[6]

Ari participated in the celebrations organized as part of the *Dia da Música Popular* (Popular Music Day) in 1939, and Carmen Miranda caused a sensation performing his song *'Boneca de piche'* ('Tar Doll'). Carmen and her sister Aurora recorded many of his sambas, and Carmen, in particular, became a good friend of his. This was also the year when his samba *'Aquarela do Brasil'* was first performed. It was sung by Araci Cortes in a *revue* at the Recreio Theatre on 16 June, but went unnoticed. It was first recorded by the famous singer Francisco Alves on 18 August for Odeon Records. The patriotism of the lyrics of this samba is obvious, but Sérgio Cabral does not see any political propaganda in it, despite the fact that the DIP were encouraging positive lyrics in praise of the nation, the family and work.[7] In fact, the DIP tried to cut the line *'Terra do samba e do pandeiro'* ('Land of samba and of tambourines'), on the grounds that it belittled Brazil. Ari was forced to visit the censors but managed to retain these words.

Ari had a deep affection for his homeland and was proud of the fact that he had made Brazil famous throughout the world with the help of his most popular songs, particularly *'Aquarela do Brasil'*. This samba became known as the *segundo hino nacional* (second national anthem). There is little doubt that he cooperated with the Vargas regime throughout its 15-year existence. A selection of his songs, including *'Aquarela do Brasil'*, were used in the show *'Joujoux e balangandans'*[8] ('Knick-knacks and Gewgaws') performed at the Municipal Theatre in June and July 1939, which raised funds for the social works of Brazil's first lady, Darci Vargas. Similarly, on 12 October of the same year, Ari appeared at the Municipal Theatre in a show dedicated to the Brazilian navy on the official *Dia do Mar* (Day of the Sea). Two of his sambas were performed alongside the national anthem and the overture from Carlos Gomes's opera *'O Guarani'* ('The Guarani Indian'). In 1941 Ari took part in the fourth anniversary celebrations of the *Estado Novo*. It would seem that from his student days onwards Ari remained a *getulista* (supporter of Getúlio Vargas), out of a conviction which was born even before the revolution of 1930. He would have been inspired by the state's brand of chauvinism, so akin to his own patriotic zeal, and this, combined with his conservative views and susceptibility to cliché, the two main characteristics of his lyrics, made him the ideal spokesman for the regime, both at home and abroad. Tárik de Souza points out the contradictions in Ari's patriotism and political persuasion, calling him *'brasileiríssimo e paradoxal'* ('Brazilian through and through and paradoxical'). Although Ari became synonymous with the patriotic spin-off of samba known as the *samba-exaltação*, which boosted the Vargas regime's image, he also took on the state when the occasion arose.[9] Above all, his stance *vis-à-vis* the regime seems to have been pragmatic. Antônio Risério calls him: '... um oportunista genial, nascido em contexto propício' ('... a brilliant opportunist, born at the right time'), who pursued public recognition more than any of his contemporaries, and whose main concern was to have a long and memorable musical career.[10]

Ari first came into contact with Walt Disney at the end of 1941. The famous cartoonist was visiting Brazil with a view to making a full-length feature film about the country. It was thought that cartoons with Latin American characters would be beneficial as part of President Roosevelt's Good Neighbour Policy towards the continent, the ultimate aim of which was to establish Latin American support for US policies in the world conflict that was brewing. Thus, the Coordinator for Inter-American Affairs for the Roosevelt Administration, Nelson Rockefeller, suggested to the State Department that it should pay for a visit to Brazil by Disney and his team, and give US$300,000 towards the production of a film with a Latin American theme. During a visit to the Grande Hotel, in the city of Belém, Disney heard North American music being played by a quartet. He asked his host Celestino Silveira if he could hear some Brazilian music and the band began to play '*Aquarela do Brasil*'. The following day the two of them caught a plane to Rio and Disney was transfixed by the scenery as they flew over Amazonia. During a stop in Barreiro, in the *sertão* or interior of the state of Bahia, he saw a collection of brightly coloured parrots and other birds in the airport, and started to play with them as he hummed the tune that he had heard the night before. In Rio he began to make plans for the animated film, which was to be called '*Alô, amigos*' ('Saludos Amigos'), the protagonist of which would be a *malandro* parrot called Zé Carioca, who would appear *gingando* (swaggering) to authentic Brazilian sambas. This was to be Disney's first contribution to the Good Neighbour Policy. When the time came to select the music for the film, Disney remembered the melody that he had heard in Belém, and Silveira tried to track Ari down as soon as they arrived in Rio, without success. Ari and Disney finally met at a cocktail party given by the film-maker in the Hotel Glória during this same visit. The film went on to be a huge success and '*Aquarela do Brasil*', renamed simply 'Brazil' by Disney, became well known all over the world. The original version was recorded by Aloísio Oliveira, but many other famous singers like Bing Crosby also recorded it.[11] Disney went on to use Ari's music in another animated film, 'The Three Caballeros' ('*Você já foi à Bahia?*') of 1945. This was the first full-length feature film to combine cartoon characters, such as Donald Duck, an Argentinian horse and Zé Carioca, with real people in the shape of Aurora Miranda. Ari became a household name in the United States overnight. When Orson Welles visited Brazil as cultural ambassador he insisted on meeting the composer of '*Aquarela do Brasil*'.

Ari finally accepted one of the many invitations that he received to go to the United States in 1944. He was commissioned to write music for a film called 'Brazil' made by Republic studios, for which he composed the samba 'Rio'. He spoke very little English and felt frustrated by his inability to communicate. He thus spent a lot of time at the home in Hollywood of Carmen Miranda, which was always full of Brazilians and the food and music of his homeland. He spent so much time in Carmen's company during his visits to the USA that rumours reached Brazil that the pair had married. Later that year Ari was asked to produce music for the film '*Três garotas de azul*' ('Three Little Girls in Blue') by Twentieth Century Fox. He thus returned to the USA and earned 1000 dollars a week for eight months, displaying a characteristically professional attitude to his work.[12] In the words of Gilberto Souto: 'Recordo muitos momentos, passados com ele, quando percebi o seu amor ao trabalho, o cuidado em apresentar somente o que de melhor pudesse produzir, a sua honestidade profissional' ('I remember many instants, spent with him, when I became aware of his love for his work, the care he took in presenting only the best he could produce, his professional honesty').[13] Unfortunately, the film 'Three Little Girls in Blue' was never made, possibly due to the intervention of the censors of the *Estado Novo* since it was to have portrayed three grasping Brazilian prostitutes, and the music Ari composed for it was never heard. He made a third visit to North America in 1948, to compose music for a Broadway musical initially named '*O trono da Amazônia*' ('The Throne of Amazonia'), but the director went bankrupt and the show was shelved. English versions of his songs featured in several other films, such as 'That Night in Rio', 'The Gang's All Here' and 'Copacabana'.[14]

Ari became very famous in the USA and was fêted in Hollywood for his professionalism, musical skill and rich, memorable melodies. Twentieth Century Fox showed their appreciation for his work by arranging a ticket for him to attend the Academy Awards Oscar ceremony in 1944. Ari himself received an award of merit for outstanding achievement from the Academy of Motion Picture Arts and Sciences on 31 December 1944 for his samba 'Rio de Janeiro', from the sound track to the film 'Brazil'. (He did not receive an Oscar, as several Brazilian journalists wrongly reported.) Ari thought that he enjoyed greater prestige among musicians in the USA than at home, yet it was largely thanks to him that samba became an export commodity for Brazil.

In 1947 Ari was voted in as a councillor on Rio city council, and two of his personal campaigns involved the building of the Maracanã stadium in preparation for the 1950 World Cup, for which he did some of the match commentaries, and the payment of copyright dues to musicians. His political career was, however, full of disappointment. In the 1950s Ari continued to perform live and took his band on tour in Uruguay and Argentina in 1955. His fiftieth birthday celebrations were attended by the then Minister of Justice, Tancredo Neves, and a host of other celebrities, and in the Rio carnival of 1955 the theme for the decorations in the centre of the city was Ari's most famous compositions. In the same year he was awarded the Order of Merit by the government in the Catete Palace, and also wrote a column in the newspaper *O Jornal*, which proved him to be a great chronicler of *carioca* night life. In June 1956 he returned to Bahia to receive the title of '*Cidadão Baiano*' ('Citizen of Bahia') for promoting the state and its capital via his music. He was also voted the fifth most important composer in the world by the US magazine *Fair-Play*. Throughout the 1950s, he set various night club shows to music, and in 1957 a show dedicated to his own life was staged at the Night and Day night club in Rio, entitled 'Mr Samba', which included many of his most famous songs. On 6 January 1958 he officially became a citizen of Rio in recognition for having written songs about numerous districts of the city. In the late 1950s he also returned to the television with great success and became head of sports for TV Tupi.

Ari was, by all accounts, a simple family man, with traditional views. Ivone remained a devoted wife throughout his life, who took care of the family while Ari enjoyed Rio's bohemian night life and travelled abroad. He had a patriarchal attitude, and was something of a moralist, being most critical of his loved ones. Most descriptions of his personality point out his shyness, superficial irritability, and his sense of humour. Often his bad temper would be nothing more than an ironic façade to enable him to have fun at someone else's expense. He appears to have taken his work very seriously, as is evidenced in a letter he wrote to Ivone from Hollywood, stating that he could not miss all the opportunities that were now open to him: 'Você deve e precisa reconhecer que todas as minhas loucuras, todos os meus desatinos, tudo o que faço de ruim e de errado, justifica-se com o que sou: um artista, um homem diferente dos outros, um predestinado, talvez' ('You should and need to recognize that all the stupid things I've done, all the madness, all the bad things I do and mistakes I make, are justified by what I am: an artist, a man who is different from others, on a predestined course, perhaps').[15] In spite of his huge commercial success, he was obliged to work to support his family throughout his life, and never became rich, largely due to the unfair system of copyright payments to musicians, against which he fought so vehemently. He earned enough money to have a three-storey house built overlooking the beaches of Leme and Copacabana, to buy a car, and to educate his children. He was a devoted Catholic, but this did not prevent him from having a great fear of death, according to his son Flávio Rubens. Ari's health began to fail in 1961. The official line was that he was suffering from hepatitis but, in truth, he had acute cirrhosis of the liver. Despite this he continued to drink alcohol and enjoy Rio's night spots. After various spells in hospital and periods of recovery, he died on 9 February 1964, carnival Sunday. 'Aquarela do Brasil' was played by the saxophonist Souza Lima at his funeral the following day, and the then president of Brazil, João Goulart, sent an official representative. Among the many compliments and homages paid to Ari, both before and after his death, the critic Sylvio Tulio Cardoso referred to him as 'o mais completo, o mais universal dos nossos compositores, a mesma significação de Villa Lobos na música erudita' ('the most complete, the most universal of our composers, with the same significance as Villa Lobos within erudite music').[16]

The discourse of the samba lyrics of Ari Barroso

Unlike most of his contemporaries, Ari does not often deal with the character of the *malandro*. Ari's avoidance of the theme of *malandragem* is not surprising, given the patriotism and pro-establishment stance that permeates most of his work, and is perhaps a consequence of his support for Vargas's work ethic, as well as his eagerness to succeed as a professional musician. It is significant that there are very few comments made in his lyrics about the poverty endured by the lower classes in the 1930s and 1940s. Occasionally, the *eu* of a song will admit to being *sem grana* (skint), such as in the samba '*E a festa Maria?*' ('And the Party Maria?') of 1938, but these asides are little more than aspects of everyday life and conversation, and add a touch of authenticity and colour. Apart from these cursory comments, life is presented as being rather idyllic and problem-free. Ari's readiness to court the establishment and to toe the official line is evidenced in his attitude to the *malandro*'s aversion to hard work. In several songs he alludes to the virtues of honest toil, through the mouthpiece of the compliant manual worker, such as in the samba '*Foi de madrugada*' ('It Was In The Early Morning') of 1936, in which a jilted male *eu* says:

Agora eu passo
No batente noite e dia
Para ver se trabalhando
Combato um pouco a nostalgia

Now I spend
Night and day labouring
To see if by working
I can combat my longing a little

In general, the lyrics of Ari Barroso's sambas written in the early 1930s are characterized by unadorned, spoken-language forms, a limited lexical range and easy rhymes. He tends to imitate casual speech and the turns of phrase typical of ordinary people, but does not stray far into their inventive *gíria* or slang, incorporating just a few typical expressions. The absence of the theme of *malandragem* partially explains the infrequent use of *morro* vernacular in his lyrics. The samba '*Amnistia!*' ('Amnesty!') of 1933, in which we see a manual worker begging a policeman to release him from his cell so that he can join in the carnival celebrations, contains abbreviated speech forms (such as *seu dotô* for *seu doutor*, a deferential form of address), the common expression *no batente* (manual labour), and prosaic detail (*comprei a prestação*, I bought in instalments):

'*Amnistia!*', 1933, Ari Barroso
Amnistia
Amnistia

Nos três dias de folia
Seu dotô
Não faça isso por favor
Na prisão
Basta só meu coração

Passo a vida no batente
Ali rente
Somente
Porque sei que o trabalho é natural
Seu dotô quer ir-se embora
É hora
Lá fora
Começou minha festa, o carnaval

Meu amor 'tá me esperando
Chorando
Passando
Um pierrot que comprei a prestação
Seu dotô por piedade
É maldade
Esta grade
Separar de mim o meu coração

'Amnesty!', 1933, Ari Barroso

Amnesty
Amnesty
During the three days of revelry
Sir
Don't do this please
In prison
My heart is enough

I spend my life doing manual work
Close by
Only
Because I know work is natural
Sir wants to go away
It's time
Out there
My party, carnival, has begun

My love is waiting for me
Crying
Wearing
A pierrot's costume I bought in instalments
Sir have pity
It's cruel
For these bars
To separate me from my heart

Authentic proverbial phrases and sayings form part of this evocation of familiar discourse. In *'O correio já chegou'* ('The Post Has Arrived') of

1933, for example, the abandoned *eu*, awaiting a letter from his lover, cites an old adage and takes pride in acknowledging his source:[17]

Longe dos olhos
Longe do coração
É o ditado mais certeiro
Deste mundo de ilusão

Out of sight
Out of mind
It's the most accurate saying
In this world of illusion

Ari skilfully brings together a selection of linguistic features associated with everyday speech. Viewed in their entirety, however, his early lyrics are relatively unimaginative and reflect his conventionality. This is best exemplified by comparing and contrasting his lyrics with those of Noel Rosa. Ari rarely employs the shockingly prosaic language favoured by Noel, preferring to stick to uncontroversial representations of stock themes and characters. The exception that proves the rule is the more mature samba *'Camisa amarela'* ('Yellow Shirt'), written in 1939, which deals with a typical scene of daily life on the *morro*, namely the romantic dalliances of a *malandro* during carnival, but does so in highly realistic detail:

'Camisa amarela', 1939, Ari Barroso

Encontrei o meu pedaço na Avenida
De camisa amarela
Cantando a 'Florisbela', oi a 'Florisbela'
Convidei-o a voltar pra casa em minha companhia
Exibiu-me um sorriso de ironia
Desapareceu no turbilhão da Galeria
Não estava nada bom
O meu pedaço na verdade estava bem mamado
Bem chumbado
Atravessado
Foi por aí cambaleando
Se acabando
Num cordão
Com um reco-reco na mão
Mais tarde o encontrei num café zurrapa
Do Largo da Lapa
Folião de raça
Bebendo o quinto copo de cachaça

Voltou às sete horas de manhã
Mas só na quarta-feira
Cantando a 'Jardineira', oi a 'Jardineira'
Me pediu ainda zonzo um copo d'água
Com bicarbonato

Meu pedaço estava ruim de fato
Pois caiu na cama e não tirou nem o sapato
E roncou uma semana
Despertou mal humorado
Quis brigar comigo
Que perigo
Mas não ligo
O meu pedaço me domina
Me fascina
Ele é o tal
Por isso não levo a mal
Pegou a camisa, a camisa amarela
Botou fogo nela
Gosto dele assim
Passou a brincadeira
Ele é pra mim

'Yellow Shirt', 1939, Ari Barroso

I found my fella in the Avenida
In a yellow shirt
Singing 'Florisbela', oh 'Florisbela'
I invited him to come back home with me
He gave me an ironic smile
And disappeared in the whirlwind of the Galeria
He wasn't good at all
My fella in truth was really tipsy
Really smashed
Irritated
He went staggering off
Ending up
In a carnival group
With a *reco-reco* in his hand
Later I found him in a seedy bar
In the Largo da Lapa square
A thoroughbred reveller
Drinking his fifth glass of *cachaça*

He came back at seven in the morning
But only on Wednesday
Singing 'Jardineira', oh 'Jardineira'
Still dizzy he asked me for a glass of water
With bicarbonate
My fella was really bad
He fell into bed with his shoes on
And snored for a week
He woke up in a bad mood
Wanting to pick a fight with me
What a fright
But I take no notice
My fella dominates me
And fascinates me

He's the greatest
So I don't take it to heart
He grabbed the shirt, the yellow shirt
And set fire to it
That's the way I like him
The fun is over
He's mine

This samba is a masterpiece of realism. The idiosyncratic portrayal of the wayward black spiv is unusually prosaic, detailed and humorous. Ari creatively brings him to life, rather than drawing heavily on the conventional language and allusions used to depict this character. In the first verse, for example, he is shown chatting up a woman, ignoring his nagging girlfriend, and staggering around in a drunken lurch from the carnival procession to a sleazy bar in Rio's bohemian night-life and red-light district. The realism of the second verse is particularly effective and comical, as we see the *malandro* reduced to a humble, pathetic figure, barely recognizable as the dapper smooth talker of the day before. The abundance of authentic slang terms (*meu pedaço*, my fella; *mamado*, tipsy; *chumbado*, smashed or sozzled; *atravessado*, angry or irritated; *café zurrapa*, a down-market bar, *zurrapa* meaning poor quality wine or plonk), the very concrete reference to bicarbonate of soda, the familiar hang-over cure, the banal mention of the man's dizziness, his bad temper and his snoring, and the two references to the flashy, yellow shirt itself, create an immediacy that is conspicuous by its absence in Ari's lyrics as a whole. Ari sets the scene both in time and in space by mentioning '*Florisbela*' and '*Jardineira*', two hit songs from the carnival of 1939, and the locations of the Avenida Central (now the Avenida Rio Branco) and the Galeria Cruzeiro in Rio's city centre. The portrayal of the long-suffering, current girlfriend here is humiliating but the humour inherent in her naïvety and devotion to a no-good play-boy prevents us from taking it all too seriously.[18] Ari could almost be quoting Noel in this song, since parallels can be drawn between the techniques which he uses here and those associated with Noel's style, such as the use of everyday, mundane images and allusions. There is a striking similarity between the reference to bicarbonate of soda here and Noel's allusion to the chemical methylene blue in the samba '*Coração*' ('Heart') of 1931 (*Viajou a procurar de norte a sul/Alguém que conseguisse encher-lhe as veias/Com azul de metileno/Pra ficar com sangue azul*, He searched from north to south/For someone who could fill his veins/With methylene blue/To give him blue blood).[19] But the vital difference lies in the fact that Ari's banal references serve to reinforce the realism of the scene, whereas Noel playfully uses his prosaic allusion to create a comic effect. '*Camisa amarela*' has all the vividness of Noel's greatest songs, but lacks the latter's linguistic playfulness. It is significant that Ari chose Araci de Almeida, Noel's good friend and favoured female singer, to record this song. Most of Ari's compositions for women were recorded by Carmen Miranda, whom Noel did not rate so highly.

There appears to be a degree of imitation, conscious or otherwise, of Noel's style by Ari. On the whole, Ari's emulation of working-class speech is less subtle than Noel's, and the lexical range and variety of Ari's lyrics are much narrower. It is revealing that the samba '*De qualquer maneira*' ('Anyway') of 1933, written by Ari in *parceria* with Noel, should have the richest lyrics of all Ari's compositions in terms of both their thematic and linguistic portrayal of Rio's *dia-a-dia*. This song is something of an exception within Ari's work, and Noel's influence is immediately obvious, particularly as regards its linguistic content. It is one of the few compositions by Ari to contain a self-referential element, evidence perhaps of a more self-conscious approach (*Vai cantar meu samba prosa*, She is going to sing my samba prose):

'*De qualquer maneira*', 1933, Ari Barroso and Noel Rosa

Quem tudo olha quase nada enxerga
Quem não quebra se enverga
A favor do vento
Eu não sou perfeito
Sei que tenho de pecar
Mas arranjo sempre jeito
De me desculpar
Eu lá na Penha agora vou estifa
Mas não vou como um cafifa
Que foi lá desacatar
Mas a força falha
Ele teve um triste fim
Agredido a navalha
Na porta de um botequim

Para ver a minha santa padroeira
Eu vou à Penha de qualquer maneira

Faz hoje um mês que fui naquele morro
E a Jú-Jú pediu socorro
Lá da ribanceira
Toda machucada
Saturada de pancada
Que apanhou de seu mulato
Por contar boato
Meu coração bateu a toda pressa
E eu fiz uma promessa
Pra mulata não morrer
Pela padroeira

Ela foi bem contemplada
Levantou do chão curada
Saiu sambando fagueira

Eu vou à Penha de qualquer maneira
Pois não é por brincadeira
Que se faz promessa
E o tal mulato
Para não entrar na lenha
Fez comigo um contrato
Pra sumir da Penha
Quem faz acordo não tem inimigo
A mulata vai comigo
Carregando o violão
E com devoção
Junto à santa milagrosa
Vai cantar meu samba prosa
Numa primeira audição

'Anyway', 1933, Ari Barroso and Noel Rosa

He who looks at everything sees almost nothing
He who doesn't snap bends
To the wind
I'm not perfect
I know that I must sin
But I always have a knack
Of excusing myself
I'm off to Penha all dressed up
But not like a pimp
Who went there out of disrespect
But things go wrong
He came to a sad end
Attacked with a knife
In the doorway of a bar

To see my patron saint
I'm going to Penha anyway

It's a month today since I went up that hill
And Jú-Jú cried for help
There on the slope
Covered in bruises
From all the blows
Dealt by her mulatto
For gossiping
My heart beat quickly
And I made a promise
So that the mulatto girl would not die
To the patron saint
And the girl was blessed
She stood up and was cured
And went off happy dancing a samba

> I'm going to Penha anyway
> Because it's not lightly
> That you make a promise
> And the said mulatto
> So as not to get a beating
> Made an agreement with me
> To disappear from Penha
> Reach an agreement and you've no enemies
> The mulatto girl is going with me
> Carrying the guitar
> And with devotion
> To the miraculous saint
> She is going to sing my samba prose
> In its first ever performance

Here the archetypal *malandro* spouts a variety of slang expressions (*jeito*, skill, knack; *estifa*, elegant or well dressed, probably from the English word stiff,[20] or formal and affected, like the typical spiv should be; *cafifa*, pimp; *entrar na lenha*, to be beaten up, and so on), and well-worn references to the *navalha* (knife), *botequim* (bar), gossiping women and domestic violence. These lyrics are enriched by the topical allusion to popular religious customs, namely the fact that the *malandro* prays to his patron saint to cure the injured woman, and then vows to go to the famous church of Penha, on a hillside on the outskirts of Rio, to pray, and makes the mulatto promise to do the same. Nevertheless, the *cotidiano* represented in this song is far removed from the warts-and-all evocations created by Noel in sambas like '*Conversa de botequim*' ('Bar Talk') and '*O orvalho vem caindo*' ('The Dew is Falling').[21] This is not one of Noel's greatest songs and the two geniuses of Ari and Noel do not appear to be compatible.

There is, in general, a watering down of street vernacular and *gíria* in Ari's work. He does not capture the authentic discourse of the *morro* or of the *malandro*, unlike Noel. As shown later in this chapter, Ari's emulations of 'black speak' draw on totally different sources. The samba '*Cabrocha inteligente*' ('Intelligent Mulatto Girl'), written in 1933, is another exception which seems to prove a rule, and in it Ari uses some of the typical slang expressions associated with the *morro*:

> '*Cabrocha inteligente*', 1933, Ari Barroso
> Que cabrocha inteligente
> Vive chorando
> Se lastimando
> Mas leva o dinheiro todo da gente
>
> Tem diploma de sabida
> A cabrocha é novidade
> Sabe temperar a vida
> Com astúcia e falsidade

Durante o dia
Está vestida de chita
Mas de noite rasga seda
Muita prosa e muita fita

'Intelligent Mulatto Girl', 1933, Ari Barroso

What an intelligent mulatto girl
She spends her life crying
Feeling sorry for herself
But takes everyone's money

She is very street-wise
The mulatto girl is trouble
She knows how to spice up her life
With cunning and deceit
During the day she's dressed in printed cotton
But by night it's silk
The gift of the gab and all show

The eponymous heroine of this samba is a gold-digging, deceitful *malandra*, and the slang expressions that Ari uses to portray her are in keeping with the speech of this mythical woman herself. She has a *diploma de sabida* (she is very street-wise), she is *novidade* (trouble),[22] she *rasga seda* (a reference to the silk she wears, but also a colloquial expression meaning to flatter or fawn over people), and she displays *muita prosa e muita fita* (she has the gift of the gab and is all show).[23]

The numerous overt references to the sexuality and the bodies of women, particularly *mulatas*, constitute a feature of Ari's lyrics which differentiates them from those of other *sambistas* writing in this era. An undercurrent of *machismo* permeates much of his work, and forms part of his conventional, even somewhat reactionary artistic personality. On the whole, women remain nameless in his songs and are defined, instead, in terms of their racial type and physical appearance. In *'Quando a noite vem chegando'* ('When Night is Drawing In') of 1933, to quote one example, the love of the *eu*'s youth is simply referred to as *'uma cabrocha que eu tinha'* ('a mulatto girl that I had'), who subsequently jilted him. In many of his sambas the gyrating hips and shaking thighs of dancing *morenas* are referred to, and the half-caste woman is portrayed as having immense sexual power, which totally entrances the male spectator. In the samba *'Maria'* we learn, for example, that *'No remelexo/A baiana é tentação'* ('When she sways/The *baiana* is a temptation'), and in *'Bahia imortal'* ('Immortal Bahia') of 1945 we are presented with the ubiquitous *'lindas baianas/Faceiras mexendo os quadris'* ('beautiful *baianas*/Show-offs wiggling their hips') and with *'As cadeiras mexendo'* ('Hips moving'), and these faceless sex objects are set against a back-drop of a masculine land ('*Bahia que nasceu/Cresceu forte e varonil*', 'Bahia that was born/And grew up strong and virile').

In the highly original '*Samba de gelatina*' ('Jelly Samba'), written for Araci Cortes in the *revue 'Concurso de beleza*' ('Beauty Contest'), Ari combines references to the erotic *mulata* with a prosaic reminder of the flip-side of the fantasy woman of the male bigot, namely the innocent virgin. The protagonist is a mulatto woman who is frenetically dancing samba and stirring passions. Her body is implicitly likened to a shaking jelly, which in turn is explicitly compared to the bosom of a young maiden. Overt references are made to the physical attributes of both women - the innocent virgin's breasts are drawn in opposition to the *mulata*'s agile and enticing hips:

'*Samba de gelatina*', 1930, Ari Barroso

Treme, treme
Requebrando
Treme, treme
Rebolando
Mulata vai devagar
Com tanta malemolência
Mulata, tenha paciência
Pode quebrar

Canjica de milho verde
Polvilhada com canela
Tremelicando no prato
Como seio de donzela

Mexo, mexo, remeleixo
Requebrando meus quadris
Ai que gelatina assim
Juro que eu nunca fiz

'Jelly Samba', 1930, Ari Barroso

Shake, shake
Wiggling
Shake, shake
Swaying
Mulatto girl take it slow
With so much soft seduction
Mulatto girl, be patient
You might break something

Maize porridge
Sprinkled with cinnamon
Trembling on the plate
Like a maiden's bosom

I shake, shake, sway
Wiggling my hips
Oh jelly like this
I swear I've never made

Ari's representation of women is strikingly sexist, although he is traditionalist in the topics that he chooses, rarely dealing with controversial issues like wife-beating, preferring to concentrate on seemingly flattering depictions of sexually intoxicating *mulatas*. The *mulata* siren is synonymous with the astute *malandra*, and Ari represents this mythical character in many of his songs. In accordance with convention, love is portrayed as man's downfall, a source of pain and economic exploitation, and often we see the collapse of the home when the faithless *malandra* deserts her partner. These self-centred *malandras* seem all the more contemptible for shattering the peace and tranquillity of the cosy *lar*. This idea of the physical disintegration of the home reflecting the emotional breakdown of the spurned, male lover was well established in samba discourse, but takes a further twist in the samba '*Se Deus quiser*' ('God Willing') of 1939, written by Ari in *parceria* with Alcir Pires Vermelho, in which the *eu* tells us that he actually tore down and set fire to his own *barracão* (shack):

> Já pus abaixo e queimei
> O meu barracão
> Já foi vendido barato
> O meu violão

> I've torn down and burned
> My shack
> I've sold off cheap
> My guitar

A distinctive feature of Ari's treatment of the theme of women and romantic love is the recurrent concept of *vingança* (revenge) and divine retribution for misdeeds, the latter always perpetrated by women. Many of these songs, which appear to be full of self-pity and bitterness, nevertheless contain a hint of optimism in their final lines, which is founded on this belief in the meting out of just deserts. A clear illustration of this can be seen in the samba '*Pobre esfarrapada*' ('Poor Ragged Woman'), a tale of an exploited *eu* who provided material wealth for his ex-lover, who subsequently turned her back on him. In the face of apparent adversity the male *eu* concludes:

> Mas teu destino está traçado
> Hei de te ver algum dia
> Só, sem ninguém, sem amor
> E com um sorriso nos lábios direi
> Eu já esqueci a minha dor

> But your destiny is set out
> I will see you one day
> Alone, with no one, without love
> And with a smile on my lips I'll say
> I've forgotten my pain

This notion of revenge and the settling of scores is most directly conveyed in the aptly entitled '*Vingança*' ('Revenge') of 1938, a so-called *samba garapa*:[24]

'*Vingança*', *samba garapa*, 1938, Ari Barroso and Alcir Pires Vermelho

Jurei
Me vingar de quem zombou de mim
Meu amor não se humilha assim
Vingança
Escuto a voz da consciência
Que me pede vingança
Sem clemência

Nosso amor quando nasceu
Era tão feliz
Tudo o que você pediu
Eu fiz
Eu fiz, você pagou com a ingratidão
Vingança
Vingança
Tenho em brasa o meu coração

'Revenge', 1938, Ari Barroso and Alcir Pires Vermelho

I swore
To take revenge on the person who mocked me
My love can't be humiliated like that
Revenge
I listen to the voice of my conscience
That asks me for revenge
Without clemency

Our love when it was born
Was so happy
Everything that you asked
I did
I did, you paid me back with ingratitude
Revenge
Revenge
My heart is on fire

Here the wronged man pours scorn on his fickle ex-girlfriend, and swears revenge, with the repeated exclamations (*vingança*, revenge) and pseudo-learned terms (*Sem clemência*, without clemency, and *em brasa*, on fire) serving to reinforce his threat. Even when love, and therefore life, turns sour, there is always a note of optimism in Ari's concluding lines. Divine retribution befalls those who cheat on their lovers and, by implication, those who do not stray from the path will be rewarded. Although Ari uses the sphere of affairs of the heart to voice his belief in *vingança*, just punishment and reward, this provides a fitting analogy for the benefits that could result from hard work, or conversely, the poverty that could stem from laziness and an unwillingness to cooperate with the Vargas regime's work ethic.

Romantic turns of phrase and scholarly discourse constitute an important facet of Ari's linguistic conservatism. Poetic clichés predominate in his sambas which deal with love, and such flowery language based on literary templates is highly appropriate for sentimental, nostalgic depictions of affairs of the heart, and for the rose-tinted, unrealistic view of life that permeates his more optimistic love songs. In the samba '*Inquietação*' ('Anxiety') of 1935, which featured in the film '*Favela dos meus amores*' ('Shantytown of My Loves'), the *eu* reflects with bitterness on the deceit and suffering that love and women cause. In an attempt to convey the depth of his feelings Ari turns to pseudo-erudite terms, such as *escravisar* (to enslave), *abismo* (abyss), *acesso da paixão* (throes of passion) and *despencar* (to tumble down or to fall from a great height), and to a lyrical metaphor (*Nas asas brancas da ilusão*, In the white wings of illusion). The latter cleverly conjures up an image of a dove in flight and is an apt and elegant representation of the way that people can lose control of their rationality when in love:

'*Inquietação*', 1935, Ari Barroso

Quem se deixou escravisar
E no abismo despencar
De um amor qualquer
Quem no acesso da paixão
Entregou o coração
A uma mulher
Não soube o mundo compreender
Nem a arte de viver
Nem mesmo de leve pode perceber
Que o mundo é sonho, fantasia
Desengano, alegria
Sofrimento, ironia

Nas asas brancas da ilusão
Nossa imaginação
Pelo espaço vai
Vai
Vai
Sem desconfiar
Que mais tarde cai
Para nunca mais voar

'Anxiety', 1935, Ari Barroso

Whoever allowed himself to be enslaved
And to tumble down into the abyss
Of any love affair

Whoever in the throes of passion
Gave over his heart
To a woman
Did not understand the world
Nor the art of living
Not even remotely can he understand
That the world is a dream, a fantasy
Disillusionment, joy
Suffering, irony

In the white wings of illusion
Our imagination
Through space goes
Goes
Goes
Without suspecting
That later it will fall
And never fly again

Similarly, the samba '*Tu*' ('You') of 1934 begins with a string of poetic metaphors inspired by the conventions of Romantic literature. The equation of the colour of the woman's lips with that of coral, and the imaginative contrast of the prosaic *engaste* (setting or mount) with the adjective *sensual* (sensual) are particularly creative:

Teu olhar
É um sonho azul
Teu sorriso
Uma promessa louca
Teus lábios
Duas jóias de coral
No engaste sensual
De tua boca

Your gaze
Is a blue dream
Your smile
A mad promise
Your lips
Two coral jewels
In the sensual setting
Of your mouth

Tried and trusted poetic images and motifs can be found in numerous songs written by Ari, such as the allusion to the *sabiá* (a songbird, usually translated into English as a thrush) in the samba '*Pra machucar meu coração*' ('To Hurt My Heart') of 1943:

'Tá fazendo ano e meio, amor
Que nosso lar desmoronou
Meu sabiá

Meu violão
E uma cruel desilusão
Foi tudo que ficou

It's a year and a half now, love
Since our home fell apart
My songbird
My guitar
And cruel disillusionment
Were all that remained

The image of the *sabiá*, a favourite songbird in Brazil, recurs throughout Brazilian literature, and is used as a symbol of the nation. The best-known example of this motif is found in the Romantic poet Gonçalves Dias's famous poem '*Canção do Exílo*' ('Song of Exile'), which was probably its original source. The poem begins:

A minha terra tem palmeiras
Onde canta o sabiá

My homeland has palm trees
Where the thrush sings

It also features in poems by several of the Modernist poets, such as Oswald de Andrade and Carlos Drummond de Andrade.[25] Likewise, the simile of the injured bird in the following lines from the samba '*Sentinela alerta!*' ('Sentry be on the Alert!') is an established image:

Sou qual pássaro ferido, caído, perdido
Por dois olhos que de maus me abandonaram[26]

I am like an injured bird, fallen, lost
For two eyes that cruelly abandoned me

The device of personification is used by Ari in several songs, such as '*Na virada da montanha*' ('Coming Round the Mountain') of 1935, in which the deserted, broken home becomes a jilted lover herself, mirroring the suffering of one of her previous inhabitants:[27]

Pobre casa abandonada
Além
No alto
Sozinha, sem ter lá ninguém
Tristonha
Caindo ao ver os prédios da cidade
Ó velha casa
Sombra eterna da saudade

Poor abandoned house
Far off
High up there
Alone, with no one there

Melancholy
Falling down on seeing the buildings in the city
Oh old house
Eternal shadow of longing

Ari's use of imagery is at its most powerful, however, when he moves away from the constraints of poetic convention and, instead, looks to everyday experience for his inspiration. In the samba *'Na parede da igrejinha'* ('On the Wall of the Little Church') of 1944, the female *eu* bemoans the departure of her *malandro* lover, and we learn that she has crossed his name off a church wall with a piece of coal. She says:

Risquei o nome dele a carvão porque
Carvão é a cor da saudade

I crossed out his name with coal because
Coal is the colour of longing

This prosaic image is highly reminiscent of Noel Rosa's observation that *'saudade não tem cor'* ('longing has no colour') from the samba *'Silêncio de um minuto'* ('A Minute's Silence') of 1935, and is something of an anomaly in Ari's work.[28] Both convey, simply yet vividly, the ineffable nature of this feeling of longing for a loved one who has departed, and yet paradoxically evoke the emptiness caused by this emotion. But Ari's image is still far closer to reality than Noel's inspirational notion. Such uncomplicated imagery is unusual in Ari's work, and he is very rarely anti-poetic in the way that Noel is, with his deliberate use of mundane language and conflicting registers.

Ari Barroso and the samba-exaltação

Ari Barroso is widely credited with having invented, or at least made his own, the sub-genre of samba known as *samba-exaltação*, with his idealized depictions of *'meu Brasil brasileiro'* ('my Brazilian Brazil', a line from his *chef-d'oeuvre 'Aquarela do Brasil'*).[29] As Sérgio Cabral says: 'Brasil brasileiro sempre foi com Ari Barroso' ('Brazilian Brazil was always Ari Barroso's preserve').[30] Towards the end of the 1930s and throughout the early 1940s Ari turned his attention to representing his nation in a flattering light, and the vast majority of his sambas from this period are noted for their overt, exaggerated patriotism or *ufanismo*, and their often boastful treatment of life in Brazil. Ari's view of his homeland centres on timeworn images and ideas taken from Brazil's literary and popular culture. Hyperbolic eulogies of the nation as a whole, and of the city of Salvador da Bahia in particular, predominate in the samba lyrics that he wrote between 1939 and 1945. In *'Aquarela brasileira'* ('Brazilian

Watercolour', later renamed *'Aquarela do Brasil'*) of 1939, we see Ari's brand of *ufanismo* at its height. According to Dalila Luciana, Ari wrote these lyrics in praise of his beloved Brazil because he was tired of songs about bars, *cachaça* (sugar cane brandy), and the promiscuity of Rio's poorer quarters. Instead he wanted to write a song that ' ... seria um hino à beleza da sua Pátria, ressaltando a Bahia, que, para Ari, era o lugar mais bonito e mais inspirador do Brasil. Era música para o mundo todo admirar.' ('... would be a hymn to the beauty of his homeland, giving special mention to Bahia, which, for Ari, was the most beautiful and most inspiring place in Brazil. It was music for the whole world to admire.')[31]

'Aquarela brasileira', *samba estilizado*, 1939, Ari Barroso

Brasil
Meu Brasil brasileiro
Meu mulato inzoneiro
Vou cantar-te nos meus versos
Ô Brasil, samba que dá
Bamboleio, que faz gingá
Ô Brasil, do meu amor
Terra do Nosso Senhor
Brasil
Brasil
Pra mim
Pra mim

Ô abre a cortina do passado
Tira a mãe preta do serrado
Bota o rei congo no congado
Brasil
Brasil
Deixa cantar de novo o trovador
À merencória luz da lua
Toda canção do meu amor
Quero ver a sá dona caminhando
Pelos salões arrastando
O seu vestido rendado
Brasil
Brasil
Pra mim
Pra mim

Brasil terra boa e gostosa
Da moreninha sestrosa
De olhar indiscreto
Ô Brasil, verde que dá
Para o mundo se admirá
Ô Brasil do meu amor
Terra do Nosso Senhor
Brasil

Brasil
Pra mim
Pra mim

Ô esse coqueiro que dá côco
Oi onde amarro a minha rede
Nas noites claras de luar
Brasil
Brasil
Ô oi essas fontes murmurantes
Oi onde eu mato minha sede
E onde a lua vem brincá
Oi, esse Brasil lindo e trigueiro
É o meu Brasil brasileiro
Terra de samba e pandeiro
Brasil
Brasil
Pra mim
Pra mim

'Brazilian Watercolour', stylized samba, 1939, Ari Barroso

Brazil
My Brazilian Brazil
My devious mulatto
I'm going to sing of you in my songs
Oh Brazil, samba that makes us
Sway and swing
Oh Brazil, the place I love
Land of Our Lord
Brazil
Brazil
For me
For me

Oh draw back the curtain from the past
Take the wet-nurse from the fields
Let the king of the Congo perform
Brazil
Brazil
Let the troubador sing again
In the melancholy moonlight
All the songs of my love
I want to see the lady of the house walk by
Through the great rooms
In her lace-trimmed dress
Brazil
Brazil
For me
For me

Brazil, a good and beautiful land
Of the headstrong mulatto girl

With the indiscreet look
Brazil, a green land
For the world to marvel at
Oh Brazil, the place I love
Land of Our Lord
Brazil
Brazil
For me
For me

Oh that coconut palm that bears coconuts
Where I hang my hammock
In the clear moonlit nights
Brazil
Brazil
Oh those murmuring springs
Where I quench my thirst
And where the moon comes out to play
Oh that beautiful dark Brazil
Is my Brazilian Brazil
The land of samba and tambourines
Brazil
Brazil
For me
For me

This world-famous samba and *tour de force* of national pride begins with what became the classic, albeit tautologous phrase *Meu Brasil brasileiro*, which is repeated in the final verse. It is significant that the first aspect of the Brazilian nation to be introduced is the mulatto, used to symbolize the nation as a whole, the *Meu* (My) serving to reinforce the idea of racial harmony and equality, as well as to objectify the figure. The mulatto is, however, *inzoneiro* (a colloquial term referring to a liar or a gossip),[32] reiterating the established caricature of the half-caste spiv. Afro-Brazilian culture, in the form of samba itself, is then revered. The movements that the music inspires, the term *bamboleio* (a swing or a sway) and the verb *gingá* (to swagger) are intimately associated with the irresistible *mulata* and strutting *malandro*. Samba is portrayed as a focus of national as opposed to class or racial pride. Brazil is an uncomplicated land, an innocent paradise created by God. The simple expression of religious faith (*Terra do Nosso Senhor*, Land of Our Lord), possibly also a reference to the Church of Nosso Senhor do Bonfim in Salvador, that so impressed Ari on his first visit there, is repeated in the third verse, but in the final verse is replaced by *Terra de samba e pandeiro* (The land of samba and tambourines), reinforcing the value of black culture to Brazil as a whole. The second verse opens with a poetic metaphor (*a cortina do passado*, the curtain from the past) which contrasts with the very Brazilian verb *botar*, meaning to put. (This is a colloquial alternative for the verb *pôr*, which is commonplace in European Portuguese but is rarely used in speech in Brazil). The high tone of this second verse is maintained, however, via the use of the poetic adjective *merencória* (melancholy) later. Traditional images of colonial Brazil are then called on, such as that of the black wet-nurse, and the *rei congo*.[33] Ari then evokes the aristocratic side of colonial Brazil, in the form of the nostalgic flash-back to a time of moonlit serenades of love and the elegant ladies of the *casa-grande* or plantation house. His choice of the term *sá dona* is significant, since it was a way of addressing the lady of the house deemed to be characteristic of black slave speech, a corruption of *senhora dona*. Ari creates a highly romanticized vision of Brazilian history, very much in keeping with the designs of the myth-mongers of the *Estado Novo*, who sought to eradicate from the media any reference to the harsh realities of the nation's past.

Ari's evocation of the lives of the white élite in this samba is reminiscent of aspects of the novels of northeastern writers like José Lins do Rego, whose semi-autobiographical novel *Menino de engenho* (*Plantation Boy*) (1932) portrays life on a sugar plantation seen through the eyes of the son of the plantation owner.[34] The examination of regional life, particularly that of the northeast, as an authentic source of national inspiration, was likewise a feature of the work of the Modernist poets from the same period. Ari appears to be influenced by this vogue for writing about the northeast, Bahia in particular, which was seen as the real Brazil. When asked why he preferred this city as a theme, he replied: 'Porque, incontestavelmente, a Bahia é um recanto de tradições e brasilidade, constituindo, assim, um motivo folclórico interessantíssimo' ('Because, undeniably, Bahia is a focal point for traditions and Brazilianness, and thus constitutes a highly interesting folkloric topic').[35] The obsessive treatment of this city in Brazilian writing was satirized by Carlos Drummond de Andrade in the poem '*Bahia*' from the section '*Lanterna Mágica*' ('*Magic Lantern*') of *Alguma Poesia* (*Some Poetry*) (1930):[36]

VIII - BAHIA

É preciso fazer um poema sobre a Bahia ...
Mas eu nunca fui lá.[37]

VIII - BAHIA

It is necessary to write a poem about Bahia ...
But I have never been there.

In 'Aquarela brasileira' Ari makes the nation female by introducing the noun *terra* (land), and his use of the adjective *gostosa* (beautiful) to describe the land, in the first line of verse three, is somewhat unusual, since it is more commonly linked to a sexually attractive woman, or tasty food. The frame of reference of the term *gostosa* seems to extend to the classic *mulata* temptress who appears in the next line (*moreninha sestrosa*, headstrong mulatto girl). Typically of Ari's *sambas-exaltação*, this song relies heavily on the Brazilian popular imagination, more specifically on the institutionalized myth of a land peopled by lazy but astute mulattos and their wily female counterparts. His vision of Brazil is clearly akin to that of the white oligarchy of colonial times, and is dominated by romanticizing condescension. In the fourth verse, Ari adopts a fictional persona and becomes a northeasterner, hanging up his hammock, once again in the moonlight, and drinking from a murmuring spring. These well-worn images combine with such banalities as that contained in the line *Ô Brasil, verde que dá* (Brazil, a green land) of the third verse, and the opening line of the fourth verse (*Ô esse coqueiro que dá côco*, Oh that coconut palm that bears coconuts) to create a trite, sentimental representation of Brazil. Ari used virtually the same images in the song *'Minha terra tem'* ('My Land Has'), written for the musical *'Vai com fé'* ('Go With Faith') of 1932 (*Tem coqueiro que dá côco/Onde estendo a minha rede*, It has coconut palms that bear coconuts/Where I hang up my hammock).[38] It is said that when he wrote *'Aquarela brasileira'*, in his home in Leme in the presence of his wife and brother-in-law, the latter, an engineer, said to him 'Você já viu coqueiro dar outra coisa?' ('Have you ever seen a coconut palm bear anything else?'), to which Ari became angry and promptly sat at his piano and wrote the melody for *'As três lágrimas'* ('The Three Tears'), as if to prove himself.[39] Ari's Brazil is a fertile land of plenty, in sharp contrast to Noel Rosa's Brazil that *'dá banana e aipim'* ('bears bananas and manioc'), two cheap staples of the diet of the poor.[40] In the final lines of this samba, Ari reminds us that the true Brazil is *trigueiro* (dark or swarthy), giving credit to blacks and mulattos for creating a symbol of national identity in the form of samba.

Like the omnipresent moonlight in the song, Ari casts a flattering glow on his Brazil. There are obvious echoes in this and other songs, as mentioned earlier in this chapter, of Brazil's unofficial 'national' poem *'Canção do Exílio'* ('Song of Exile') by Antônio Gonçalves Dias. The northeastern thematic flourished in Brazilian narrative in the 1930s, but unlike the often gritty realism of the regional novels, Ari looks to the templates of nineteenth-century Romantic literature in order to portray his rural idyll. As is characteristic of much of his work, this samba portrays the Brazilian people as being united by a common, uncontroversial history and religious faith, and draws heavily on the myths of the docile national character, the prosperity and beauty of the land, and racial harmony.[41]

Ari's eulogies of black Brazil are full of references to the mulatto, who is venerated as the quintessential Brazilian, the epitome of *brasilidade*, an embodiment of the nation's glorious colonial past. Ari is especially full of admiration for mulatto women, and their mythical sensuality and lasciviousness. Allusions to *morenas bonitas* (pretty dark girls) abound in Ari's later work, in particular. An amalgam of the two dominant forces that shaped Brazil's history, the white European and black African, the *mulata* is the symbol of the nation and her beauty is a reflection of Brazil itself. Teófilo de Queiroz Júnior traces the evolution of this myth through Brazilian literature, and finds elements of it present in the work of the poet Gregório de Matos (1636?-96). He also examines the presence of the *mulata* in the lyrics of popular carnival song, and says that '*Quem inventou a mulata?*' ('Who Invented the *Mulata*?') by Ernesto de Souza, which was performed in the carnival of 1903, was the first to include a direct reference and tribute to this stock type. By the 1920s and 1930s she was established as irresponsible, amoral, irresistible, envious and irreverent. She was used as a symbol of 'Brazilianness', just as the native Indian had been in the Indianist movement in literature.[42]

In the samba '*Faixa de setim*' ('Strip of Satin') of 1940, Bahia is venerated and allusions to elements of Afro-Brazilian culture abound, such as the local Catholic beliefs and customs of the *povo*, the forms of address used by black slaves towards their masters and the white women of the plantation house (*Ioiô* and *Iaiá*), the loving, black wet-nurse of the plantation, and the lower town of the city of Salvador, which is synonymous with the black community. Salvador da Bahia is portrayed as the nation's birthplace in many of these patriotic sambas, and Afro-Brazilian cultural products and religious beliefs, naturally intimately linked to this city, which was the main port of entry for African slaves in colonial times, are used as symbols of Brazil as a whole. Ari wrote '*Faixa de setim*' as a tribute to the Senhor do Bonfim, and when he finished writing the lyrics he said to his wife: 'Será que já paguei minha promessa? Esgotei todos os temas em homenagem ao santo. Está na hora de parar' ('Have I now paid off my promise? I have exhausted every theme in homage to the saint. It's time to stop').[43]

'*Faixa de setim*', 1940, Ari Barroso

Bahia
Terra de luz e amor
Foi lá onde nasceu
Nosso Senhor
Bahia
De Iaiá e de Ioiô
Da Mãe Preta carinhosa

Que no berço me embalou
Quando eu nasci na cidade baixa
Me enrolaram numa faixa
Cor de rosa de setim
Quando eu cresci
Dei a faixa de presente
Pra pagar uma promessa
Ao meu Senhor do Bonfim

Pedi que me abrisse o caminho
Da felicidade
Pedi que me desse um carinho
Pra minha mocidade
Sou feliz
Ninguém mais feliz que eu
Bahia
Senhor do Bonfim me atendeu

'Strip of Satin', 1940, Ari Barroso

Bahia
Land of light and love
It was there where
Our Lord was born
Bahia
Of *Iaiá* and of *Ioiô*
The loving black wet-nurse
Who rocked me in my cradle
When I was born in the lower city
They wrapped me in a strip
Of pink satin
When I grew up
I gave the strip as a present
To pay for a promise
To my Lord of Bonfim

I asked him to pave the way
For my happiness
I asked him to show me affection
In my youth
I'm happy
There's no one happier than me
Bahia
The Lord of Bonfim answered my prayers

Popular religion is a recurrent motif in Ari's sambas, and constitutes one of the most characteristic features of his representation of daily life. His lyrics are peppered with references to God and to the Catholicism of the people, as well as to Afro-Brazilian cult practices. In addition to the commonplace veneration of the church of Nosso Senhor do Bonfim, where a procession of the faithful culminates every January, often seen in his patriotic glorifications of Salvador da Bahia, Ari seeks to show the religious convictions of the most humble Brazilians, whose everyday discourse is full of references to the Catholic faith. Antonio Candido explains how the Catholic revival of the 1930s was closely linked with right-wing politics.[44] It would seem to be no coincidence that Ari continually asserted his own religious devotion and that of the *povo* through his lyrics, and was also an ardent supporter of the Vargas regime. People are portrayed as being contented with their lot, grateful for all that God has given them. This is a logical extension of Ari's blatant, pro-establishment rhetoric in his *sambas-exaltação*. He presents the typical Brazilian as a law-abiding, God-fearing individual, and does not seek to expose the reality of his life.

Hackneyed references to aspects of Bahian culture are used over and over again in Ari's work. It is important to note, however, that Ari created idealized depictions of colonial life and its legacies from the early 1930s onwards, long before the nationalistic fervour of the *Estado Novo* began to exert an influence on song lyrics. In *'Terra de Iaiá'* ('Land of *Iaiá*') of 1931, for example, Ari incorporates typical allusions to the black wet-nurse, the church of Nosso Senhor do Bonfim, *Iaiá* and *Ioiô*, Bahian food and typical Afro-Brazilian dishes, and attractive *baianas*, thematic constants which reappear in his later work, from the beginning of the 1940s in particular.

In the samba *'Terra seca'* of 1944, Ari deals explicitly with the harshness of slavery, and adopts the persona of an African slave. He caricatures the speech of the captive by referring to himself in the third person for the most part, by failing to pluralize nouns (*Essas terra, estes rio, estas mata, estes campo,* and so on), and by using the corrupted deferent form of address associated with 'slave-speak' in the popular imagination (*meu sinhô* for *meu senhor*), and supposedly simplified pronunciation (*moiado* for *molhado, trabáia* for *trabalha, nêgo* for *negro, véio* for *velho,* and so on):[45]

'Terra seca', 1944, Ari Barroso

O nêgo 'tá moiado de suó
Trabáia, trabáia, nêgo
Trabáia, trabáia, nêgo

As mão do nêgo 'tá que é calo só
Trabáia, trabáia, nêgo
Trabáia, trabáia, nêgo
Ai meu sinhô, nêgo 'tá véio
Não aguenta
Essa terra tão dura, tão seca, poeirenta
Trabáia, trabáia, nêgo

Trabáia, trabáia, nêgo
O nêgo pede licença pra falá
Trabáia, trabáia, nêgo
O nêgo não pode mais trabaiá

Quando nêgo chegou por aqui
Era mais vivo e ligeiro que o saci
Varava estes rio, estas mata, estes campo sem fim
Nêgo era moço, e a vida, brinquedo pra mim

Mas esse tempo passou
Essa terra secou...ô ô
A velhice chegou e o brinquedo quebrou
Sinhô: nêgo véio tem pena de tê-se acabado
Sinhô, nêgo véio carrega este corpo cansado

'Dry Earth', 1944, Ari Barroso

The negro is bathed in sweat
Work, work, negro
Work, work, negro

The negro's hands are just calluses
Work, work, negro
Work, work, negro
Oh master, the negro is old
He cannot take it
That earth so hard, so dry and dusty
Work, work, negro
Work, work, negro
The negro asks permission to speak
Work, work, negro
The negro can work no more

When the negro arrived here
He was more lively and agile than the *saci*[46]
He would cross these endless fields, woods, rivers
The negro was young, and life was easy for me

But that time passed
That land dried up
Old age arrived and the easy life stopped
Master, the old negro is sorry he's finished
Master, the old negro is dragging his tired body

This was Ari's favourite composition, and Dalila Luciana says that he was inspired to write about scenes of slavery after seeing blacks working hard in the fields of the interior when he was returning, by train, from a trip in 1944. He was angered by the cruelty of the landlords of the plantations, and felt a tenderness towards the indefatigable slaves of colonial times who overcame their suffering to create music and dance.[47]

Ari's treatment of Brazil's racial composition picks up on the most obvious myths and stereotypes which permeated Gilberto Freyre's seminal work *Casa-grande e senzala* (*The Masters and the Slaves*), published in 1933. For Freyre, Brazil's colonial history was essentially a harmonious uniting of races, which resulted in the imagined racial democracy of the early twentieth century, the flesh and blood symbol of which was the mulatto himself. By drawing on his own memories of his childhood on a plantation and the observations of nineteenth-century travellers, rather than any scientific or reliable documentary evidence, Freyre naturally fell into the trap of romanticizing the past. His theories give us a clear insight into the national mythology of the 1930s and the paternalism of the Vargas regime. In an attempt to counteract increasing centralization, the northeastern regionalist movement, led by Freyre, set out to assert the importance of the traditions of the region, and to emphasize the positive legacy of miscegenation in order to instil a sense of pride in the population as a whole. Despite his efforts to dispel many existing prejudices and preconceptions concerning the African contribution to the formation of Brazilian culture, Freyre perpetuates certain myths, such as that of the licentious *mulata*, and is equally guilty of patronizing blacks and their heritage. His blatant simplifications of social relations and naïve representations of the negro and the mulatto, like any stereotype, contributed to the marginalization of black Brazilians long after his book was published, in spite of his efforts to create a more positive impression of blacks. Ari's condescending depiction of black Brazil is in tune with that of the white plantation aristocracy, to which Freyre belonged, which looked back with nostalgia to the old order of the rural plantation society when faced with political and social instability and uncertainty in the 1930s and early 1940s.[48]

Whilst appearing to acknowledge the importance of the African legacy, and presenting blacks and their traditions as the exotic 'other' that makes Brazil different, the caricatural formulas that Ari adopts in his lyrics conspire to tame Afro-Brazilian culture and to dilute its distinctiveness and power as an identity marker. He sanitizes examples of black cultural production and Brazil's colonial history to make them more palatable for the increasingly white, middle-class audiences for whom he was writing. Against a backdrop of the *branqueamento* (whitening) policy, the marginalization of blacks in relation to the mainstream urban-industrial society of the Vargas era, and the transformation of black popular art forms into the harmless picturesque or folkloric, Ari chooses to represent Afro-Brazilians not in contemporary life, where they are a stigmatized, undesirable element, but in the sentimentalized context of the colonial plantation, where they can exist as quaint, side-show curiosities, frozen in time.

Ari Barroso was a traditional, Catholic, family man, and a consummate professional musician. The impact of his conservative values and his pragmatic approach to his career can be seen in the lyrics of his sambas, which are characterized by their simplicity and conventionality of theme and form. Ari abided by the unwritten rules of the samba genre, to create fine examples of the established norms, such as the use of poetic language in sambas of the *lírico-amoroso* type, and of ready-made, spoken language forms in his portrayals of the *dia-a-dia*. Only very occasionally did he stray from this safe treatment of traditional topics, inching towards the unexpected realism and spontaneity perfected by Noel Rosa. Ari's great skill lay in his exploitation of linguistic and thematic cliché, and his adoption of the templates of erudite literature, particularly the hackneyed images of nineteenth-century Romantic poetry, and of the northeastern thematic that flourished in the 1930s in the novel. As a respectable, white celebrity, he played a key role in enhancing the image of the Brazilian nation, both at home and abroad. The lyrics that he wrote during the *Estado Novo* period clearly reflect the attempts made by the state's propaganda machine to extol the virtues of Brazil and to invent a single, unifying national identity. Ari's own patriotic zeal complemented the nationalistic drive of the political regime, and was thus given free rein by the censors of the DIP to endorse the state's populist mythology. The Utopian Brazil that he depicted was welcomed as a perfect propaganda tool, and he thus enjoyed considerable commercial success and an official stamp of respectability. His lyrics glorify Brazil's past, papering over racial tensions and social and economic inequalities, and they emphasize the idea that all Brazilians are united by a common, uncontroversial history, and religious faith. Not only was he the ideal vehicle for disseminating the propaganda of the Vargas regime, but he also played right into the hands of the myth-mongers of Hollywood, drawing on his love for his *pátria* to create lasting, grandiloquent depictions of the picture-postcard Brazil that the United States, in the context of the Good Neighbour Policy, was only too keen to publicize. He was one of Brazil's most important 'exports' to Hollywood and a key player in the cultural exchange between the USA and Latin America promoted by President Roosevelt. There is no question that he developed samba lyrics in a new direction, influenced by changing tastes among the record-buying public, by the image-makers of both the New State and Hollywood, but most importantly by his own moral values, ideological leanings and patriotic fervour.

Notes

1. Cabral, S. (1994), p. 406.
2. Luciana, D. (1970), I, p. 269.
3. Ibid., pp. 181-2.
4. Moraes, M. de (1979), pp. 112-21.
5. Cabral, S. (1994), pp. 48, 118.
6. Tinhorão, J. R. (1972), p. 214.
7. Cabral, S. (1994), pp. 179-80.
8. A *balangandã* (or *balangandam*) is an ornamental silver buckle with amulets and trinkets attached, and forms part of the typical attire of Bahian women which was adopted by Carmen Miranda. McGowan, C. and Pessanha, R. (1998), p. 31.
9. Souza, T. de (1983), p. 28.
10. Risério, A. (1985), p. 40.
11. According to Dalila Luciana, 46 different versions were recorded in Egypt alone. Luciana, D. (1970), I, p. 266.
12. Between 1938 and 1941, 18,000 copies of the record of his samba *'Na Baixa do Sapateiro'* were sold in Brazil, for example, and 55,000 in the USA. Ibid., p. 242.
13. Ibid., p. 253.
14. McGowan, C. and Pessanha, R. (1991), p. 12.
15. Luciana, D. (1970), I, p. 326.
16. Souza, T. de (1983), p. 29.
17. Ataúlfo Alves makes similar use of ready-made sayings, see pp. 76-7. Noel Rosa also uses proverbs and set phrases, but distorts them to create a comic effect. In *'Malandro medroso'* ('Fearful *Malandro*') of 1930, pp. 124-5, for example, the *malandro eu* spouts the commonplace phrase *se Deus quiser* (God willing) but does so to create ironic linguistic acrobatics: *Eu devo, não quero negar/Mas te pagarei quando puder/Se o jogo permitir/Se a polícia consentir/E se Deus quiser* (I owe, there's no denying/But I'll pay you when I can/Gambling permitting/The police consenting/And God willing).
18. Compare Ataúlfo Alves's samba *'Ai, que saudades da Amélia'*, pp. 63-4, which gives a similarly humorous and affectionate depiction of an exploited woman.
19. See pp. 131-2 for the entire lyrics of this samba.
20. Máximo, J. and Didier, C. (1990), p. 185.
21. See pp. 98-9 and 126-7.
22. According to the *Novo dicionário da gíria brasileira*, *novidade* means either a difficulty, a quarrel, a fight, an irregularity or a problem. Viotti, M. (1957), p. 306.
23. According to the *Dicionário da gíria brasileira*, *rasgar seda* is a slang term for *bajular* (to fawn over, to flatter). Silva, E. C. da (1973), p. 174.
24. *Garapa* was a popular term used to mean a good thing.
25. See p.127 for details of similar allusions found in Noel Rosa's lyrics .
26. This image also appears in the following lines from the samba *'Laura'* of 1944, by Ataúlfo Alves: *'Sem ela sou uma ave ferida/Caída, sem força para voar'* ('Without her I am an injured bird/Fallen, without the strength to fly'), p. 77.
27. There are echoes of Noel's samba *'Meu barracão'* ('My Shack') of 1933, pp. 113-14 in Ari's *'Na virada da montanha'*; in both songs the humble shack is personified and becomes a spurned female lover.
28. See pp. 132-3.
29. This sub-genre of samba is also referred to as *samba-de-exaltação, samba-cívico* and *samba-apoteose*.

30. Cabral, S. (1994), p. 101.

31. Luciana, D. (1970), I, p. 266.

32. It is worthy of note that the term *inzoneiro* was not a common slang term, and when Francisco Alves recorded this samba he mistakenly sang the invented word *rizoneiro* instead. This is a clear illustration of Ari's recreation of a stylized vernacular, as opposed to the real-life slang of the *povo,* employed so skilfully by Noel Rosa. According to José Ramos Tinhorão, Ari was never an outstanding lyricist and was criticized for his easy rhymes, such as *inzoneiro/brasileiro,* and banalities like *coqueiro que dá côco.* Tinhorão, J. R. (1972), p. 212.

33. The so-called king, queen and imaginary court of the Congo have traditionally been worshipped by blacks in the northeast of Brazil since the time of slavery. The coronation of the 'kings of the Congo' was carried out by blacks at the church of Nossa Senhora do Rosário in the seventeenth century, and was celebrated by a procession, dancing and simulated warfare. The 'King of the Congo' was also commonly represented in Portugal, particularly in the church of Nossa Senhora do Rosário in Oporto. Cascudo, L. da C. (1980), pp. 242-4.

34. Rego, J. Lins do (1984).

35. Luciana, D. (1970), I, p. 316.

36. Andrade, C. Drummond de (1930).

37. It is interesting to note that Noel Rosa also deals with the theme of Bahia in his samba *'Na Bahia'* ('In Bahia') of 1936, although in a characteristically light-hearted and farcical way (*Aonde foi que Jesus pregou sua filosofia?/Na Bahia! Na Bahia!* Where did Jesus preach his philosophy?/In Bahia! In Bahia!).

38. Cabral, S. (1994), p. 123.

39. Luciana, D. (1970), I, p. 265.

40. From *'O orvalho vem caindo'* ('The Dew is Falling') of 1933, written by Noel Rosa and Kid Pepe, pp. 126-7.

41. The samba *'Rio de Janeiro'* (*'Isto é o meu Brasil'*, 'This is My Brazil') of 1944, written for the film 'Brazil', produced by Republic Pictures, and recorded in the United States, equally epitomizes the sub-genre of the *samba-exaltação.* Its simplistic language and ideas, naïve, stock descriptions of the landscape, flora and fauna, straightforward rhymes and syntax, lexical repetition, the personification of Brazil, and references to popular religion, all conspire to create an uncomplicated vision of Brazil that has little to do, in fact, with the then capital. The sub-title of this song is far more appropriate, since the lyrics deal with an imagined, Utopian Brazilian nation, in keeping with the ideas and intentions of the image-makers of Hollywood, who were only too happy to reinforce the myths of the Vargas regime. According to João Máximo, this songs was originally recorded in English ('Give in and give Rio a chance, you'll see what Rio does to you ...'). He believes that Ari's *fase de exaltação* (patriotic phase) was his least creative, and that his earlier sambas in particular were of far greater quality. Máximo, J. (1984), 'Ary Barroso 20 anos depois', p. 1.

42. Queiroz Júnior, T. de (1975), pp. 69, 73.

43. Luciana, D. (1970), I, p. 316.

44. Antonio Candido (1987), p. 188.

45. Gilberto Freyre identifies and explains the effects that the African slaves had on the Portuguese language in Brazil, in his opinion. As well as adding new lexical items such as *batuque, cachimbo* (pipe), and *candomblé,* they shortened the infinitive form to give, for example, *mandá* instead of the purist form *mandar* (to send), brought the object pronoun before the verb (*me deixe,* as opposed to the standard

182 THE SOCIAL HISTORY OF THE BRAZILIAN SAMBA

European Portuguese form *deixe-me*), and simplified consonant clusters, giving *muler* and *coler* as opposed to *mulher* (woman) and *colher* (spoon). Freyre, G. [n.d.], pp. 319-24.

46. In Brazilian folklore the *saci* is a mythical one-legged black man, who ambushes travellers.

47. Luciana, D. (1970), I, pp. 297, 308.

48. In the *marcha 'Cena de senzala'* ('Scene from the Slave Quarters'), of 1941, Ari draws heavily, as he does elsewhere, on the myths of plantation life and of the supposedly paternalistic and benevolent slave system instituted by the Portuguese in the Tropics. Echoes can be heard here of the concept of Luso-Tropicalism, the theory that the colonization of Brazil was essentially a harmonious process, due to the absence of racial prejudice on the part of the Portuguese and their tolerant attitude towards the culture of the African slaves, developed by Gilberto Freyre in *Casa-grande e senzala*. The central figure of this song is that of a nostalgic but placid *Pai João* (literally Father John, the Brazilian equivalent of Uncle Tom), who calls out for his home town of Luanda in Angola, and is consoled by music performed on African, indigenous and European percussion instruments and dances his samba with pride.

Conclusion

After 1930 the Brazilian samba developed in line with the reformulation of the class structure in the city of Rio de Janeiro. A product of the *carioca* proletariat, mostly of Afro-Brazilian descent, samba was, however, defined by the socio-economic rather than racial background of its first creators. As a result, the genre could be easily assimilated by lower-middle-class whites, unlike its virtual contemporary, jazz, in the United States, whose white performers were considered inauthentic imitators. Paradoxically, although social divisions had been accentuated by changes in the appearance of the city introduced from the beginning of the century, resulting in the alienation of the emerging social groupings, class divisions became increasingly blurred throughout the 1930s, largely due to continued urbanization and industrialization. The commercial- ization of popular music, within this wider context of industrialization, played a crucial role in both reflecting and reinforcing these social changes.

The discourse of the lyrics of sambas written in the Vargas era was affected by the relationship between their creators and the target audience. In the 1930s samba was adapted for middle-class tastes, giving rise to the sentimental lyrics of the *samba-canção* and orchestral arrangements for sambas such as '*Aquarela brasileira*' by Ari Barroso. The evolution of both the musical aspects and the lyrics was directly linked to the notion of ascension of the social ladder. Bourgeois samba differed from its proletarian forerunner in that it emphasized melody rather than rhythm, and added more complex harmonies and more sophisticated lyrics. The former was perfected by 'upwardly mobile' *sambistas*, such as Ataúlfo Alves, Noel Rosa and Ari Barroso, all of whom belonged to the first generation of professional composers born of the radio and the record industry. The different types of samba which coexisted in this period reflected the respective social groupings and aspirations of their creators. In reaction to the growing respectability of commercial samba, the lesser-known popular composers of the *morros* and poorer quarters of the city of Rio de Janeiro made their samba more syncopated, creating the sub-genre of *samba-de-breque*, with its satirical, anti-establishment lyrics.

If we accept that any form of popular culture is a means of negotiation between dominant and subaltern groups, the lyrics of samba can be interpreted as a vehicle for establishing a musician's stance in relation to the power structure of the Vargas regime. Although Ataúlfo Alves, Noel Rosa and Ari Barroso are all examples of the new breed of professional composers who emerged in this era, their lyrics differ significantly, and these differences provide telling indications of their respective social positions. There is a direct correlation between their willingness to comply with tradition in their songs and the degree to which they were inclined to be coerced by authority.

Ataúlfo Alves, who started out as a musician in the shantytowns of the city of Rio, was to epitomize the ambitious, pragmatic black *sambista* of the 1930s, and in many ways his response to the wealth of opportunities open to popular musicians for the first time was that of the streetwise *malandro* himself. Yet, in order to be acceptable for middle-class tastes he steered clear of the ethos of *malandragem* in his lyrics, preferring to write sambas with safe romantic themes. The discourse of his lyrics is charged with socio-cultural significance in that the antagonisms created by his use of pseudo-erudite motifs and poetic devices alongside the plain talking and simple language which came to him naturally, reflect the unstable status of samba itself in this period. Ataúlfo sought to gain cachet from the inclusion of learned turns of phrase and literary techniques, and took great pains to polish up his lyrics for a more discerning audience. The blatant clashes of linguistic register and rather kitsch effects that sometimes stem from his endeavours are important reminders of the tension within the genre as a whole. They also reflect his uncertain, shifting position; like many poor blacks in the 1930s he was unsure of his place within a society whose structure was rapidly changing.

Noel Rosa was instrumental in foregrounding the lyrics of samba and elevating the status of popular music as a whole. He explored the potential of language to the full, and pushed the frontiers of convention to their limits. Although he was a lower-middle-class white, Noel remained fascinated by Rio's low life, especially the underworld of *malandragem*. No other popular musician has captured the prosaic realities of the *cotidiano* with such wit and powers of observation. Like the ambiguous spiv himself, he associated freely with both the *morro* and the *cidade*, and his lyrics bear witness to his fluency in their contrasting frames of discourse: the complex *gíria*, colloquialisms and even grammatical slips of the inhabitants of the shantytowns, and the skilful wordplay and learned allusions of the educated middle class. The incorporation of these linguistic contrasts into his lyrics is self-conscious and both registers are cleverly intertwined. Noel's education, social class and personal eccentricity enabled him to play around with samba's unspoken rules, both thematic and linguistic, to create highly original lyrics. Unlike

Ataúlfo, who made every effort to abide by the rules in order to gain respectability and acceptance, Noel was a loner, a 'one off', who cocked a snook at authority via his unwillingness to conform and who had a total disregard for economic success. His attitude to tradition mirrored his antagonistic position with respect to the political regime, and his popularity stemmed from his unique genius, which ensured that he was appreciated in spite of his scathing attitude towards the ruling élite, and his reluctance to espouse its ideals. Noel captured the essence of what it meant to be Brazilian in this era with a graphic, often unflattering, realism. Although his alternative vision of national identity contradicted the official line and may not have been tolerated by the censors after 1937, it struck a chord with the average Brazilian, perhaps more so than the platitudinous patriotism of Ari Barroso's *sambas-exaltação*.

Unlike Noel, Ari Barroso thrived on convention and cliché, and his use of trite themes and hackneyed language in his lyrics reflected his willingness to conform and comply with the propaganda-mongers of the *Estado Novo* and Hollywood. His cooption by the Vargas government as a mouthpiece for mythologizing the nation, both at home and abroad, was facilitated by his genuine patriotism and belief in the regime. Ari represents the antithesis of Ataúlfo Alves, in that he was a highly respected, university-educated, white musician and media celebrity, whose main artistic concern was to create lyrics which would ensure his acceptance as an authentic *sambista* among as wide an audience as possible. To this end, Ari strove to emulate an imagined, stylized 'black-speak' or adopted the persona of the Afro-Brazilian in many of his sambas, in direct opposition to Ataúlfo's attempts to 'whiten' his lyrics. The Brazil that Ari depicted, however, is far removed from the real *dia-a-dia* of the lower classes. He avoided polemical topics and prosaic slang expressions. Instead, he capitalized on the political mood of the era and reworked many of the myths of the popular imagination, deftly incorporating images from Romantic poetry and the northeastern literary thematic into his lyrics. His version of the nation's identity is inextricably bound up with that of the state's image-makers; it is an artificial, glamorized, phoney *brasilidade*, which reflected the increasing cooption of popular culture, particularly music, by the *Estado Novo*, and was also symptomatic of the transformations of the samba genre and its creators throughout the first half of the twentieth century.

Glossary

baiana
An Afro-Brazilian woman from the northeastern state of Bahia, usually from the state capital of Salvador da Bahia, who wears the traditional dress of a hooped skirt, lace blouse, turban, necklaces and amulets. Such women are often street vendors who sell food of African origin. The costume of the *baiana* was adopted by Carmen Miranda in the late 1930s.

bairro
A district or neighbourhood of a city.

bamba
A slang term for a tough guy or someone with a particular skill. This term was often used to refer to the leading samba composers of a particular district of the city of Rio de Janeiro.

bandolinzinho
A kind of mandolin, sometimes called a *bandolim*.

barracão
A humble shantytown dwelling, usually translated as a shack.

batucada
A percussion jam session.

batuque
The generic name given to circle dances and their percussion accompaniment, performed by slaves on Brazil's colonial plantations from the seventeenth century onwards.

bloco carnavalesco
An early carnival group, the forerunner of the *escola de samba*.

bombo/bumbo
A large drum used by military bands and in popular music, particularly in early carnival processions.

bonde

The electrified tram, an essential component of the public transport system of the city of Rio de Janeiro in the first decades of this century, particularly as a vehicle for taking poor factory workers from the shantytowns to their places of employment in Rio's *Zona Norte*.

bota-abaixo

Literally 'knocking down', this was the term used to refer to the savage urbanization of the city of Rio de Janeiro which commenced in 1904 under the direction of the then mayor of Rio, Pereira Passos, and President Rodrigues Alves. The city centre was the object of a massive renovation campaign, which drove out the poor to the hillside shantytowns.

botequim

A down-market bar.

branqueamento

Literally 'whitening', this was the ideology which underpinned the Vargas administration's immigration policy, and vaunted the advantages of encouraging mass white immigration from Europe to counterbalance and ultimately to outweigh the black and mulatto population.

brasilidade

Literally 'Brazilianness', the term which became synonymous with national identity in the 1930s and 1940s.

cachaça

A type of liquor made from sugar cane, a favourite alcoholic drink among the poor.

calundu

A dance of African origin that was performed by slaves in Brazil in the late eighteenth and early nineteenth centuries. It is more frequently referred to as the *lundu*.

candomblé

A syncretic religious cult practice, which combines elements of Christianity and various African belief systems. It originated on the plantations of Brazil's northeast, where African slaves would use the Christian icons and traditions as a cover in order to continue to worship their own deities.

capoeira
A mixture of dance and martial art, which was developed by Angolan slaves on Brazil's colonial plantations in the eighteenth and nineteenth centuries, partly as physical training for slave rebellion. It developed in urban areas after the abolition of slavery in 1888, and is a popular sport/performance art form in Brazil today.

carioca
An adjective used to refer to someone or something thing from the city of Rio de Janeiro.

carnaval
Carnival.

casa-grande
The plantation house where the white patriarchal family lived in colonial times.

cavaquinho
A small, four-string guitar of European origin, similar to the ukelele.

caxias
A stickler for discipline or someone who abides by the rules. The Duque de Caxias, Luís Alves de Lima e Silva (1803-80) was the head and patron of the Brazilian army.

chanchadas carnavalescas
Light musical comedies produced by Brazilian film studios in the 1930s and '40s, which incorporated hit songs from the annual carnival and were often modelled on Hollywood movies of the same era.

choro
The *choro* was a slow, sentimental musical genre, which combined elements of the polka, the waltz, and the *maxixe*, and was performed by groups of musicians in Rio de Janeiro from the end of the nineteenth century. Although its origins were more bourgeois than those of the samba, and it enjoyed greater respectability than the latter, both genres were developed by blacks and mulattos.

cidade
Literally 'city', this term was used in samba lyrics to distinguish between the humble *morro*, *favela*, or *bairro*, and the more affluent but less

colourful areas of the city of Rio de Janeiro.

compadrito
The macho, violent peasant character who featured in the lyrics of the Argentinian tango in the first decades of the twentieth century.

cotidiano
Everyday life, sometimes referred to as the *dia-a-dia*.

crônica/cronista
A newspaper column/columnist. The *crônica* is a characteristically Brazilian genre, which has been adopted by many of the country's greatest writers, including Machado de Assis, Manuel Bandeira and Carlos Drummond de Andrade. The *crônica* is a vehicle for commenting on everyday events and apparently trivial aspects of life, often in a humorous and tongue-in-cheek way.

cuíca
A percussion instrument, often translated into English as a friction drum.

curro
A kind of Cuban version of the *malandro* who appears in the nineteenth-century novel *Cecilia Valdés* by Cirilo Villaverde. It is no coincidence that the slave-based societies of both Brazil and Cuba should produce a mythical black figure who rejects demeaning manual work and challenges his inferior social position.

desfiles
Carnival processions.

dia-a-dia
See *cotidiano*.

DIP
The acronym for the *Departamento de Imprensa e Propaganda* or Press and Propaganda Department, the lynch-pin of the propaganda machine of the Vargas regime, whose remit was particularly focused on censorship and cooption of the arts and popular culture.

entrudo
An early form of carnival celebration which originated in the Azores, and which became popular in Portugal in the fifteenth and sixteenth centuries.

It was taken to Brazil in the early colonial period.

escola de samba
Literally 'samba school', this term refers to the groups of musicians and dancers who compete with each other during the annual carnival celebrations in the city of Rio de Janeiro. The first *escola de samba* was created in the poor district of Estácio de Sá in 1928, and was called 'Deixa Falar' ('Let Them Speak').

Estado Novo
The New State, the authoritarian regime established by Getúlio Vargas in 1937, and which governed Brazil until 1945.

eu
Literally 'I' in Portuguese, this term is used throughout this book to refer to the persona or voice of a particular set of lyrics.

favela
A hillside shantytown, characteristic of the city of Rio de Janeiro.

gafieira
A dance hall predominantly frequented by the black inhabitants of the city of Rio de Janeiro at the beginning of the twentieth century, an imitation of the balls of the white élite In the 1930s the latter began to take an interest in the *gafieiras* and gained access to what was essentially a black stronghold. In the 1960s these dance halls were rediscovered by university students and members of the middle class.

gingar
Literally 'to sway', this term refers to the characteristic gait of the *malandro* and to the movements involved in *capoeira*.

gíria
Slang.

iaiá
The form of address used by slaves when addressing the white women and girls from the plantation house. It is derived from *sinhá*, itself a corruption of *senhora* (lady or madam).

inzoneiro
A rarely used colloquial term which refers to a liar or a gossip.

ioiô
The male equivalent of *iaiá*. It is derived from the word *sinhô*, which in turn is a corruption of *senhor* (sir).

jeito/jeitinho
The art of subverting the law for personal advantage, or overcoming some problem, often of a bureaucratic nature, by means of a shady or underhand act. People who *têm jeito* (have the knack) are particularly good at pulling off such acts. This concept is typically Brazilian, and is considered an unofficial institution. It is sometimes translated into English as string-pulling.

lar
Home.

lírico-amoroso
Literally 'lyrical-romantic', this term is used to describe certain song lyrics which typified the samba and the *samba-canção* in the 1930s and 1940s. Such lyrics usually deal with the theme of women and love affairs.

lundu
See **calundu**. Also a term used to refer to a solo song form which developed from the middle of the nineteenth century, and was influenced by the *modinha*.

malandra
The female equivalent of the lazy, debauched *malandro*, a rebellious, fun-loving *femme fatale*, who was frequently the focus for the more melancholy lyrics of sambas of the *lírico-amoroso* type and especially of the *samba-canção* in the 1930s and 1940s.

malandragem
The ethos of idleness, fast living and petty crime which is embodied in the figure of the *malandro*, and which constituted one of the key themes of samba lyrics in the 1920s and 1930s.

malandro
The black or half-caste spiv or hustler, who became a common feature of Rio's poorer quarters at the beginning of this century, and who gained mythical hero status in the lyrics of samba until the end of the 1930s.

malandro regenerado

The *malandro*'s reformed counterpart who pursued an honest, hard-working existence, and who replaced the subversive spiv in the lyrics of samba from the end of the 1930s, largely due to the cooption of popular songwriters by the Vargas regime.

marcha carnavalesca/marchinha

One of the two genres of popular music used to accompany the early carnival celebrations in the city of Rio de Janeiro in the first decades of the twentieth century. Unlike the samba, the carnival march was of bourgeois origin and was inspired by Portuguese marches, which had been passed on to Brazil via music hall.

maxixe

An urban dance form and instrumental accompaniment which emerged in the city of Rio de Janeiro between 1870 and 1880, and drew on elements of the polka, the habanera and African rhythms.

mestiço

An adjective used to refer to someone of mixed race.

mil-réis

The currency used in Brazil until 1942, when it was replaced by the *cruzeiro*.

mineiro

An adjective used to refer to someone or something from the state of Minas Gerais, in Brazil's southeast.

Modernist/ Modernismo

The Modernist literary movement, which emerged from the Modern Art Week of 1922, a cultural event held in the Municipal Theatre of the city of São Paulo, which brought together writers, artists and intellectuals, one of the most important of whom was the poet and musicologist Mário de Andrade. The Modernist movement centred on a group of poets, such as Oswald de Andrade and Carlos Drummond de Andrade, who wanted to make poetry more accessible and to portray the realities of life in Brazil in their work.

modinha

A type of urban popular song, which first appeared in the mid-nineteenth century, and was traditionally accompanied by the *violão*.

morena
A dark-skinned woman, usually of mixed race.

morro
Literally 'hill', but synonymous with the hillside shantytowns of the city of Rio de Janeiro. This term is used widely in samba lyrics from the Vargas era.

operário
The factory worker, who emerged in urban Brazil as the Vargas regime pursued its policy of industrialization, and found his way into samba discourse in the late 1930s and early 1940s as part of the glorification of the new work ethic.

orixás
The deities worshipped in *candomblé*.

otário
A loser, mug or sucker, the antithesis of the street-wise *malandro*. This law-abiding, hard-working figure was ridiculed in the lyrics of samba in the Vargas era, but with the increasing cooption of songwriters by the state he was transformed into the sensible, respectable manual worker.

pandeiro
Tambourine.

parceiro/parceria
Literally 'partner/partnership', these terms were used to refer to co-writers/co-writing of sambas. *Parceria falsa* or false partnership was the term used to describe the common practice of selling a samba to someone, often a singer, so that his name would feature on the record and sheet music as the creator, or one of the creators, of a given composition.

partitura
Sheet music.

paulista
An adjective used to refer to someone or something from the state of São Paulo.

povo
Ordinary people, usually the poor masses.

prestamista

The loan shark, who targeted the more humble districts of Rio de Janeiro at the beginning of the twentieth century, and was often a European immigrant. This figure is attacked in some of Noel Rosa's lyrics.

reco-reco

A percussion instrument, usually translated into English as a scraper.

samba-canção

The *samba-canção* was the slower, more orchestrated sub-genre of samba, with more melancholy lyrics, which appeared in the 1930s and was well suited to performance by dance bands. It is sometimes referred to as the Brazilian blues. It is often also called the *samba-de-meio-de-ano*, literally 'mid-year samba' as opposed to carnival samba, written at the beginning of the year.

samba-de-breque

This sub-genre of samba was created by the singer Moreira da Silva (born 1902), and was characterized, as its name suggests, by the inclusion of pauses or breaks in the performance of a song to allow the singer to make a comment, often ironic or humorous, on the situation described in the lyrics. Moreira da Silva's 1938 recording of the samba *'Acertei no Milhar'* ('I've Won the Lottery'), written by Wilson Baptista and Geraldo Pereira, came to epitomize this vocal style.

samba-de-enredo

The percussion-based samba which provides the accompaniment for the carnival processions in Rio de Janeiro today.

samba-de-morro

Literally 'the samba from the hill', this was the sub-genre of samba that was written and performed by the poor, predominantly black *sambistas* of Rio's shantytowns, and which placed great emphasis on percussion accompaniment. It is sometimes referred to as the *samba-de-batucada*.

samba-exaltação

The sub-genre of samba which emerged during the *Estado Novo* years, and was typified by its overtly patriotic and often clichéd lyrics. Ari Barroso was the chief exponent of the *samba-exaltação*, and his ultra-famous *'Aquarela do Brasil'* ('Watercolour of Brazil') of 1939 is one of the best examples of this variant of samba.

samba malandro
This type of samba was characterized by its anti-establishment lyrics, which relied heavily on the quick wit and ironic comments of the *malandro* protagonist. Such songs predominated in the 1920s and early 1930s, before the Vargas regime introduced its clamp-down on the thematics of samba lyrics.

sambista
A samba composer, who usually also performs his own songs.

saudade
A combination of sadness and longing or nostalgia for the past, and often for a lost love. It is said that this term is unique to the Portuguese language.

sertanejo
An adjective used to refer to someone or something from the *sertão* or barren hinterland of Brazil's northeast.

sinhá
Derived from the word *senhora* (lady or madam), this was the form of address used by African slaves when speaking to the ladies of the plantation house, the wives or daughters of the plantation owner.

surdo/tambor surdo
Bass drum.

tamborim
A small, cymbal-less drum-like tambourine, which is struck with a stick.

terreiro
The place of worship of *candomblé*.

tintureiro
Literally the 'dry cleaner's', this was also a slang term used in Rio de Janeiro in the 1930s to refer to the police van which was used to arrest suspected criminals and vagrants.

ufanismo/ufanista
The noun and corresponding adjective used to describe the hyperbolic patriotism of the Vargas era, and in particular the lyrics of the *samba-exaltação*.

umbigada

A blow or bump with the *umbigo* or belly button, a movement which characterized the *batuque* circle dances, and which came from the dances of the Congo and Angola, where it was the culmination of the marriage ceremony.

valente

The peace-keeper of the hillside shantytowns in the first decades of the twentieth century, who enforced a moral code of practice in an effort to ensure internal harmony. This figure was often synonymous with that of the *malandro*.

vingança

Revenge, often the theme of sambas which dealt with the failure of love affairs and the treachery of women.

viola

A type of guitar first taken to Brazil from Portugal by the Jesuits.

violão

Six-string guitar.

Zona Norte

Literally the 'North Zone', this is the umbrella term used to refer to the working-class northern suburbs of the city of Rio de Janeiro, such as Vila Isabel, Estácio de Sá and São Cristóvão.

Zona Sul

Literally the 'South Zone', this is the umbrella term used to refer to the affluent, beachside districts in the south of the city of Rio de Janeiro, such as Copacabana, Ipanema, Flamengo and Botafogo.

Bibliography

Adamo, S. C. (1983), 'The Broken Promise: Race, Health and Justice in Rio de Janeiro 1890-1940', unpublished PhD thesis, University of New Mexico.

Alencar, E. de (1984), *Claridade e sombra na música do povo*, Francisco Alves, Rio de Janeiro.

Alencar, E. de (1981), *Nosso Sinhô do samba*, Funarte, Rio de Janeiro.

Alencar, E. de (1985), *O carnaval carioca através da música*, 2 vols, Francisco Alves, Rio de Janeiro.

Almirante (Domingues, H. F.) (1977), *No tempo de Noel Rosa,* Francisco Alves, Rio de Janeiro.

Alvarenga, O. (1982), *Música popular brasileira*, Duas Cidades, São Paulo.

Alves, H. L. (1976), *Sua excelência o samba*, Símbolo, São Paulo.

A Modinha, October 1935; September 1942; December 1943; February 1944.

Andrade, C. Drummond de (1930), *Alguma Poesia*, Pindorama, Belo Horizonte.

Andrade, O. de (1966), *Poesias reunidas de Oswald de Andrade,* Difusão Européia do Livro, São Paulo.

Antônio, J. (1982), *Noel Rosa*, Abril Educação, São Paulo.

Antônio, J. (1966), 'Noel Rosa: um poeta do povo', *Revista Civilização Brasileira*, no. 8.

Antonio Candido (Antonio Candido de Mello e Souza) (1970), 'Dialética da malandragem: caracterização das *Memórias de um sargento de milícias'*, *Revista do Instituto de Estudos Brasileiros*, no. 8.

Antonio Candido (1987), 'A revolução de 1930 e a cultura', in *A educação pela noite e outros ensaios*, Ática, São Paulo.

Antonio Candido (1992), 'A vida ao rés-do-chão', in *A crônica: o gênero, sua fixação e suas transformações no Brasil*, Editora da Unicamp, Campinas.

Appleby, D. P. (1983), *The Music of Brazil*, University of Texas Press, Austin.

Aragão, D. (1984), 'Ataúlfo Alves 15 anos depois', *Jornal do Brasil*, 24 April.

Aratanha, M. de (1991), 'Brasil: caleidoscópio de sons', *O Correio da Unesco*, no. 5.

Araújo, A. (1983), 'O samba e o negro no Brasil', *Estudos Afro-asiáticos*, nos. 8-9.

'As atividades culturais do DIP'(1942), *Cultura Política*, no. 20.

Assis, J. M. Machado de (1962), *Obra completa*, vol. 3, Aguilar, Rio de Janeiro.

Augusto, S. (1993), *Este mundo é um pandeiro: a chanchada de Getúlio a JK*, Companhia das Letras, São Paulo.

Augusto, S. (1983), 'Getúlio Vargas em versos e trovas', *Folha de São Paulo*, 20 November.

Barbosa, L. N. de H. (1995), 'The Brazilian *Jeitinho*: An Exercise in National Identity', in Hess, D. J. and Matta, R. A. da (eds), *The Brazilian Puzzle: Culture on the Borderlands of the Western World*, Columbia University Press, New York.

Barbosa, O. (1978), *Samba: sua história, seus poetas, seus músicos e seus cantores*, Funarte, Rio de Janeiro.

Barros, O. de (1968), *A Lapa do meu tempo 1909-1914*, Pongetti, Rio de Janeiro.

Bello, J. M. (1968), *A History of Modern Brazil 1889-1964*, Stanford University Press, Stanford, CA.

Berlinck, M. T. (1976), 'Sossega leão!: algumas considerações sobre o samba como forma de cultura popular', in *Contexto*, Hucitec, São Paulo.

Bloch, P. (1965), 'O Rio de Noel', *Manchete*, 10 April.

Bloch, P. (1964), 'Pedro Bloch entrevista Ismael Silva', *Manchete*, 20 June.

Borges, B. (1982), *Samba-canção: fratura e paixão*, Codecri, Rio de Janeiro.

Bourne, R. (1974), *Getúlio Vargas of Brazil 1883-1954: Sphinx of the Pampas*, Charles Knight, London.

Brandão, D. (1956), 'Ataúlfo é sambista de verdade', *Manchete*, 21 January.

Britto, J. M. de (1966), *Do modernismo à bossa nova*, Civilização Brasileira, Rio de Janeiro.

Brookshaw, D. (1986), *Race and Colour in Brazilian Literature*, The Scarecrow Press, Metuchen, NJ and London.

Burns, E. B. (1980), *A History of Brazil*, Columbia University Press, New York.

Cabral, S. (1979), *ABC do Sérgio Cabral: um desfile dos craques da MPB*, Codecri, Rio de Janeiro.

Cabral, S. (1974), *As escolas de samba: o quê, quem, como, quando e por quê*, Fontana, Rio de Janeiro.

Cabral, S. (1975), 'Getúlio Vargas e a música popular brasileira', in *Ensaios de opinião*, Inúbia, Rio de Janeiro.

Cabral, S. (1972), 'Noel Rosa, 200 músicas em 26 anos, 4 meses e 23 dias de vida', *Cadernos de Opinião*, no. 2.

Cabral, S. (1990), *No tempo de Almirante: uma história do rádio e da MPB*, Francisco Alves, Rio de Janeiro.

Cabral, S. (1994), *No tempo de Ari Barroso*, Lumiar, Rio de Janeiro.

Cabral, S. (1963), 'O desconhecido Ismael Silva', *Correio da Manhã*, 17 February.

Cabral, S. and Tinhorão, J. R. (1962), 'Estácio foi escola de samba: Ismael era o professor e Francisco Alves só assinava o nome', *Jornal do Brasil*, 2 February.

Caetano, P. (1988), *54 anos de música popular brasileira: o que fiz, o que vi*, Pallas, Rio de Janeiro.

Caldeira, J. (1987), *Noel Rosa: de costas para o mar*, Brasiliense, Brasília.

Carone, E. (1977), *O Estado Novo 1937-1945*, Difel, Rio de Janeiro.

Carvalho, L. F. M. de (1980), *Ismael Silva: samba e resistência*, José Olympio, Rio de Janeiro.

Cascudo, L. da Câmara (1980), *Dicionário do folclore brasileiro*, Melhoramentos, São Paulo.

Castelo, M. (1942), 'O samba e o conceito de trabalho', *Cultura Política*, no. 2.

Castelo, M. (1941), 'O samba e o trabalho', *Vamos Ler!*, no. 275.

Chediak, A. (1991), *Songbook: Noel Rosa*, 3 vols, Lumiar, Rio de Janeiro.

Costa, N. (1965), *Rio através dos séculos: a história da cidade no seu IV centenário*, O Cruzeiro, Rio de Janeiro.

Cruls, G. (1949), *Aparência do Rio de Janeiro*, vol. 2, José Olympio, Rio de Janeiro.

Dias, A. Gonçalves (1969), *Poesia*, Agir, Rio de Janeiro.

Dicionário da gíria brasileira (1973), Bloch, Rio de Janeiro.

Edmundo, L. (1957), *O Rio de Janeiro do meu tempo*, 2 vols, Conquista, Rio de Janeiro.

Efegê, J. (1980), *Figuras e coisas da música popular brasileira*, 2 vols, Funarte, Rio de Janeiro.

Efegê, J. (1982), *Figuras e coisas do carnaval carioca*, Funarte, Rio de Janeiro.

Ellmann, M. (1979), *Thinking about Women*, Virago, London.

Ferreira, Aurélio Buarque de Hollanda (1986), *Novo dicionário da língua portuguesa*, Nova Fronteira, Rio de Janeiro.

Ferreira, J. L. (1990), 'A cultura política dos trabalhadores no primeiro governo Vargas', *Estudos Históricos*, vol. 6.

Freyre, G. (1933), *Casa-grande e senzala*, José Olympio, Rio de Janeiro.

Freyre, G. ([n.d.]), *Casa-grande e senzala*, Livros do Brasil, Lisbon.

Fry, P. (1982), 'Feijoada e "soul food": notas sobre a manipulação de símbolos étnicos e nacionais', in *Para inglês ver: identidade e política na cultura brasileira*, Zahar, Rio de Janeiro.

Gambini, R. (1977), *O duplo jogo de Getúlio Vargas: influência americana e alemã no Estado Novo*, Símbolo, São Paulo.

Giacomini, S. M. (1988), *Mulher e escrava: uma introdução histórica ao estudo da mulher negra no Brasil*, Vozes, Petrópolis.

Giani, L. A. A. (1987), *Noel Rosa: o coração do samba*, Sesc, Rio de Janeiro.

Gilbert, S. and Gubar, S. (1979), *The Madwoman in the Attic: The Female Writer and the Nineteenth-Century Literary Imagination*, Yale University Press, New Haven, CT and London.

Gledson, J. (1994), *Brazil: Culture and Identity*, University of Liverpool, Institute of Latin American Studies, Working Paper 14.

Gledson, J. (1981), *Poesia e poética de Carlos Drummond de Andrade*, Duas Cidades, São Paulo.

Goldwasser, M. J. (1975), *O palácio do samba: estudo antropológico da escola de samba Estação Primeira de Mangueira*, Zahar, Rio de Janeiro.

Gomes, B. F. (1985), *Wilson Batista e sua época*, Funarte, Rio de Janeiro.

Goulart, S. (1990), *Sob a verdade oficial: ideologia, propaganda e censura no Estado Novo*, Marco Zero, São Paulo.

Guimarães, F. (1978), *Na roda do samba*, Funarte, Rio de Janeiro.

Heitor, L. (1939), 'Música em discos', *Revista Brasileira de Música*, no. 6.

Holanda, N. de (1970), *Memórias do Café Nice: subterrâneos da música popular e da vida boêmia do Rio de Janeiro*, Conquista, Rio de Janeiro.

Jornal de Modinhas, 8 January 1931; 19 August 1931; 24 June 1932; 22 November 1932.

Kubik, G. (1979), 'Angolan Traits in Black Music, Games and Dances of Brazil: A Study of African Cultural Extensions Overseas', *Estudos de Antropologia Cultural*, no. 10.

Lago, M. (1976), *Na rolança do tempo*, Civilização Brasileira, Rio de Janeiro.

Lesser, J. (1994), 'Immigration and Shifting Concepts of National Identity in Brazil during the Vargas Era', *Luso-Brazilian Review*, vol. 31, no. 2.

Lesser, J. (1995), *Welcoming the Undesirables: Brazil and the Jewish Question*, University of California Press, Berkeley.

Lira, M. ([n.d.]), *Brasil sonoro*, A Noite, Rio de Janeiro.

Lopes, G. da C. (1987), 'Dama do cabaré admite que foi pivô da polêmica', *O Fluminense*, 4 May.

Luciana, D. (1970), *Ary Barrozo ... 'um turbilhão!'*, 3 vols, Freitas Bastos, Rio de Janeiro.

Maia, J. (1936), 'A história triste das melodias bonitas', *O Carioca*, 18 July.

Martins, L. (1964), *Noturno da Lapa*, Civilização Brasileira, Rio de Janeiro.

Mathias, H. G. (1983), *Getúlio Vargas*, Tecnoprint, Rio de Janeiro.

Matos, C. (1982), *Acertei no milhar: malandragem e samba no tempo de Getúlio*, Paz e Terra, Rio de Janeiro.

Matos, C. (1986), 'O malandro no samba: de Sinhô e Bezerra da Silva', in Vargens, J. B. M. (ed.), *Notas musicais cariocas*, Vozes, Petrópolis.

Matos, C. (1978), 'Seu Getúlio vem', unpublished Master's dissertation, Pontifícia Universidade Católica, Rio de Janeiro.

Matos, C. (1989), 'Singular e/ou plural: uma reflexão sobre o estudo das literaturas menores e sua possível contribuição para uma nova historiografia', *34 Letras*, vol. 4.

Matta, R. Da (1979), *Carnavais, malandros e heróis: para uma sociologia do dilema brasileiro*, Zahar, Rio de Janeiro.

Máximo, J. (1984), 'Ary Barroso 20 anos depois', *Jornal do Brasil*, 9 February.

Máximo, J. (1984), 'Um mestre que mereceu bem mais', *Jornal do Brasil*, 24 April.

Máximo, J. and Didier, C. (1990), *Noel Rosa: uma biografia*, Linha Gráfica, Brasília.

McGowan, C. and Pessanha, R. (1991), *The Billboard Book of Brazilian Music: Samba, Bossa Nova and the Popular Sounds of Brazil*, Guinness Publishing, Middlesex.

McGowan, C. and Pessanha, R. (1998), *The Brazilian Sound: Samba, Bossa Nova, and the Popular Music of Brazil*, Temple University Press, Philadelphia.

Medina, C. A. de (1973), *Música popular e comunicação*, Vozes, Petrópolis.

Menezes, E. D. B. de (1982), 'Elitelore versus folclore, ou de como a cultura hegemônica tende a devorar a cultura subalterna', *Cadernos*, vol. 17.

Moraes, M. de (1979), *Recordações de Ari Barroso*, Funarte, Rio de Janeiro.

Moreira, S. V. and Saroldi, L. C. (1984), *Rádio Nacional: o Brasil em sintonia*, Funarte, Rio de Janeiro.

Muniz Jr, J. (1976), *Do batuque à escola de samba: subsídios para a história do samba*, Símbolo, São Paulo.

Muniz Jr, J. ([1976(?)]), *Sambistas imortais: dados biográficos de 50 figuras do mundo do samba*, vol. 1, Impres, São Paulo.

Murce, R. (1976), *Bastidores do rádio: fragmentos do rádio de ontem e de hoje*, Imago, Rio de Janeiro.

Nascentes, A. (1953), *A gíria brasileira*, Livraria Acadêmica, Rio de Janeiro.

Nasser, D. (1966), *A vida trepidante de Carmen Miranda*, O Cruzeiro, Rio de Janeiro.

Nasser, D. (1983), *Parceiro da glória: meio século na MPB*, José Olympio, Rio de Janeiro.

'Noel Rosa: o jovem e inspirado compositor de sambas, disse ao Diário de Notícias "com que roupa" irá brincar no Carnaval' (1931), *Diário de Notícias*, 15 February.

'Noel Rosa, o "philósofo" do samba, fala a "A Pátria" sobre as suas últimas produções que vae apresentar no Carnaval de 1935' (1936), *A Pátria*, 4 January.

Nosso século 1930/1945: a era de Vargas (1982), Abril Cultural, São Paulo.

Novo dicionário da gíria brasileira (1957), Tupã, Rio de Janeiro.

Oliven, R. G. (1987), 'A mulher faz e desfaz o homem', *Ciência Hoje*, vol. 37.

Oliven, R. G. (1984), 'The Production and Consumption of Culture in Brazil', *Latin American Perspectives*, vol. 40, no. 2.

Pacheco, J. (1955), *Noel Rosa e sua época*, G. A. Penna, Rio de Janeiro.

Pacheco, J. (1958), *O cantor da Vila*, Edições Minerva, Rio de Janeiro.

Paezzo, S. (1972), *Memórias de Madame Satã*, Lidador, Rio de Janeiro.

Pereira, J. B. B. (1970), 'O negro e a comercialização da música popular brasileira', *Revista do Instituto de Estudos Brasileiros*, no. 8.

Pereira, J. B. B. (1983), 'O negro no rádio e na televisão brasileira', *Estudos Afro-asiáticos*, vols 8-9.

Perrone, C. A. (1988), *Letras e letras da música popular brasileira*, Elo, Rio de Janeiro.

Perrone, C. A. (1989), *Masters of Contemporary Brazilian Song: MPB 1965-1985*, University of Texas Press, Austin.

Phonarte, no. 37 (1930), pp. 2-7.

Pinto, L. A. C. (1953), *O negro no Rio de Janeiro: relações de raças numa sociedade em mudança*, Companhia Editora Nacional, São Paulo.

Pires, A. (1989), 'Olhar(es) sobre o modernismo brasileiro II', *Brotéria*, vol. 129, no. 6.

Queiróz Júnior, T. de (1975), *Preconceito de cor e a mulata na literatura brasileira*, Ática, São Paulo.

Rangel, L. (1953), 'Noel Rosa: letra e música', *Manchete*, 26 December.

Rangel, L. (1962), *Sambistas e chorões*, Francisco Alves, Rio de Janeiro.

Rego, J. Lins do (1984), *Menino de engenho*, Nova Fronteira, Rio de Janeiro.

Rego, J. Lins do (1941), 'Noel Rosa pede um biógrafo', *Diretrizes*, 24 April.

Revista da Música Popular, October 1954-February 1995; September-December 1955; April 1956; June 1956.

Risério, A. (1985), 'Notas para uma antropologia de ouvido', *Folha de São Paulo*, 28 December.

Rodrigues, A. M. (1984), *Samba negro, espoliação branca*, Hucitec, São Paulo.

Rowe, W. and Schelling, V. (1991), *Memory and Modernity: Popular Culture in Latin America*, Verso, London.

Sales, F. (1984), *MPB em pauta*, José Olympio, Rio de Janeiro.

Sales, H. (1954), 'O parceiro esquecido de Noel', *O Cruzeiro*, 4 September.

Sandroni, C. (1990), 'O feitiço decente', *Opus*, vol. 2, no. 2.

Sandroni, C. (1992), 'Panorama et évolution de la musique populaire brésilienne', conference paper given at the Fête du Brésil, La Garde, 13 June.

Sant'anna, A. Romano de (1978), *Música popular e moderna poesia brasileira*, Vozes, Petrópolis.

Sayers, R. S. (1956), *The Negro in Brazilian Literature*, The Bell Press, Denver.

Schwarz, R. (1987), 'A carroça, o bonde e o poeta modernista', in *Que horas são?*, Companhia das Letras, São Paulo.

Schwarz, R. (1992), *Misplaced Ideas: Essays on Brazilian Culture*, Verso, London and New York.

Severiano, J. (1983), *Getúlio Vargas e a música popular*, Editora da Fundação Getúlio Vargas, Rio de Janeiro.

Severiano, J. and Homem de Mello, S. (1997), *A canção no tempo*, Editora 34, São Paulo.

Sharpe, S. (1976), *Just Like a Girl: How Girls Learn to be Women*, Penguin, Harmondsworth.

Silva, E. de C. e (1939), 'O samba carioca', *Revista Brasileira da Música*, no. 6.

Silveira, J. (1941), 'Não quero choro nem vela', *Diretrizes*, 4 September.

Sodré, M. (1988), *O terreiro e a cidade: a forma social negro-brasileira*, Vozes, Petrópolis.

Sodré, M. (1983), 'O território do samba', *Estudos Afro-asiáticos*, nos 8-9.

Souza, O. de (1991), 'As vozes e o gênio', *Veja*, 25 December.

Souza, T. de (1983), *O som nosso de cada dia*, L&PM, Porto Alegre.

Spender, D. (1980), *Man-made Language*, Routledge & Kegan Paul, London.

Tinhorão, J. R. (1962), 'Bando dos Tangarás trouxe para o rádio com "Na Pavuna" o samba que era das ruas', *Jornal do Brasil*, 9 February.

Tinhorão, J. R. (1990), *História social da música popular brasileira*, Caminho, Lisbon.

Tinhorão, J. R. (1981), *Música popular: do gramofone ao rádio e TV*, Ática, São Paulo.

Tinhorão, J. R. (1982), *Música popular: mulher & trabalho*, Senac, São Paulo.

Tinhorão, J. R. (1976), *Música popular: os sons que vêm da rua*, Tinhorão, Rio de Janeiro.

Tinhorão, J. R. (1972), *Música popular: teatro e cinema*, Vozes, Petrópolis.

Tinhorão, J. R. ([n.d.]), *Música popular: um tema em debate*, JCM Editores, Rio de Janeiro.

Tinhorão, J. R. (1977), 'Nos anos de ouro nos auditórios', *Jornal do Brasil*, 1 May.

Tinhorão, J. R. (1969), *O samba agora vai ...: a farsa da música popular no exterior*, JCM Editores, Rio de Janeiro.

Tinhorão, J. R. (1988), *Os sons dos negros no Brasil: cantos, danças, folguedos - origens*, Art, São Paulo.

Tinhorão, J. R. (1986), *Pequena história da música popular: da modinha ao tropicalismo*, Art, São Paulo.

Tota, A. P. (1980), 'A glória artística nos tempos de Getúlio', *Isto É*, 2 January.

Treece, D. (1996), 'Melody, Text and Luiz Tatit's *O Cancionista*: New Directions in Brazilian Popular Music Studies', *Journal of Latin American Cultural Studies*, vol. 5, no. 2.

Vasconcelos, A. (1964), *Panorama da música popular brasileira*, vol. 2, Livraria Martins, São Paulo.

Vasconcelos, G. (1977), *Música popular: de olho na fresta*, Graal, Rio de Janeiro.

Velloso, M. P. (1990), 'As tias baianas tomam conta do pedaço: espaço e identidade cultural no Rio de Janeiro', *Estudos Históricos*, vol. 6.

Vianna, H. (1973), 'Nascimento e vida do samba', *Revista Brasileira de Folclore*, vol. 35.

Villaverde, C. (1972), *Cecilia Valdés;* or, *La loma del ángel: novela de costumbres cubanas*, Porrúa, Mexico City.

Voz da Mocidade, 22 January 1932; 18 February 1933.

Williams, D. (1994), 'Ad perpetuam rei memoriam: the Vargas Regime and Brazil's National Historical Patrimony, 1930-1945', *Luso-Brazilian Review*, vol. 31, no. 2.

Index

DEMCO